James Payn

Minutes of the Committee of Defence of Philadelphia

1814-1815

James Payn

Minutes of the Committee of Defence of Philadelphia
1814-1815

ISBN/EAN: 9783337006952

Printed in Europe, USA, Canada, Australia, Japan

Cover: Foto ©ninafisch / pixelio.de

More available books at **www.hansebooks.com**

MEMOIRS

OF THE

HISTORICAL SOCIETY

OF

PENNSYLVANIA.

VOLUME VIII.

CONTAINING THE

MINUTES

OF THE

Committee of Defence of Philadelphia.

1814–1815.

PHILADELPHIA:
J. B. LIPPINCOTT & CO.
FOR THE
HISTORICAL SOCIETY OF PENNSYLVANIA.
1867.

Entered, according to Act of Congress, in the year 1867, by

J. B. LIPPINCOTT & CO.,

In the Clerk's Office of the District Court of the United States for the Eastern District of Pennsylvania.

PREFATORY NOTE.

The following pages are copied from the original minutes in the handwriting of the late JOHN GOODMAN, Esq., of the Incorporated Northern Liberties of Philadelphia, who was Secretary of the Committee. A few years before his decease he presented the original manuscript to the Historical Society of Pennsylvania.

March, 1867.

PROCEEDINGS

OF THE

CITIZENS OF PHILADELPHIA

AND

ADJOINING DISTRICTS

AT A

TOWN MEETING

Held on the 26th of August, 1814,

AND THE

PROCEEDINGS OF THE GENERAL COMMITTEE

APPOINTED BY THE CITIZENS AT THE SAID MEETING.

TOWN MEETING.

At an unusually large and respectable meeting of the citizens of Philadelphia and adjoining districts, convened on the 26th of August, 1814, in the State House yard,

Thomas McKean was unanimously called to the Chair, and Joseph Reed appointed Secretary.

The following named gentlemen were appointed a Committee, viz.: Jared Ingersoll, Charles Biddle, John Sergeant, John Goodman, Robert McMullin, Thomas Leiper, and John Barker, to consider and report what measures ought, in their opinion, to be adopted for protection and defence. Having retired, they soon after reported the following resolutions, which were unanimously adopted:

Resolved, That Charles Biddle, Thomas Leiper, Thomas Cadwalader, General Jno. Steel, George Latimer, John Barker, Henry Hawkins, Liberty Browne, Charles Ross, Manuel Eyre, Jno. Connelly, Condy Raguet, Wm. McFaden, Jno. Sergeant, Jno. Geyer (Mayor), Joseph Reed,

For the City of Philadelphia;

Colonel Jonathan Williams, John Goodman, Daniel

Groves, John Barclay, John Naglee, Th. Snyder, J. W. Norris, Michael Leib, Jacob Huff, Jas. Whitehead,

For the Northern Liberties and Penn Township;

James Josiah, R. McMullin, Jno. Thompson, E. Ferguson, Jas. Ronaldson, P. Miercken, R. Palmer, P. Peltz,

For the District of Southwark, and the Townships of Moyamensing and Passyunk;

be a Committee for the purpose of organizing the citizens of Philadelphia, of the Northern Liberties, and Southwark, for defence, with powers to appoint committees under them, to correspond with the Government of the Union and of the State, to receive the offers of service from our fellow-citizens in other parts of the State and Union, to make arrangements for supplies of arms, ammunitions and provisions, to fix on places of rendezvous and signals of alarm, and to do all such other matters as may be necessary for the purpose of defence.

Resolved, That our fellow-citizens who have been drafted under any requisition of the President of the United States, or have offered their services, be requested to consider themselves subject to the directions of the said Committee, provided that the directions of the said Committee shall in no respect contravene the orders of the General or State Government.

Resolved, That the Committee be authorized to make such applications as they may deem necessary, for the purpose of procuring an adequate disbursement of the funds provided by the Commonwealth for military purposes.

Resolved, That the Committee be authorized to call upon the City Councils, and upon the Corporations in the Northern and Southern Districts, in the name of the citizens, to make such appropriations as may be necessary for the purposes aforesaid.

Resolved, That the Committee be authorized and requested to make provision for the families of such of the drafted militia and volunteers as, during their absence on service, may be in want of assistance.

    (Signed) THOMAS McKEAN,
               Chairman.
(Signed) JOSEPH REED,
       Secretary.

NOTES.

Thomas McKean, the Chairman of the town meeting, was a native of Chester County, Pennsylvania. He settled in "the three lower counties," now the State of Delaware, where he filled many important offices. He was a member of the Congress of 1768, and of that which adopted the Declaration of Independence, for which he voted. In 1777 he was appointed Chief Justice of Pennsylvania, an office which he held for twenty-two years. In 1799 he was chosen Governor of Pennsylvania, being the candidate of the Republican party, re-elected in 1802, and again in 1805, on which last occasion he was the candidate of the Federal party, in opposition to Simon Snyder, the Republican candidate. He was eighty years of age in 1814. In 1817 he died.

Joseph Reed, the Secretary of the town meeting, was a native of Philadelphia, being the son of General Joseph Reed, of the army of the Revolution. He was a member of the bar, and for many years the Recorder of the City of Philadelphia. In politics he was a Democrat.

Jared Ingersoll was a native of Connecticut, and occupied a prominent position at the Philadelphia bar for a long period. He was once the candidate of the Federal party for Vice-President of the United States. Hon. Charles J. Ingersoll and Hon. Joseph R. Ingersoll, both members of Congress from Philadelphia, were two of his sons.

Charles Biddle was Vice-President of the Supreme Executive Council of Pennsylvania under the first constitution of the State, and the father of Nicholas Biddle, the President of the Bank of the United States. He was a merchant, and a member of the Democratic party.

John Sergeant, a very eminent member of the Philadelphia bar, was several times a member of Congress. He was one of the envoys to the Congress of Panama. During the existence of the Whig party he was once their candidate for Vice-President of the United States, being placed upon the same ticket with Henry Clay.

John Goodman served during the war of the Revolution, and was for many years a very prominent member of the Democratic party, frequently serving in the Legislature from Philadelphia County. He was for a long time an alderman in the Northern Liberties, and was distinguished for the soundness of his decisions. He lived to an advanced age.

Robert McMullin was a native of the District of Southwark, and by trade a shipwright. He was an active member of the Democratic party, and a man of much influence generally.

Thomas Leiper was born in Scotland. His business was that of a tobacconist. He was very prominent in the Republican, or Democratic party. Mr. Jefferson was nominated for the Presidency at his house in Philadelphia. In 1814 he was President of the Select Council of Philadelphia.

John Barker served during the Revolution in the Pennsylvania militia. He was a gentleman of social habits and great personal popularity. At town meetings he was an acceptable speaker. He filled the offices of Mayor of the City of Philadelphia and Sheriff of the City and County. He was a Democrat, and a zealous supporter of the war of 1812 with Great Britain. His son, James N. Barker, a man of much literary talent, was a captain in the army during that war, and afterwards was an alderman of Philadelphia, and mayor. President Jackson appointed him Collector of the Port of Philadelphia.

Henry Hawkins, originally a sea-captain, and thence known as Captain Hawkins, was a merchant, and probably a member of the Federal party.

Thomas Cadwalader was the son of General Cadwalader of the revolutionary army, and commanded the forces raised in Philadelphia for the defence of that place in the war of 1812. He was a lawyer by profession, and a member of the Federal party. Judge John Cadwalader and General George Cadwalader are two of his sons.

John Steele was a native of Lancaster County, Pennsylvania, and represented that county in the Legislature. President Jefferson appointed him Collector of the Port of Philadelphia, which office he held during several succeeding administrations until advanced in years, when he resigned. In politics he was a Democrat.

George Latimer was a merchant, and belonged to the Federal party. He represented the City of Philadelphia in the Pennsylvania Legislature.

Liberty Browne was a silversmith, and carried on business on Chestnut Street near Third Street. He was an active Democrat, and frequently a candidate of that party for a seat in the City Councils. In 1814 he was President of the Common Council.

Charles Ross was Captain of the First City Troop, which performed active duty between Philadelphia and Baltimore in 1814. In politics he was a Federalist.

Manuel Eyre was a merchant, of a family eminent as shipwrights for many years in Kensington. For a long period he was one of the directors of the Bank of the United States. In politics he was probably a Democrat in 1812. He was the son-in-law of John Connelly, next mentioned.

John Connelly was an auctioneer, appointed by Governor Snyder. He was a prominent Democrat, and represented the City of Philadelphia in the State Legislature during several sessions.

Condy Raguet, originally a merchant, and subsequently a lawyer, was a distinguished writer upon political economy and finance. He was in 1814 a member of the Federal party, and served in the Legislature of Pennsylvania. He edited the *Philadelphia Gazette,* the *State Rights' Advocate,* and the *Journal of Banking,* in the latter years of his life.

William McFaden was originally a sea-captain. He served during the revolutionary war. In politics he was a Democrat.

John Geyer, a native of Philadelphia, was a printer, carrying on business for many years in Third Street above Race Street, where he published a German newspaper. At the date of the town meeting he was Mayor of Philadelphia.

Colonel Jonathan Williams was a grand-nephew of Dr. Franklin, and born in Boston in 1750. He was brought up a merchant, and during the Revolution was in France, where he was of great service to his native country. In 1785 he returned to the United States. In 1800 he was appointed major of artillery in the regular army, and shortly afterwards became colonel of engineers, and was placed at the head of the Military Academy at West Point. After leaving the army he settled in Philadelphia, where he was elected a member of Congress in 1814, but he died before taking his seat.

Daniel Groves was a native of the Northern Liberties, by trade a bricklayer and stone-mason. He represented the County of Philadelphia for four years in the State Senate, and also served in the Board of Commissioners of the Northern Liberties. In politics he was a Democrat.

John Barclay was a native of Bucks County, Pennsylvania, and at one period was one of the associate judges of that county. He afterwards removed to the Northern Liberties, where he continued to reside until his death, filling for some time the presidency of the bank of that district. In politics he was a Federalist.

John Naglee was born in the Northern Liberties, where he carried on an extensive business as a lumber-merchant for many years. In the campaign of 1814 he commanded the Northern Liberties Artillery Company, attached to General Cadwalader's Advanced Light Brigade of Volunteers. He was a prominent Democrat. One of his sons was a brigadier-general in the late war.

Thomas Snyder was a native of the Northern Liberties; a brickmaker by trade. He was an active Democrat, and commanded a brigade of militia at Marcus Hook in the campaign of 1814.

Isaac W. Norris was a descendant of one of the early settlers of Philadelphia. He carried on business as a ship-chandler. Originally he was a Federalist, but subsequently acted with the Democratic party. In the campaign of 1814 he served in the infantry company of State Fencibles.

Michael Leib was of German origin, born in Philadelphia. He was a very active member of the Democratic party, frequently serving in the Legislature. He was at one time Senator of the United States, which office he resigned on being appointed Postmaster at Philadelphia.

Jacob Huff was a victualler by trade, and a warm Democrat. He commanded a rifle company during the war of 1812.

James Whitehead was a grocer, carrying on business on Second Street below Callowhill Street. He was an influential member of the Federal party.

James Josiah was a resident of Southwark, a sea-captain by profession. He commanded the Andrew Doria, and is said to have been the first person whose vessel displayed the American flag in the port of London after the revolutionary war. He married a daughter of Col. Marsh, a soldier of the Revolution, but left no children. In politics he was a Democrat.

John Thompson, a shoemaker by trade, was a prominent Democrat in the District of Southwark. He served several times in the State Legislature, and was afterwards one of the County Commissioners.

Ebenezer Ferguson, it is believed, was born in Ireland. He was for many years a magistrate in the District of Southwark, and an active member of the Democratic party.

James Ronaldson was a native of Edinburgh, in Scotland. After coming to this country he entered into partnership with Archibald Binney, another Scotchman, and founded a type-foundry in Shippen Street west of Ninth Street, one of the earliest in the United States. He afterwards established the Philadelphia Cemetery, at Ninth and Shippen Streets, and, in concert with his brothers, created the marine railway in Southwark. He was a public-spirited and energetic citizen, and did much for the improvement of Moyamensing by building and otherwise. In the early part of his life he was a Democrat, afterwards he joined the Whig party. He served in the Board of Commissioners of Moyamensing. His death occurred in the spring of 1841.

Peter Miercken was a sugar-refiner in Southwark, his place of business and residence being in Shippen Street above Second Street. He was an active and influential Federalist. During Freas's insurrection, in Northampton County, he was a member of the First City Troop. At one time he was an inspector of the Walnut Street Prison.

Richard Palmer was a prominent Democrat in Southwark. He was the son of Mrs. Ann Palmer, a cake-baker in Chestnut Street, after whom the well-known Philadelphia tea-cake, the A. P., was called. Mr. Palmer was for some years the Prothonotary of the Court of Common Pleas of Philadelphia, and afterwards an alderman in Southwark.

Philip Peltz was a farmer and gardener, residing in Passyunk

Township. He filled the office of county commissioner and some other positions of a public nature. He belonged to the Democratic party.

The present Receiver of Taxes in Philadelphia is his grandson.

₊ The Historical Society of Pennsylvania is indebted to the venerable Peter Hay, Esq., Alderman, a soldier of the war of 1812, for much of the information contained in the above notes.

The following are from the newspapers of the day:

(From the Philadelphia Gazette.)

At length our citizens appear to be aroused from their delusive slumbers. The forbearance of the enemy had not only deceived the mass of the people, but had likewise deluded the Government into an idea of complete safety. This fatal delusion is now dissipated; and the capital of our country, which was last week occupied by the President and the heads of departments, is now in the hands of the enemy! We can have no correct account of the actual force of the enemy; but surely it cannot be of magnitude sufficient to keep possession of Washington for any length of time. We rather ought to believe that the spirit of our Southern fellow-citizens would rise up in its mightiest force, and by a well-concerted and unanimous operation, either totally overwhelm or disgracefully expel the audacious invaders of our country.

While we are all burning with solicitude to hear of the progress of the enemy, and deeply sympathizing with our fellow-citizens who are now experiencing all the horrors of invasion, do we sufficiently examine into our own situation? Do we recollect that it may next, and that very soon, too, be our turn to meet the brunt of battle? Have we active and intelligent officers at the head of this military district? Is there reciprocal confidence subsisting between the United States and the State's authorities?

(From the Aurora.)

THE TOWN MEETING.

It will be remarked that the proceedings at the town meeting held yesterday do not comprehend any very particular expression of sentiment on general principles, but that they merely announce the formation of a committee of safety. Let it not therefore be supposed that the meeting showed any indifference relative to the questions involving the destinies of the nation. There are no printed resolutions of devotion to the country, because, as Governor McKean well said, "this is not a time for speaking, but a time for acting;" there are no declarations of oblivion of the past, because, as Governor McKean also correctly said, "we have now nothing to do with the past—we must only think of the present and of the future." Neither are there any resolutions to suppress party contentions, because, as Governor McKean also told the meeting, "there are now but two parties, our country and its invaders."

We have no doubt that the people will heartily concur in all the measures which the Committee of Safety may propose; and we have no doubt that the Committee will suggest such measures only as shall be calculated to protect, uphold, and gratify their constituents.

Every man who can ought to aid in a prompt and efficient organization of the militia; every man liable to militia duty ought to acquire the knowledge of firing with precision; no officer ought to flatter himself with having knowledge enough, but should search for information from every accessible source.

Those whose houses are to be defended by men in humble life—those who have wealth—should aid the wives and children of such as are in want of it. A wise man, said Dr. Franklin, will throw a few barrels of water into a pump in order to be able to make ample use of the well.

As some alien enemies are permitted to remain among us, it will of course be their duty and their interest to be perfectly quiet. To run about in search of news, and to openly exult at American distresses, is putting human patience to a trial rather too severe.

PROCEEDINGS OF THE GENERAL COMMITTEE.

FIRST MEETING.

PHILADELPHIA, *August* 26*th*, 1814.

The Committee appointed at a meeting of the citizens of Philadelphia and adjoining districts convened this day in the State House yard, met, pursuant to notice given, at the City Hall.

PRESENT (27):

Charles Biddle,	Wm. McFaden,	Charles Ross,
Jno. Barker,	John Geyer,	T. Cadwalader,
Jno. Sergeant,	Jos'h Reed,	Liberty Browne,
Jno. Goodman,	Jacob Huff,	Eben'r Ferguson,
Robt. McMullin,	Richard Palmer,	Henry Hawkins,
Thos. Leiper,	Daniel Groves,	Manuel Eyre,
George Latimer,	Jas. Ronaldson,	James Josiah,
Michael Leib,	John Thompson,	Peter Miercken,
Condy Raguet,	Jas. Whitehead,	Jno. Naglee.

Charles Biddle was appointed Chairman, and John Goodman, Secretary.

On motion, the proceedings of the town meeting were read. Whereupon

Resolved, That a committee be appointed to correspond with the Government of the Union and of this State. Messrs. Latimer, Sergeant, and Reed were appointed as said committee.

Resolved, That Michael Leib, Jacob Huff, John Goodman, John Thompson, Ebenezer Ferguson, Jno. Connelly, and Liberty Browne be a committee to make arrangements for supplies of arms, ammunition, and provisions, to fix on places of rendezvous, and signals of alarm, and for other purposes.

Resolved, That Henry Hawkins, James Josiah, Wm. McFaden, John Naglee, and Peter Miercken be a committee for defence on the Delaware, and to procure seamen, &c.

Resolved, That Jno. Steele, Thos. Cadwalader, Charles Ross, Thos. Snyder, Jonathan Williams, Manuel Eyre, Condy Raguet, Eben'r Ferguson, and Daniel Groves be a committee for organizing the citizens of the city and adjoining districts into military bodies, for directing measures of public defence, and for making proper inquiry relative to men and arms, to receive the offers of service, and to report from time to time.

Resolved, That a committee be appointed to procure adequate funds, provided by the Commonwealth, to defray the necessary expense in placing the city and districts in a proper state of defence. This subject was referred to the Committee of Correspondence.

Resolved, That John Geyer, Jno. Goodman, and Robert McMullin be a committee to apply to the corporations of the city and adjoining districts for the appropriate funds to answer immediate demands for the accomplishment of the objects expressed in town meeting.

Resolved, That Jno. Connelly, Jno. Barclay, Jno. Steele, Henry Hawkins, and Liberty Browne be a committee to make provision for the families of such of the drafted militia and volunteers as, during their absence on service, may be in want of assistance.

Resolved, That the Committee of Correspondence immediately draft a letter to the Governor on subject of defence, and requesting his Excellency to visit the city. The Committee, after a short time, reported a draft of a letter, which was ordered to be signed by the Chairman, and countersigned by the Secretary; and Thomas Leiper and James Ronaldson were appointed a committee forthwith to proceed and present the said letter to the Governor, and to forward the views of the Committee as expressed in the letter.

Resolved, That four citizens be appointed in each ward of the city, twenty-one for the Northern Liberties and Penn Township, and twenty-six for the Districts of Southwark, Moyamensing, and Passyunk, whose duty it shall be to apply to each free, able-bodied inhabitant in their respective wards and districts, to promote and encourage the immediate formation of volunteer companies, and the organization of those companies into regiments and battalions with all possible speed, and that every exertion be made to provide arms and accoutrements, and to stimulate the officers to muster their respective commands in marching order, and to drill them at least two hours in every day.

Whereupon the following citizens were appointed for said purpose, viz.:

Alexander McCaracher, Daniel Miller, Peter Hertzog, and John Miller—*Upper Delaware Ward*.

Conrad Wile, Joseph Hertzog, James D. Pratt, and Frederick Eringer—*Lower Delaware Ward*.

Jacob Chrystler, Benj'n Reynolds, Daniel Oldenbaugh, and Randall Hutchinson—*High Street Ward*.

Samuel Carswell, Richard Fox, Richard Tybout, and Samuel Meeker—*Chestnut Ward*.

Wm. Smiley, Chas. C. Watson, Matthew McConnell, and George Bartram—*Walnut Ward*.

Joseph S. Lewis, Benj'n B. Howell, Wm. Dilworth, and Benj'n Chew, Jun'r—*Dock Ward*.

Wm. Etris, Dan'l Smith, J. W. Thompson, and Robert Wharton—*New Market Ward*.

George Summers, Benj'n Lyndall, Alphonso C. Ireland, and Joseph Watson—*Cedar Ward*.

Andrew Pettit, Abram Shoemaker, Jr., Bayse Newcomb, and Walter Ker—*Locust Ward*.

James Ash, James Harper, Jr., William Newling, and Jno. L. Leib—*South Ward*.

Thomas M. Souder, Jno. Markoe, Charles Barrington, and Peter Lyle—*Middle Ward*.

Joshua Sullivan, Saml. Hodgdon, Wm. Montgomery, and Daniel Denman—*North Ward*.

Nicodemus Lloyd, Sam'l Richards, George Alexander, Wm. Mandrie. Jno. Dennis and Jacob Kugler added. See p. 46—*South Mulberry Ward*.

Doctor Elisha Griffith, Alex'r Cook, Edward Penington, Doctor Glentworth—*North Mulberry Ward.*

Benj'n Naglee, Geo. Meyers, Charles Harper, Wm. Binder, Joseph P. Zebley, Charles Wheeler, Michael Collar, Jacob Souder, Joseph Grice, Capt. Peter Brown, Sam'l McFeran, Sam'l Bowers, Henry Lentz, Henry Probasco, Wm. Duncan, Henry A. Beck, Sebastian Zimmerman, Henry Nixon, Peter Hotz, Andrew C. Barclay, Geo. Loudensleger—*For the Northern Liberties and Penn Township.*

Jno. Hunter, James Lafferty, Geo. Reese, Michael Freitag, John Lentz, Jr., James Engle, Joshua Raybold, Richard Renshaw—*For Moyamensing and Passyunk.*

Daniel Guiry, Jos'h P. McCorkle, Archibald Binney, John Huber, Geo. Ord, Thomas Maitland, Thos. Elliot, Richard Palmer, Jno. Lentz, Cornelius Stevenson, Capt. Paul, Geo. Morton, Geo. Weaver, Daniel Bussier, Jno. Young, Garret Buckhorn, Henry Engle, Jno. Curtis—*For Southwark.*

Resolved, That George Latimer be, and he hereby is, appointed Treasurer, to receive and pay over such moneys as the Committee from time to time may direct.

Resolved, That the resolution under which the ward committees for the city and adjoining districts were appointed, for the purpose of forming and organizing volunteer companies, &c., be published, together with the names of the citizens composing the several committees, and that the said Committee report from time to time to the Sub-Committee heretofore appointed by the General Committee.

Resolved, That James Whitehead, James Josiah, and Peter Miercken be a Committee to inquire into the state of the State magazine, and to take such measures relating thereto as they may deem necessary for the safety of the city.

Whereupon adjourned to meet on the 27th, at 7 o'clock, at the same place.

JNO. GOODMAN,
Secretary.

SECOND MEETING.

PHILADELPHIA, *August* 27*th*, 1814.

The Committee met.

Present:—Messrs. Biddle, Goodman, Sergeant, Latimer, Thompson, Palmer, Williams, Groves, McFaden, Peltz, Raguet, Ferguson, McMullin, Eyre, Reed, Naglee, Cadwalader, Josiah, Ross, Whitehead, Miercken.

The Committee of Correspondence reported that they had written to the Governor of the State of Delaware, to a gentleman in Wilmington, and likewise to one in Chester, relative to the present state of affairs and the measures adopted, and that they will also send communications to, and correspond with, the Governor of the State of New Jersey. The above received as a report in part, and the Committee continued.

The Committee of Arrangement reported progress in their inquiry respecting arms, &c., and were continued.

The Committee for the Defence of the Delaware and procuring Seamen reported in writing as follows, viz.:

"That they have applied to Commodore Murray for such gun-boats and barges as are not immediately in service, to be officered and manned by them with volunteers; that he has offered the Committee three gun-boats and one barge, completely fitted with their armament; that the Marine Artillery, commanded by Captain Ansley, amounting to seventy men, have offered their services to man them; that they have given notice in the public papers to masters, mates, pilots, and seamen to come forward and volunteer their services in the defence of the Delaware; that the families and wives of such as are in want shall be supplied while in service.

"Your Committee also recommend that a survey be immediately taken of the breadth of the channel over the bar near Fort Mifflin; that a sufficient number of small vessels be procured to stop the same, to be filled with scuttles and ballast, ready to sink on the approach of the enemy.

"Likewise that application be made to the Governor of New Jersey for permission to erect a fort near Red Bank, on the Jersey shore. Volunteers to the number of sixty have already offered their services for that duty.

"That your Committee be authorized to order the shipping to be removed from the wharves up the river."

Whereupon ordered, that the above Committee take measures to sound the channel and make inquiry respecting vessels to be sunk, when necessary, and that they report as soon as practicable. The other recommendations in their report were ordered to lie on the table for the present.

The Committee of Public Defence and for organizing the Citizens and Military Bodies made a report, whereof the following is a copy, viz.:

"The Committee of Defence appointed under the authority of the General Committee, begs leave respectfully to report that the following measures have been taken:

"Your Committee has given written instructions to the brigade-majors of the two brigades of the First Division of militia, forthwith to furnish the Committee with abstracts of the effective force of their respective brigades, and to muster their brigades for inspection as speedily as possible, in order that any deficiencies in arms or accoutrements may be noted and provided for.

"Your Committee waited upon General Bloomfield, and made an arrangement for proceeding, on Monday next, attended by the officers of engineers in this quarter, to examine the approaches to the city, in order to fix upon such positions as it may be advisable to strengthen by the voluntary labor of the citizens. For this purpose Captain Babcock and the other officers of engineers are to be immediately ordered to the city, and placed under the direction of your Committee.

"In answer to the inquiries of your Committee as to the force of regulars, volunteers, and militia intended to be employed in defence of the city and its environs, the General stated the—

Regulars fit for duty.. 256
Volunteers marched or marching 502
Drafted militia marching 430
Volunteers to march on Tuesday, about 300

The two brigades, amounting to 3000 effectives, including the above corps, are to be encamped as soon as possible.

"Your Committee impressed upon the General the expectation and wish of the citizens, that the volunteers and militia from this quarter shall not be so far detached as to deprive the city and its environs of their co-operation in case of the sudden appearance of the enemy, and the General has engaged to impart that expectation and wish to the General Government.

"Your Committee has agreed with the General, that in case of sudden alarm the rendezvous of the enrolled citizens shall be in Broad Street, with their right on Chestnut Street, extending southwardly.

"Signals of alarm will be published in general orders, as requested by your Committee.

"In compliance with the request of your Committee, the General will immediately order that no vessel or boat shall pass the fort without examination, and that a boat shall row guard at night.

"In case of a sudden muster in consequence of the expected approach of the enemy, muskets will be delivered to the militia at the rendezvous, and musket cartridges, there being 5000 stand of arms of excellent quality in the U. S. Arsenal; fixed ammunition is also in preparation there: 2000 rifles wanting repair, and

1000 sabres, may at any time be had on the requisition of the Committee.

"At the request of your Committee the General has ordered on duty thirty men of the First Troop of Cavalry, under Captain Ross, who is to march to-morrow to form a chain of videttes from the city to Port Penn, on the Delaware, and the mouth of the Elk River, in order that intelligence may be rapidly conveyed of the enemy's movements.

"An application having been made by certain of our fellow-citizens, to obtain a warrant from your Committee authorizing them to raise one or more companies of infantry for the defence of the city and its environs, and to organize those companies into a battalion or regiment, to act under their own officers, subject to the directions of the Committee. Such a warrant was accordingly granted; and it is the intention of your Committee to promote such associations as far as may be practicable.

"General Bloomfield having declared to your Committee that no moneys of the United States are now under his control, it becomes necessary that immediate provision be made, by the direction of the Committee of Finances, to place a considerable fund in the hands of the Treasurer, as expenses will be immediately incurred."

The above report was accepted, and the Committee continued.

The Committee appointed to apply to the corporations of the city, Northern Liberties, and Southwark, reported that applications were made to those of the city and

Northern Liberties, and that they will apply to that of Southwark, Moyamensing, and Spring Garden on Monday. Report accepted, and Committee continued.

On motion,

Resolved, That a committee be appointed to procure a room in a central part of the city as an office for the transaction of the business of the General Committee, and that they be empowered to employ a person to assist the Secretary in recording the transactions of the said Committee. Whereupon Messrs. Thompson and McMullin were appointed.

The Committee appointed to inquire into the state and condition of the State magazine, reported as follows, viz.:

"The State magazine contains about 900 to 1000 barrels of powder, or quarter casks 4000, the property of, viz.:

United States, about	1200
Wm. Rogers	800
Geo. Hunter	800
S Gratz & Brothers	175
James Twaddell	350
Michael Dixon	240
A. McCall	300
In small parcels	1135
	5000

"Forty quarter casks, the property of State of Pennsylvania, in the name of F. Facring.

"The United States magazine contains a very large quantity of powder."

The said Committee also reported a written communication from Jno. Keemle, Keeper of the State magazine, which is placed on file.

The following general orders of the commander of the district were read, viz.:

FOURTH MILITARY DISTRICT.
HEADQUARTERS,
PHILADELPHIA, *August* 27*th*, 1814.

GENERAL ORDERS.—Captain Ross, with thirty men of his troop of cavalry, are called into service, to act as vidcttes between this city and the Delaware and the Chesapeake.

The signal for alarm will be six guns, fired in quick succession, at Fort Mifflin, at the Navy Yard, and at the Arsenal, and by the drums of the city and Northern Liberties beating "to arms." And immediately thereupon all the militia will parade equipped completely for the field, right upon Chestnut Street, extending southwardly on Broad Street.

The officers of the Topographical Department and Corps of Engineers will report themselves on Monday next to General Jonathan Williams, who is pleased to undertake the superintendence of the erection of works in and near this city for its defence.

By order of
GENERAL BLOOMFIELD.

(Signed)   WM. DUANE,
            Adjutant-General.

A letter from John Purden, relative to defence and propositions for the means, was read, and referred to the Committee of Defence for the Delaware.

A communication from A. J. Dallas, Esq., relative to the organization of the citizens, was read, and referred to the committee appointed for that purpose.

Resolved, That a committee be appointed to report rules and regulations for the government of this body. Whereupon Messrs. Sergeant, Leib, and Reed were appointed for that purpose.

Resolved, That a committee be appointed immediately to proceed to the Department of War, and confer with the Secretary upon the subject of the defence of this district, and that said committee make the necessary inquiries of the Secretary of the Navy relative to the men employed in the building of the seventy-four in the Delaware, and on other subjects which may appear proper and necessary. Whereupon Messrs. Eyre and Cadwalader were appointed the committee.

Ordered, That all warrants to be drawn on the Treasurer be signed by the Chairman and Secretary.

Resolved, That Messrs. Cadwalader and Eyre be a committee to wait upon General Bloomfield, the commanding officer of this district, and inquire of him his reasons for issuing his after-orders dispensing with the services of the militia of the Second Brigade, and that they report, if practicable, immediately.

The Committee having retired, after some time reported:

"That General Bloomfield, to their inquiries, replied, that he had issued no counter-orders with respect to the Second Brigade, and that Brigade-Inspector Tryon must have mistaken him. 'That the Second Brigade had not been included in his orders.'"

Approved, and Committee discharged.

Resolved, That the Chairman and Secretary wait upon General Bloomfield and request him to call out the draft of the Second Brigade.

The Chairman announced to the meeting the resolutions of the Directors of the Bank of Pennsylvania, offering the loan of a sum of money to the Committee.

Mr. Brown stated that the City Councils had this evening appropriated 300,000 dollars for the defence of the city.

Adjourned to meet on the 28th instant, at 3 o'clock P.M.

JNO. GOODMAN,
Secretary.

THIRD MEETING.

PHILADELPHIA, *August* 28*th*, 1814.

The Committee met.

Present:—Messrs. Biddle, Goodman, Leib, Brown, Palmer, Peltz, Latimer, Ferguson, Sergeant, Thompson, Reed, Raguet, Whitehead, Snyder.

The minutes of the last meeting were read.

The Committee appointed to report a system of rules and regulations for the government of the General Committee, reported that they had made some progress in the business committed to them, and were continued.

The Committee appointed to procure a room, reported that they have procured a room for the sittings of the General Committee in the County Court-house, which will be ready to morrow for the reception of the Committee; which was approved, and the Committee were discharged. With respect to *the second part* of the resolution under which the said Committee was to act, relating to the appointment of an assistant secretary, that subject was referred to the Secretary of this Committee.

The Committee of Correspondence reported that they had written to the Governor of New Jersey.

Resolved, That a committee of accounts be appointed, to consist of three persons. Messrs. Hawkins, McMullin, and Whitehead were appointed.

The Committee for that purpose appointed, reported the following detail of property, belonging to the State of Pennsylvania, in the City of Philadelphia and its vicinity, independent of muskets distributed to the different regiments in the First Division of Pennsylvania Militia, viz.:

		qrs.	lbs.
40 kegs powder, wg.	10	0	0
9 do. musket-balls.	14	3	15
3 do. buckshot.	5	0	0

A quantity of iron shot of different sizes in the State House cellar.
1 chest of iron shot at the late dwelling of Ct. Biddle, Esq., deceased.
4 boxes musket-balls, in same residence.
A quantity of old cartouch-boxes, rifle-pouches, &c., left since the revolutionary war.
1280 muskets and bayonets, in complete order for service.
1500 cartouch-boxes and belts, in complete order for service.
1500 bayonet scabbards.
1000 brushes and wires.
1000 wipers.
120 screw-drivers.
120 ball screws.
200 camp-kettles, all in complete order.
About 20 brass field pieces, 4-pounders (one of them 6-pounder).
2 brass field pieces, 12-pounders.
6 or 8 old iron guns.
32 wall tents, and flies for ditto.   All new.
160 common tents.   All new.
10 bell tents.   "
1 hospital tent.   "
Poles for the above.   "
74 old common tents.
A quantity of old tents at the City Hospital.

(F. F.)

Ordered, That the Secretary publish the names of the Standing Committees, with the respective duties, for the information of the public.

Ordered, That the following note be signed by the Chairman and Secretary, and published, with the names of the members of which the Sub-Committee is composed, viz.:

"The Committee of Defence, desirous of embodying all the physical force of this section of the State as promptly as possible, give notice that any number of individuals who may be desirous of organizing companies, battalions, and regiments, will receive their authority for such organization on application to the Sub-Committee."

Resolved, That the Committee for Supplies of Arms. Ammunition, &c., be instructed to call upon the Deputy Quartermaster-General of this Commonwealth, and, in conjunction with him, and, if necessary, with any other officers of the State or Union, to have the guns. arms. ammunition, and stores belonging to this Commonwealth, immediately put in a state of complete preparation for service.

Resolved, That two members be added to the present number of the Sub-Committee of Defence. Messrs. Palmer and Whitehead were appointed for that purpose.

Resolved, That a committee be appointed to prepare an address from the committee to the citizens of this district, requesting them immediately to hold meetings for the purpose of making the necessary arrangements for volunteer enrolments for military purposes; also for making arrangements for forming fatigue parties for the works intended to be erected under the directions of the General Committee; and further

Resolved, That in order to promote the important objects above expressed, the same committee be directed to call meetings of the citizens of the several wards and townships, at such times and places as they may deem most expedient, and to request one member at least of each of the ward and district committees already appointed, to attend there with their colleagues. Messrs. Reed, Leib, Palmer, Sergeant, and Groves were appointed a committee to carry the two above resolutions into execution.

A member stated that one of the gun-boats, manned with volunteers, had gone down the Delaware.

Resolved, That the stated meetings hereafter be at 4 o'clock P.M., daily.

Adjourned.

JNO. GOODMAN,
Secretary.

FOURTH MEETING.

PHILADELPHIA, *August* 29*th*, 1814.

The Committee met at the County Court-house room.

Present:—Messrs. Biddle, Goodman, Connelly, Latimer, Brown, Groves, Miercken, Huff, Peltz, Leib, Palmer, Sergeant, Williams, Ferguson, Reed, Naglee, Whitehead, Geyer, Leiper, Ronaldson, McFaden, Thompson, McMullin, Josiah.

A letter was read from James Ronaldson, dated Lancaster, 27th inst., concerning the condition of the gun-carriages at Fort Mifflin, and recommending the citizens of Philadelphia to write to their friends in the country towns to have meetings called, for the purpose of bringing the whole militia into action for the defence of Philadelphia. Ordered to lie on the table.

The Committee for the Supply of Arms, &c., reported as follows: a letter signed by Timothy Banger, for Callender Irvine, Commissary-General, of this date, informing that there are in the U. S. Arsenal about 9000 American, French, English, and German muskets fit for service, and about 6000 muskets of above kind, part of which could soon be made ready to issue; also field ordnance and howitzers, fixed ammunition, musket-balls, cartridges, cartouch-boxes and belts, bayonet scabbards and belts, gun slings, screw-drivers, brushes and wires, ball screws.

Camp equipage as follows, viz.: fascine hatchets, tents and flies, shovels, camp-kettles, mess-pans, axes and slings, broad-axes, spades; also a very large quantity of powder.

The said letter also referring the Committee to Lieut. Baker, who represents the Commissary-General of Ordnance, for information whether the above, except camp equipage, can be placed at the disposal of the Committee of Defence; also for further information concerning the condition of the above; also informing the Committee that on requisition made for the purpose of defence, sanctioned and signed by General Bloomfield, the quantity of camp equipage required will be furnished by the Commissary-General, so far as in the arsenal. For the particulars of this information see the above letter, which was referred to the Committee of Defence.

The Committee for organizing the Citizens, &c., reported a letter from Daniel Sharp, Brigade-Inspector, of 28th inst., to Jonathan Williams, Chairman of said Committee, informing that the following is the effective force of the First Brigade, First Division, Pennsylvania Militia, viz.:

6527 cavalry, artillery, infantry, and militia.

Artillery 180
Volunteer infantry 280
Militia 600
                                                                        ———
                                                                        1060

In actual service, leaving 5467 effective men in the First Brigade.

Copy of above letter ordered to lie on the table.

The Sub-Committee of Defence reported as follows. viz.:

"That it is their intention immediately to erect field fortifications on the heights and most important passes to the entrances of the city, to wit, from the west side of Schuylkill, commencing at such places as General Williams, and the United States engineers under his command, shall deem proper, and for this purpose the aid of the citizens and the necessary tools will be wanted. The Committee therefore take the liberty of offering the following resolutions, viz.:

"*Resolved*, That the Sub-Committee of Defence be authorized to call to their assistance such topographical engineers and men of science, whether professional or not, as may be willing to afford their services; and that if the said Sub-Committee should want the aid of any officer or soldier in the corps that have marched, or may hereafter march, they be authorized, in the name of the Committee, to ask of the commanding general a furlough for such officer or soldier; also,

"*Resolved,* That the said Committee be authorized to purchase intrenching tools, instruments and implements for the purpose of erecting fortifications."

The said Committee made further report, viz.:

"That General Snyder offers the services of such part of the County Brigade as is held in requisition, to take the field whenever called on; That Mr. Frederick Eckstein, No. 71 Locust Street, offers his services, in case the topographical department should have occasion for them; that Mr. Patterson, professor, &c., offers his services, in anything he is competent to, to the Committee."

Whereupon the Chairman of the Sub-Committee of Defence was directed to associate Mr. Patterson with the topographical department.

The Committee for the Defence of the River Delaware reported a communication from General Williams as follows, viz.:

"The Chairman of the Sub-Committee, by invitation of the Committee for the Defence on the Delaware, went down the river this day with them. The weather was too boisterous to sound, &c., but a position was examined on the Jersey shore bearing within half a mile of the place where obstructions may be placed. It is the opinion of the Chairman that a battery might be thrown up here which would effectually command that point, and prevent the enemy from taking up the obstructions, at same time being capable to protect itself against a landing on its flank and attack in its rear from such a force as might come in boats.

"August 28th, 1814."

The Committee for the Defence of the River Delaware also made the following report, viz.:

"That they (accompanied by General Williams, who politely offered his service) have surveyed the channel over the bar at Fort Mifflin, and to the westward of the fort, and the different sites for erecting a fort; that the breadth of the channel over the bar 300 fathoms, and it will take 12 vessels from 100 to 200 tons to stop the same, and 3 others of a smaller size to stop the channel lately made to the eastward of the pier sunk in the middle of the river; that a battery of 4 heavy guns may be erected on the pier, which would command the channel and be covered from an attack by Fort Mifflin; that a fort erected about one mile above the mouth of Mantua Creek, on the Jersey shore, will annoy the enemy on their approach up the river, and command the channel, which, with Fort Mifflin put in order, will prevent the enemy from approaching the city by water. The channel to the westward of the fort is shallow and narrow, having only 12 feet water at high tide within half a mile of the fort; that a small battery on the wharf at the hospital on Province Island, and one at the picket-guard at Fort Mifflin, with a gun-boat in the channel, would prevent the enemy's boats from getting into the Schuylkill; that it will be necessary to have a small vessel, with two row-boats, a captain, and ten hands kept in constant pay to attend to them, to be under the control of your Committee, for the purpose of transporting men and material."

A letter, accompanied with a draft for the defence of the Delaware, was read, and referred to the Committee for the Defence of the Delaware.

An application from Wm. Armour, stating that he had been drafted into the military requisition from the President of the United States, and requesting the Committee to grant him the privilege of joining a volunteer corps, under marching orders, being read, the following resolution was adopted by the Committee, viz.:

Resolved, That in the opinion of the Committee any militiaman who is drafted, and under the present requisition from the President of the United States, and who shall perform a tour of duty in any volunteer corps under the present call, ought not to be fined in the militia.

On motion,

Resolved, That the Chairman and Secretary be a committee to wait upon General Bloomfield and request of him that no part of the garrison of Fort Mifflin be removed therefrom; also to request that he will give orders for the immediate removal of all powder not likely to be wanted in this quarter, from the U. S. Arsenal to some convenient place of safety.

Resolved, That the different committees appointed by the Board be authorized to accept the services of as many of their fellow-citizens as may tender them, to aid them in the execution of such plans as they may think proper for the same purposes.

The Committee adjourned for half an hour, in order to afford the Chairman and Secretary an opportunity to wait on General Bloomfield, to make the request contained in the resolution preceding the foregoing. The Chairman and Secretary having returned, the Committee resumed their duties, and the Chairman made report—

"That the Committee appointed for the purpose had waited on General Bloomfield, who assured them that none of the force at Fort Mifflin would be withdrawn; that he had ordered some infantry troops away from the Lazaretto to Kennet's Square, and that the powder in the U. S. Arsenal Magazine that was not likely to be wanted would be removed as fast as possible, that considerable quantities had been already removed."

Whereupon the Committee was discharged.

General Williams stated that he had received a letter in French on the subject of defence, which was translated and read in English. The letter was referred to the Committee of the Delaware.

Resolved, That the Committee of Defence take measures for having the ordnance in the State Arsenal put in complete order, and for having some of the heavy ordnance put on carriages. The Committee appointed for the purpose reported a set of rules and regulations for the government of the General Committee at their meetings, which were ordered to lie on the table.

An anonymous letter on the subject of defence was read, and referred to the Committee for the Defence of the Delaware.

Mr. McMullin stated that the corporation of the District of Southwark had appropriated $20,000 towards defraying the expense of defending the city and districts.

Mr. Leiper and Mr. Ronaldson, the Committee appointed to proceed with a letter from this Committee to the Governor of Pennsylvania, and for other purposes, reported that they had performed the duties assigned to them, and presented a letter from the Governor, directed to Charles Biddle, Esquire, which was read, and of which the following is a copy, viz.:

HARRISBURG, 28th August, 1814.

SIR:

Impressed with the importance of the subject of your communication under date of the 26th inst., and of information previously received through other channels, I have issued general orders (of which I do myself the honor to inclose a copy) for the assembling at Philadelphia a military force which, I trust, will prove sufficient to protect the City of Philadelphia, and for the repelling of any enemy that may be thrown on our shore. The other matter contained in your communication, in the nature of queries, can be answered when an investigation and closing of the accounts by the Adjutant-General has been had; nor can I perceive it to be of importance to know whether a portion of any specified appropriation is to be applied for the defence of any particular section of the State. The present militia law, however imperfect in many of its parts it is discovered to be, in its 29th section has made provision commensurate with any necessary expenditure connected with the militia system. So soon as the necessary arrangements are here made to permit my absence I shall have the honor to visit Philadelphia. I beg you to accept for the Committee of Defence, and for yourself personally, assurances of consideration and esteem.

(Signed)   SIMON SNYDER.
To CHARLES BIDDLE, ESQUIRE.

The above letter, and copy of general orders inclosed, are on file.

A letter from the city corporation to the Secretary of War, and his answer thereto, were read, and ordered to lie on the table. The following are copies of said letters, viz.:

To THE SECRETARY OF WAR.
SIR :

As a Committee of the Select and Common Councils of this city, we have before had the honor of communicating with you on the subject of the defence of the Bay and River Delaware, and we have lately had a conference with Captain Babcock, of the Corps of Engineers, on the same subject. We find, from his statement, that he does not think himself justified in doing more than constructing two martello towers. We have this afternoon had a meeting of our Councils, and have laid the plan of constructing such towers before them, and also stated to them that you had left it optional with the corporation either to have these erected or to establish permanent fortifications, using the towers as auxiliary works. The members of the Councils and all those citizens with whom we have conversed, are decidedly averse to the construction of martello towers only. We therefore take the liberty of suggesting that if you will authorize us to construct a fortification consisting of a battery of thirty-two 24-pounders on the Pea Patch, and suitable fortifications on Newbold's Point and Red Bank, we shall be enabled, after the example of our sister city of New York, with the assistance of volunteer service from our citizens, to defend our city and the shores of the Delaware with much less expense, and altogether to our satisfaction, than it is possible for the United States to do. Such expense, however, as may be incurred, we should expect that the United States would reimburse. We will only add how anxious our citizens are on this subject of defence, and how satisfactory it would be to us to have a speedy communication from you on the subject of this letter.

We have the honor to be, respectfully, &c.

(*Copy of the answer.*)

MONTGOMERY COURT-HOUSE,
25*th August*, 1814.

GENTLEMEN :

I have received your letter, and, as you request, commit the business of fortifying the Delaware to yourselves.

If Captain Babcock is unnecessary to your plans and operations, I wish him to repair immediately to Baltimore, where he may be much wanted, and you will oblige me by making this known to him.

I am, gentlemen, very respectfully,
Yr. obedt. servant,
(Signed)   JOHN ARMSTRONG.
Messrs. Leiper, Brown and others, Philadelphia.

The Committee adjourned.
JNO. GOODMAN,
Secretary.

FIFTH MEETING.

Philadelphia, 30*th August*, 1814.

The Committee met.

Present:—Messrs. Biddle, Goodman, Sergeant, Leiper, Leib, Ferguson, Peltz, Brown, Miercken, Williams, Reed, Josiah, Ronaldson, Steel, Groves, McFaden, Thompson, Geyer, Connelly, Palmer.

The minutes of the last meeting were read.

A letter from Wm. Duncan and Henry Lentz, inquiring of the Committee whether they considered the enrolling of the citizens generally (on the plan progressed in) to be superseded by the general orders of the Governor of Pennsylvania of the 27th inst., being read, it was

Resolved, That the Sub-Committee for the Northern Liberties and Penn Township be directed to proceed with their enrollments, and in the organization of the companies, as soon as possible.

A letter from M'l Eyre and Th. Cadwalader, on the subject of the present state of defence at Baltimore, was read, and ordered to lie on the table.

A letter from General Bloomfield, and one inclosed from Robert McKoy, contractor with the Government of the United States, requesting a loan of money to enable him to perform his contract, were read. These letters were referred to the Committee of Supplies to make report thereon. After some time they were taken up by special order, and the said Committee requested to take them under consideration immediately. The Committee retired, and after some time reported, verbally, that the contract of Mr. McKoy is confined to supplies for the Pennsylvania troops, and that there would be no risk in loaning the money either to Mr. McKoy or General Bloomfield. Whereupon it was

Resolved, That the Committee of Supplies be authorized to advance to Robert McKoy, contractor, or to the commanding general, the sum of five thousand dollars, upon such terms and in such manner as they may think proper, and that the Chairman be authorized, upon the requisition of the said Committee, to draw upon the Treasurer for said sum of five thousand dollars.

A letter from Tench Coxe, on the subject of blankets, and embracing other objects, was read, and laid upon the table.

A letter from Charles W. Hare, accompanied with documents, relating to a dispute with John Barker, was read, but the reading of the documents was postponed. The letter and documents were ordered to lie on the table.

Mr. Thompson stated that the fixed ammunition had been ordered from the U. S. Arsenal to York, and suggested the propriety of obtaining assistance to make up cartridges. A member also stated that one thousand stand of arms are also about to be sent off by the order of the Adjutant-General.

The subject of the above information was referred to the Committee of Correspondence, who were instructed to write to the Governor, requesting him not to send off any ammunition, arms, &c., from this city or its vicinity. A letter to said purport was written by the said Committee to the Governor, a copy of which is on file.

A letter from Lewis Rush and Joseph Hertzog, tendering the services of the Philadelphia Senior Military Association to this Committee, was read, and referred to the Sub-Committee of Defence.

Letters from Capt. Ross and Lieut. Rush, of the videttes established between Philadelphia and Port Penn and Elkton, were read, and ordered to lie on the table.

Resolved, That a committee be appointed to inquire into the state of the telegraph on the Delaware. Referred to the Committee of Defence on the Delaware.

A letter from Dr. John C. Otto, offering his services to the Committee as physician, was read, and referred to the Committee appointed to distribute aid to the wives and children of those who are in service.

Resolved, That the Committee for Supplies, &c., be authorized and instructed to call to their assistance, immediately, as many persons willing to give their services as they shall deem necessary; also,

Resolved, That the said Committee be instructed to take immediate measures for having in readiness medical supplies of all sorts, and for forming a medical and chirurgical staff.

Resolved, That John Dennis and Jacob Kugler be added to the Committee for raising Volunteers in South Mulberry Ward.

Resolved, That the Secretary be excused from serving as a member of the Committee of Supplies, on account of the other duties he has to perform, and that Mr. Ronaldson be substituted in his place as a member of said Committee.

Resolved, That Messrs. Sergeant, Connelly, and Groves be a Committee to procure a store-house and storekeeper, and, as soon as the same are provided, to request contributions from the citizens in the name of this Committee.

A letter from Thomas Lloyd, on the subject of a topographical map of the country between the cities of Washington and New York, was read, and ordered to lie on the table.

The Sub-Committee of Defence made report as follows, viz.:

"That they have taken into consideration the letter in French addressed to the General Committee by Mr. M. L. Merlin; that the writer of said letter makes a proposition to have organized a legion of people of color, to be called the Black Legion, and to be commanded by white officers; that it seems improper to the Committee to have the proposed legion organized at this time, when there is so short a supply of arms and accoutrements for our white citizens; but the Committee think, that under a proper regulation, these people of color might be employed as fatigue parties on the works, to act in a manner detached from the white citizens who may be so employed."

This report was referred to the same sub-committee, with orders to act on it as they shall see proper.

An anonymous letter (signed Archimedes) was read, and referred to the Committee of Defence.

A letter from John E. Addiks, of which the following is a copy, was read, and referred to the Committee of Supplies, viz.:

PHILADELPHIA, 30*th August*, 1814.

CHARLES BIDDLE, ESQUIRE.

SIR:—Presenting you with a sample of a parcel of muskets, I beg you to observe that the quantity is about 3000, and the price $14½. The whole of them are made at Philadelphia by Mr. Kunkle, whose name is stamped on the locks of them, and who has, since a number of years, manufactured, under contract, for the Government of the United States. The muskets are proved, have the U. S. calibre, and are warranted to be new and of the best quality. Should the Committee of Safety think proper to effect a purchase of them, you'll be sensible of the necessity of doing so without loss of time, since the scarcity of arms, and the general demand for them, prevents me from giving a refusal.

I am, respectfully, &c.,

(Signed)   JOHN E. ADDIKS.

P.S.—Any communication I request to be left at the bar of the Coffee-house, Second Street.

I have about 60 muskets, second-hand, at $11, but in good order, and send also a sample of them if desired.

(Signed)   J. E. A.

Resolved, To meet in future at the Common Council chamber.

Adjourned.

JNO. GOODMAN,
Secretary.

SIXTH MEETING.

PHILADELPHIA, 31*st August*, 1814.

The Committee met.

Present:—Messrs. Biddle, Goodman, McFaden, Whitehead, Connelly, Brown, Thompson, Leiper, Palmer, McMullin, Groves, Steel, Latimer, Reed, Sergeant, Ronaldson, Williams, Josiah, Barker, Ferguson, Naglee.

Resolved, That the word "Topographical," in the resolution concerning Topographical Engineers, &c., passed on the 29th inst., be struck out, and the word "Military" be inserted in its place. (See resolution, page 35.)

General Williams, from the Sub-Committee of Defence, reported that they had made the following appointments, in pursuance of the above-mentioned resolution, viz.:

Military Engineers.

Chief—General Williams.
Second—Colonel Foncin.

For the Topographical Department.

Dr. Patterson,
Mr. Strickland,   } And assistants.
Mr. John Biddle,

For the Direction of Labor.

Messrs. Souder, Wesener, Eckstein, Belon, Eckfeldt, Cloud.

For Occasional Agencies.

Messrs. Kingston, Evers, &c.

A letter from B. Chew, Jr., Lieutenant of the Franklin Flying Artillery, requesting a loan from the Committee of $500, was read, and referred to the Committee of Supplies.

A letter from N. G. Dufief, inclosing a plan of defence, was read, and ordered to lie on the table.

A letter from Wm. Davy, offering blue cloth, coatings, and blanketing for sale, was read, and referred to the Committee of Supplies.

A letter, signed "Experience," recommending the employment of riflemen, was read, and ordered to lie on the table.

Letters from Drs. Heylin, Hewson, Kugler, and Calhoun, and a verbal offer from Dr. Gillespie (through Mr. Latimer), of services as a physician or surgeon, were referred to the Committee of Supplies, and for forming a medical and chirurgical staff.

A letter, dated at the Philadelphia Navy Yard, from Joseph Chambers, concerning repeating arms, was read, and referred to the Sub-Committee of Defence.

REPORTS OF COMMITTEES.

The Sub-Committee of Defence made report, that applications are frequently made to them for arms and accoutrements; that they therefore request the attention of the General Committee to this object, in such manner as they may deem most proper; but so that the possession of the arms and accoutrements intended to be distributed to the volunteers, in the order of their organization, may be in the General Committee of Defence; and so that there may be no doubt either as to the place of deposit of said arms, &c., or as to the power over them.

Whereupon it was

Resolved, That Messrs. Latimer, Groves, and Ronaldson be a Committee to wait on General Bloomfield, and inquire of him upon what terms the arms and accoutrements now in the U. S. Arsenal may be procured, so as to be placed under the direction of this Committee, or such part of said arms, &c., as belonged to the Lady Johnson's cargo.

The said Committee of Defence made further report, that Mr. Mellon had waited on them with a military machine, which in their opinion deserves attention. It was

Resolved, That the said subject be referred to the Committee of Supplies.

On the recommendation of the said Sub-Committee of Defence, it was

Resolved, That the offer made by the Senior Military Association of their services be accepted, and that the Chairman of the General Committee be instructed to inform the said Association thereof.

The Committee of Supplies reported as follows, viz.:
"That they have appointed Mr. Carswell a temporary commissary, to furnish rations to a corps of volunteers which arrived yesterday in this neighborhood. That they have appointed a committee to apply to all the gunsmiths in the city and suburbs to ascertain what amount of arms they have to repair, and how soon they could be fit for service.

"That they have directed the Committees of Enrollment of the respective wards and districts, to collect the public arms within their several bounds, and deposit them in the store-house of the General Committee.

"That they have applied to Drs. Wistar, Cathrall, Barton, Chapman, and Otto to aid them in the organization of a medical staff.

"That they have applied to the Board of Health and to the President of the Board of Inspectors of the Prison, for the use of the hospital and the new prison for barracks for the troops which may arrive here."

The applications were granted.

"That they have appointed a committee for preparing and mounting artillery, and procuring the necessary apparatus.

"That they have agreed to place the 5000 dollars voted by the General Committee on the application for Mr. McKoy, U. S. contractor, in the hands of General Bloomfield."

The Committee of Supplies also reported that "The Chairman of the General Committee had advanced the 5000 dollars for Mr. McKoy, taking General Bloomfield's note to Mr. Biddle at 30 days; that had also advanced 300 dollars to Captain Ross, for the use of the videttes." Whereupon,

Ordered, That a warrant be drawn in favor of said Chairman, for the said 5000 dollars and 300 dollars.

The Committee for the Defence of the Delaware reported:

"That sixty carpenters have volunteered their services at the Navy Yard, and are now employed in making the gun-carriages and preparing the stuff for the platforms at Fort Mifflin; that the platforms will be ready to be sent down on Friday morning; that Mr. Thomas Davis is directed to repair the pier, where the battery is to be erected, and they anticipate in a few days to have it ready for the engineers; that Mr. Flanagan, pilot, has offered his boat, and volunteered his own services to the Committee, for transporting men and materials; and General Steel has tendered to them the two barges belonging to the Custom-house. The expense of the above will be—

2 officers at $30..	$60
12 hands at $15	180
	$240 per month.

"That $30,000 will be wanting to purchase fifteen vessels to stop the channel; they will sell for as much, if not used, as the first cost, the materials for one-third the price."

The above report was ordered to lie on the table.

The Committee appointed to procure a Store-house and employ a Store-keeper, and to give notice that the Committee are ready to receive Donations, made report:

"That they have procured for a store-house the room in the east wing of the State-house, intended for a courtroom; that they have employed James McGlathery as store-keeper, and have given notice in the newspapers that they are ready to receive 'Donations.'"

Ordered to lie on the table.

The Committee of Correspondence reported:

"That they have written to the Governor of Pennsylvania on the subject of the fixed ammunition and arms ordered to be sent off from the Arsenal, and that they had taken other measures relative thereto."

A copy of the above letter is on file.

Mr. Connelly and General Williams were permitted to withdraw for the rest of the day.

Resolved, That Captain Huff be excused from serving on the Committee of Supplies, and that Mr. Reed be added, as a member, to said Committee.

A letter from Captain Ross was read by the Chairman.

Resolved, That the Chairman be instructed to write to the Secretary of War, and, through his agency, endeavor to obtain immediately a supply of arms and accoutrements from Albany, Harper's Ferry, and any other place from which they may be obtained.

Resolved, That the Committee of Supplies be instructed to inquire into the expediency of providing biscuit and salt provisions, to supply any demands that may be made upon them by the troops which may arrive in this neighborhood, and for whom provision is not made by the General or State Government.

Resolved, That the sum of one thousand dollars be placed in the hands of the Committee for the Defence of the Delaware, and that the Chairman draw an order accordingly.

Resolved, That the Committee of Supplies take into consideration the propriety of arming with pikes, and if approved, to procure any number not exceeding two thousand.

Resolved, That the following article concerning the banks be inserted in the newspapers of this city, viz.:

"The General Committee of Defence, after a careful attention to the recent measure adopted by the different banks in this city, of suspending the issue of specie, are satisfied that there is nothing in this measure which ought to occasion alarm, or produce a doubt, in the minds of their fellow-citizens, as to the solidity of these institutions; on the contrary, they believe it to be a measure of wise precaution, which gives them an additional claim to public confidence.

"The Committee have also the satisfaction to announce, that the Bank of Pennsylvania has this morning agreed to advance the sum of three hundred thousand dollars, if required, for the public service, and they have reason to believe that the other banks will, if there should be occasion, make similar advances.

"The patriotic feelings of our fellow-citizens cannot fail to appreciate the value of such a disposition of the moneyed institutions, and to discern in it the grounds of a very strong claim to the public support.

"The Committee therefore earnestly call upon their

fellow-citizens, by all means to support the measure that has been thus adopted by the banks.

     " (Signed) CHARLES BIDDLE,
                "*Chairman.*
" (Signed) John Goodman,
      "*Secretary.*
"Aug. 31st, 1814."

Copies of the above were sent to the *Democratic Herald*, and to Messrs. Bronson and Jackson.

Adjourned.
           JNO. GOODMAN,
             Secretary.

SEVENTH MEETING.

     Philadelphia, *September* 1*st*, 1814.

The Committee met.

Present:—Messrs. Biddle, Goodman, Whitehead, Steel, Palmer, Peltz, Sergeant, McFaden, Latimer, Huff, Leiper, Williams, Josiah, McMullin, Miercken, Leip, Thompson, Geyer, Groves, Naglee, Brown, Palmer.

The minutes of the last meeting were read.

A letter from Manuel Eyre and Thos. Cadwalader, dated Georgetown, 29th August, was read, and ordered to lie on the table.

A letter from General Bloomfield, in answer to the inquiries yesterday ordered to be made, concerning the manner of procuring the arms and accoutrements in the

U. S. Arsenal, was read, and referred to the Committee of Supplies.

A letter from E. Gordon, Chairman, and Joshua Jones, Secretary, of a meeting of the Townships of Oxford, Lower Dublin, Byberry, &c., and making inquiries concerning supplies of arms, was read. Also a letter from W. Guier, J. M. Wallace, Jr., and T. B. Zantzinger, a Committee of the Philadelphia Grenadiers, inquiring whether arms can be had for said company, was read. Whereupon,

Resolved, That the Chairman be requested to inform those who have applied, or may apply, for arms, that the Committee has taken measures to procure supplies of them, and will answer their inquiries in the course of a few days.

A letter from Dr. Waterhouse, offering his services as a surgeon, was read, and ordered to lie on the table.

A letter signed Martin Thomas, was read, and ordered to lie on the table.

An anonymous letter was read, and ordered to lie on the table.

A letter from C. A. Rodney, Esq., dated at camp near Elkton, 30th ult., was read, and ordered to lie on the table.

A letter from Governor Pennington, of New Jersey, in answer to the Sub-Committee of Correspondence, was read, and referred to the Sub-Committee of Defence.

Resolved, That the sum of one thousand dollars be

placed in the hands of the Sub-Committee of Defence, and that the Chairman be directed to draw an order accordingly.

Resolved, That Doctor John Redman Coxe be enrolled on the medical staff, in consequence of his offer of services through the Chairman of the Sub-Committee of Defence.

Resolved, That Mr. Robert Brooke's name be enrolled on the list of military engineers, in consequence of his offer of services.

Resolved, That the Chairman and Secretary be a Committee to wait upon the Governor of Pennsylvania, on the part of this Committee, and that they be particularly instructed to inquire what measures will be taken to procure supplies of ordnance, arms, ammunition, accoutrements, and provisions, and for procuring medical supplies.

Resolved, That the Postmaster of Philadelphia be, and he hereby is requested, upon the application of the Commanding General, the District Judge, or District Attorney for this District, to stop and open any letter or letters that may come, or have come, into the Post-office, and which may be supposed to be treasonable, or to be intended to aid or inform, or in any manner to further the views of the enemy.

Resolved, That Messrs. Latimer, Groves, and Ferguson be a Committee to consider and report on some efficient plan for detecting spies.

The following resolution was proposed and seconded, but the consideration of it postponed until to-morrow, viz.:

Resolved, That the Committee of Supplies be instructed to purchase any number of muskets they can procure, not exceeding five thousand stand.

A letter from Captain Ross, of the videttes, was read by the Chairman.

A letter from Mr. Pettibone, making proposals to supply 1000 pikes, was read, and referred to the Committee of Supplies.

The Committee of Supplies reported, that a place in the Navy Yard had been procured, and other arrangements made, to prepare fixed ammunition.

A statement of donations received, by James McGlathery, storekeeper, dated this day, amounting to 22 blankets and 1 rug, was read.

John Connelly was discharged from the Committee for providing for the Wives and Children of those in Service, and John Geyer appointed, by the Committee, in his place.

The Committee appointed to take into consideration Mr. Purden's plan of defence, reported, recommending the postponement of it for the present.

*Resolved, That a committee be appointed to proceed, when they may think proper, to the encampment at

Kennet's Square, and, with the consent of the commanding officer, there to inquire into the situation of the troops of this district, and make report to this Committee.

*The above resolution was not passed, the consideration of it postponed for the present.
Adjourned.
FRANCIS S. COXE,
Assistant Secretary.

EIGHTH MEETING.

PHILADELPHIA, *September* 2d, 1814.

The Committee met.

Present:—Messrs. Biddle, Goodman, Miercken, Brown, Steel, Leiper, Whitehead, Leib, Connelly, Sergeant, Latimer, Josiah, McMullin, Groves, Naglee, Reed, Ronaldson, McFaden, Ferguson, Williams, Cadwalader, Eyre, Palmer, Barker, Thompson.

The minutes of the last meeting were read.

A letter from N. B. Boileau, Esquire, Secretary of the Commonwealth, in answer to the inquiries made of the Governor of Pennsylvania, was read, and referred to the Committee, to consider and make report thereon. Committee, Messrs. Williams, Leib, and Josiah.

A letter from Richard Bache, Captain of Franklin Flying Artillery, was read, and referred to the Committee of Supplies.

A letter from "A Citizen," was read, and ordered to lie on the table.

A letter from John Randall, Race Street, was read, and referred to the Committee of Defence for the Delaware.

A copy of a resolution by the Tammany Society, to aid in manual labor on the works to be erected near the Schuylkill or Delaware, was read, and ordered to lie on the table. Delivered to Sub-Committee of Defence.

REPORTS OF COMMITTEES.

"*The Sub-Committee of Defence* have taken into consideration the letter of the Governor of New Jersey to George Latimer, Esq. (of Committee of Correspondence). which was referred to them by the General Committee, and do thereon make the following report:

"Governor Pennington observes that 'General Lewis has required of him, by his letter of the 30th of August, the whole of the five thousand men *to assemble* in the vicinity of New York.'

"These five thousand men, it appears, form the whole number called for by the requisition of the Government of the United States; and it also appears that the commanding general of this district has made his claim to General Elmer's brigade, being a part of the five thousand men in question.

"The Sub-Committee observe that the Governor of New Jersey refers the decision of this question to the General Government, which seems to imply a suspension of the call of this force till further orders.

"In the opinion of the Sub Committee, the defence of the Delaware is equally important with that of the Jersey shores of New York harbor, and ought (especially in the present position of the enemy) to demand and receive a full proportion of the force of New Jersey.

"The Committee have been further led to remark that the call on the militia of New York and New Jersey has been *to assemble*, while the call of the Pennsylvania militia has only been *to be ready* to assemble. Conceiving, as they do, that the formation of camps of discipline and instruction ought always to precede camps of actual service, whenever there is time for such formation, they beg leave to propose to the General Committee to make application to the executive authority to have camps immediately formed, in proper positions, so that the double object may be answered, of making the militia an efficient body and enabling them to move forward towards the enemy whenever he shall appear to aim an attack in any part of the State. To effect these objects, the Sub-Committee invite the attention of the General Committee to the high grounds over Gray's Ferry, extending on the right of the Darby Road, between three and four miles from the city, which offer very advantageous and salubrious positions.

"(Signed)   JON. WILLIAMS,
"*Chairman.*"

The above report ordered to lie on the table.

The Committee appointed to consider and report *on some efficient plan for detecting spies*, report:

"That perhaps one of the best methods for detecting those vital enemies would be, that the citizens generally should be invited to report all persons of suspicious character to the mayor of the city, or some justice of the peace in the county, to be legally proceeded against. Your Committee are of opinion that this method would be highly efficacious, inasmuch as it would make every citizen the guardian of his own rights, and strike terror into the minds of those incendiaries which now infest our city with impunity. As an auxiliary measure, your Committee would recommend that the Committee of Correspondence be instructed to write to all the keepers of stage-offices and commanders of steam-boats, requesting them to furnish such person as may be appointed by the Committee of Defence, with a list of such passengers as may arrive or depart from the city; and further, that all ferrymen and toll-gatherers be requested to detain any person who cannot give a good account of himself, until information thereof can be given to the mayor or some justice of the peace."

Ordered to lie on the table.

The Committee appointed on the night of the 27th August, to proceed to the Department of War, and to confer with the Secretary of War on the subject of the defence of this district, and also to confer with the Secretary of the Navy, &c., report:

"That they left Philadelphia at 12 o'clock the night of their appointment, and arrived at Baltimore at 11 o'clock the next night, where they held a conference of about two hours with Commodore Rodgers, who stated that he then had an organized force of fourteen hundred men, divided into two regiments, the first commanded by Captain Porter, the other by Captain Perry; that he would afford all the aid in his power for the defence of our city and district; that under present circumstances he could bring only part of his forces to our assistance, unless the Committee could obtain discretionary orders for him from the Secretary of the Navy, in which case he would do all in his power, with his force, to protect us from the enemy, and would act with all practicable dispatch. The Commodore further declared, that he should be pleased at all times to co-operate with the General Committee.

"Your Committee left Baltimore about 4 o'clock on Monday morning, and arrived at Washington about 2 o'clock P.M., passing over the field of battle, and beholding with poignant mortification the effects of want of foresight, and fit organization of the measures of defence for the district.

"During the afternoon your Committee waited upon the President, the Secretary of War (then John Armstrong), the Secretary of State, the Secretary of the Navy and the Attorney-General, who had then all returned to the City of Washington, but without any fixed residence. They all conversed freely on our business, appeared to be convinced of its importance, and declared their readiness to grant us all the protection in their power consistent with their resources and the claims of other quarters of the Union. On Tuesday morning we addressed letters to the Secretary of War and Secretary of the Navy, copies of which you have herewith, Nos. 1 and 2, and proceeding to deliver the letters, we found that Mr. Armstrong had departed, at an early hour, for New York, and Mr. Monroe was acting as Secretary of War, to whom we gave our communication No. 1.

"During the afternoon we again waited on Mr. Monroe. He informed us that our communication was then before the President, that he did not think it practicable to give us a written answer that evening, as the heads of the different departments were scattered, without their papers to refer to; and arrangements being in preparation, in consequence of the enemy's being then at Alexandria, that other business of importance required their immediate care; but that the President was well aware of our situation, and had every disposition to comply with our wishes and expectations; that our communication should receive the earliest attention, and an answer forwarded to Philadelphia, to prevent our being delayed at Washington.

"We waited upon the Secretary of the Navy, and conversed freely with him upon the objects of our appointment. He told us that Commodore Rodgers was ordered to Washington, with a detachment of his forces, for a particular object, which would be terminated in a few days, when he should return to the command of our district, and would be instructed to act agreeably to the wish expressed by us; that he would also send, by post, to Philadelphia, a written answer to our communication, and would do all in his power, should he be consulted by the President, to aid the objects embraced in our letter to the Secretary of War, which was read to him. We also received, from the Secretary of the Navy, an order for the cannon mentioned in our letter to him. Mr. Rush, the Attorney-General, also engaged to use his influence to the same effect.

"The subject of discharging the men employed upon the seventy-four, now building in this port, would be taken into consideration, and orders in relation thereto would be issued.

"Upon the whole, your Committee confidently trust that the answers expected from the two departments will be satisfactory to the General Committee.

(Signed)   "MANUEL EYRE,
"THO. CADWALADER.

"Since the foregoing report was prepared we have received an answer from the Department of War, which is handed herewith, marked No. 3.

"(Signed as above.)

"Copies of papers referred to in the above report:

"No. 1.

"GEORGETOWN, D. C.,

"TO THE HONORABLE   *August* 30*th*, 1814.
"THE SECRETARY OF WAR.

"SIR:—At a public meeting of the citizens of Philadelphia, and of the incorporated districts northward and southward of the city, held on the 26th instant, a General Committee was appointed to provide for the public safety, and the defence of the city and its environs, and we have been delegated by that Committee to confer with the General Government on the highly important subjects committed to our care and directions.

"Our Committee must be well aware that, threatened as our country is in every quarter, the General Government does not possess the means of making adequate provision for the security of each particular district, and that much will necessarily be left to be supplied by local exertion and vigor. We have a right to expect, however, that our exertions will receive the best aid in the power of the Government to supply, and that our vigor will be applied to the best effect under the direction of the most able military commanders the Government can select.

"In behalf of our constituents, therefore, we request that Major-General Izard be assigned to the command of our district, and if that officer cannot be called from the frontier at this time, that Brigadier-General Miller be immediately ordered to Philadelphia. We, moreover, request that in the mean time Brigadier-General Swift be put on duty at Philadelphia, without displacing the officer now commanding. Our constituents calculate on receiving the ready co-operation of the officers of the United States in Philadelphia and its vicinity, and we request that orders to that effect be issued, and that the arms and military stores collected in and near Philadelphia be made subject to the requisition of the General Committee on any sudden emergency. It is also the expectation of our constituents that the garrison at Fort Mifflin be immediately strengthened, and that a fit proportion of artillerists be detailed for that service, under an experienced officer, and that the guns and all the necessary munitions of war be put in a fit state of preparation. Our fellow-citizens also deem it essentially requisite for their security that works be immediately erected on the Pea Patch, of sufficient strength to defend the entrance of the river. If orders to that effect be not already issued, we have to request that arrangements be made for commencing the works and completing them without loss of time, and that the officer charged with that duty be directed to report to, and from time to time to confer with, the Committee.

"A chain of videttes is established between Philadelphia and Elkton, and the officer at the outpost will be ordered to receive and transmit with all expedition, any dispatches communicating important intelligence, and we request that such dispatches be forwarded to Elkton by a special messenger.

"By the report of the general commanding at Philadelphia, it appears that the regulars fit for duty in and near Philadelphia amount to only 256 men. With so small a force allotted to us by the United States, we do not hesitate to request that the volunteers and drafted militia, from the eastern counties of our State, be at no time so far detached as to deprive us of their aid and co-operation in case of a sudden attack.

"The wealth and consequence of our city, its vast importance to the Union, and the immense collection of public property in our vicinity, afford attractions to the enemy of so powerful a nature that we make no apology for the urgent manner in which we have advanced our claims for protection. You will readily believe that we have no wish to impose unnecessary trouble or expense on the Government.

"We have the honor to be, &c.,
(Signed) "MANUEL EYRE,
"THOS. CADWALADER.

"No. 2.

"(COPY.) GEORGETOWN, D. C.,
"To the Hon. WM. JONES, "30th *August*, 1814.
SECRETARY OF NAVY.

"DEAR SIR:—As a Committee from the Grand Committee of Defence for the City and County of Philadelphia, we are authorized to call on you for such aid in resisting any attack of the enemy as will be consistent with the duties of your department to grant. Considering the aid of our naval resources, and the personal services of the navy officers, seamen, and marines will be most essentially necessary for the protection of the ships and public property in Philadelphia and its vicinity, as well as for the safety and defence of the City of Philadelphia, and the Bay and River Delaware, we hope the crews of the flotilla will at no time be so far weakened as to endanger its safety and leave that avenue to the city unprotected. As Commodore Rodgers has now a very respectable force under his command, we are desirous that you should give him immediate instructions to employ the whole or any part of that force at his discretion, for the defence of the City of Philadelphia and its approaches, should the enemy's force at any time, in that quarter, require it. Having the fullest confidence in the abilities, courage, and discretion of Commodore Rodgers, we rely upon his using his force at those points where it is most essential for the good of our country. We therefore wish his instructions to be as general as you can make them, consistent with the public welfare. Should Commodore Rodgers' services be required by you at this time, distant from the Delaware, the important interest we represent calls upon us to ask of you the immediate appointment of Captain Porter to the command of our district, still calculating upon the aid of Commodore Rodgers and his force, under the discretionary orders above referred to. We thank you for the offer of the public ordnance under your control, and will accept of the four guns now lying in Baltimore, of the description you mentioned, and we shall make use of them if the occasion requires it. We assure you, on behalf of the General Committee, that we shall be pleased to co-operate most cordially with you in repelling, within our military district, every invasion of the enemy.

"With respect, &c.,
(Signed) "MANUEL EYRE,
"THOS. CADWALADER.

"No. 3.

"(COPY.)   WAR DEPARTMENT,
"GENTLEMEN: *August* 31*st*, 1814.

"Your letter of the 30th inst. has been received. The important command which has been assigned to General

Izard renders it impracticable to order him to Philadelphia at this time.

"Brigadier-General Miller cannot be removed from the frontier without injury and inconvenience to the service.

"General Swift has been directed to meet the Committee at Philadelphia, and will furnish plans and give the necessary orders for erecting such works as the Committee may please to adopt, under the unlimited authority communicated by this department on the 27th inst.

"General Bloomfield has been directed to put Fort Mifflin in the best possible state of defence, and to communicate with the Committee relative to other arrangements for the protection and security of the district.

"I have the honor to be, gentlemen, &c.,

(Signed) "JAMES MONROE.
"MESSRS. EYRE AND CADWALADER."

The above report ordered to lie on the table.

Messrs. Reed, Ferguson and Ronaldson obtained leave of absence for the rest of the day.

Resolved, That the Committees appointed in the different wards of this city, and in the districts adjoining, to enroll the inhabitants, &c., be requested to make a report, forthwith, of their rolls, to this Committee; and that this resolution be published, signed by the Chairman and Secretary.

Resolved, That no anonymous communications be received by this Committee.

Ordered to be published, signed by the Chairman and Secretary.

Resolved, That five hundred dollars be placed at the disposal of the Committee, for providing for the wives and children of those in service, and that the Chairman draw an order accordingly.

Resolved, That the Sub-Committee of Defence be directed to order up from Baltimore the four gunnades offered by the Secretary of the Navy.

The following resolution was moved, and postponed until to-morrow, viz.:

Resolved, That the Committee to whom was referred the correspondence with the Secretary of War, be instructed to request that two thousand regulars be immediately encamped near the City of Philadelphia, with the volunteers and militia called out from Pennsylvania.

A letter from Wm. Duncan, Henry Lentz, and Ch. Wheeler, Committee for Northern Liberties, was read, and referred to the Sub-Committee of Defence.

Resolved, That the Committee appointed to wait on General Armstrong, &c., be instructed to inquire again, of the Secretary of War, respecting the means of procuring the disposal of arms, accoutrements, &c.

Resolved, That the Committee for Defence of the Delaware be instructed to employ men to complete the works at and near Fort Mifflin; and, if practicable, to obtain from General Bloomfield his authority for the same purpose, so as to make the Government of the United States chargeable with the expense.

The Committee having retired, after a short time returned, and reported that General Bloomfield had promised to give his order for work to be done at the fortifications in and about Fort Mifflin, to-morrow morning.

Resolved, That the Committee for the Defence of the Delaware be instructed to purchase a sloop of 45 to 50 tons, at not more than $1100.

Adjourned.

JNO. GOODMAN,
Secretary.

NINTH MEETING.

PHILADELPHIA, 3d *September*, 1814.

The Committee met.

Present:—Messrs. Biddle, Goodman, Reed, McFaden, Williams, Steel, Groves, Leiper, Eyre, Brown, Palmer, Thompson, Sergeant, Ferguson, Latimer, Leib, Connelly, Cadwalader, Josiah, Ronaldson, McMullin, Whitehead, Huff.

The minutes of the last meeting were read.

A letter from Richard Rush, Esquire, to the Mayor of Philadelphia, dated Washington, 1st inst., informing that Admiral Cochrane had given notice to the Government of the United States (in a dispatch dated 18th ultimo, received by the Secretary of State the 31st ultimo), that it was his intention to issue to the naval force under his command, an order "to destroy and lay waste such towns and districts upon the coast as may be found assailable."

A motion was made that said letter be published in handbills, which was postponed; and the letter was referred to a committee of three, consisting of Messrs. Leib, Reed, and Connelly, who were ordered to withdraw, and report on it immediately.

A letter from Judge Peters, concerning the insulating of the Schuylkill middle bridge, was read, and referred to the Sub-Committee of Defence.

A letter from the proprietors of the Vauxhall Gardens was read, and ordered to lie on the table.

A letter from Tench Coxe, concerning pikes, was read, and referred to the Committee of Supplies. A sample of a pike accompanied this letter.

A letter from James Gailand to Jared Ingersoll was read, and referred to the Sub-Committe of Defence.

A letter from Matthew Carey was read, and ordered to lie on the table. Some printed inclosures were ordered to be distributed to the chairmen of the different committees.

A second letter from M. Carey was read, and ordered to lie on the table.

A letter from Wm. Graham, dated Chester, 1st inst., was read, and referred to the Committee of Correspondence. See their answer on file.

A letter from the Sub-Committee for the Northern Liberties (Samuel Macferran, Chairman), was read, and ordered to lie on the table.

A letter from Joseph Thomas, M.D., offering his services as a surgeon, was referred to the Sub-Committee of Defence.

REPORTS OF COMMITTEES.

The Committee to which was referred the letter from the Secretary of the Commonwealth to the Chairman of the General Committee of Defence, dated Philadelphia, September 2d, 1814, report:

That for the sake of perspicuity, they have preferred the plan of interrogatories and answers, and they accordingly have subjoined, as part of their report, the interrogatories of the Secretary and the answers of the Committee.

1*st Interrogatory of the Secretary.*—What is the present state of defence, other than that authorized by Government, as to men, arms, ammunition, equipments, and camp equipage?

Answer by the Committee.—The Committee have not made, nor do they contemplate any defence unauthorized by the Government. They have encouraged the enrollment of volunteers under the terms of the militia law. *Time* has not permitted the completion of these enrollments; the Committee are therefore unable to state the number of men that may appear on an emergency. The Committee are daily employed in devising means to procure arms, ammunition, and camp equipage, and no efforts or expense, will be spared for these objects; but the Committee have abundant reason to solicit all the aid the Government can supply, having really no arms, ammunition, equipments, or camp equipage under their exclusive control.

2d Interrogatory.—How many men, and what species of force are, under the present information as to the enemy, deemed necessary for defence?

Answer.—The Committee have no other information respecting the enemy than what is contained in the public papers. But should he land on the shores either of the Chesapeake or the Delaware, and march toward the city, with a force of ten thousand men, we ought to have at least twenty thousand men to oppose him. Of this force, as much as possible should be field artillery, on positions which may be found in the course of his march on his flanks. To aid this species of force, your Committee have directed the occupancy of the heights west of the Schuylkill; they have sent topographical engineers to point out every position between this and Chester, and they mean to continue these preliminary measures to the ultimate points where the enemy may land, that, when he does appear, we may be able to dispute the ground with him at every pass. The Committee take this opportunity of observing that if camps of discipline and organization were established at the various heights and encamping grounds, from 3 to 10 miles distant from the city, the measure would have a tendency to enable us to meet the enemy with a smaller force, and with far less probable loss than must otherwise be the unavoidable consequence. But the Committee are obliged to confine themselves to the expression of their regret that the measure is not within the compass of their power.

3d Interrogatory.—Have any plans of defence been agreed upon by the Committee, independently of or in conjunction with the United States Government; and how far (if any have been agreed upon) have they been executed, and what is expected from the Commonwealth?

Answer.—A defence of the River Delaware has been agreed upon, in the following manner: Fort Mifflin is to be put in complete order by the General Government, aided by citizen artificers, and every other means in the power of the Committee. A battery on Davis' pier, in the middle of the river, is constructing, to bear its force on the channel over the bar, where it is contemplated sinking hulks, and thereby obstructing the passage. A position on the Jersey shore, within 220 yards of this passage, is also contemplated, and the United States engineer is daily expected for this, and such other parts of the river defence as may be judged expedient. The gun-boats in the river will doubtless retire before the enemy, if they cannot oppose him, and form their ultimate point of defence behind these obstructions.

It is expected from the Commonwealth, that its resources of men and money will be employed in defending this metropolis, an essential part of the whole; the constituted authorities of the State having pledged themselves to the nation to employ all the energies of the

Commonwealth in support of the war and against the common enemy.

4th Interrogatory.—What provision is made by the Committee, or by the United States, for the volunteers from the country, as to quarters, rations, and forage?

Answer.—A small supply of rations, consisting of eight hundred barrels of beef and pork, near three hundred barrels of biscuit, and twenty barrels of vinegar, have been already purchased, or ordered to be purchased, together with a hundred barrels of whisky, and twenty barrels more of vinegar; but the Committee hold all these in reserve for an emergency, not deeming it proper to issue them on ordinary occasions. Means have been taken to provide straw, and the hospital belonging to the Board of Health, and the New Prison, are provided as quarters. The Committee are unacquainted with the provision made by the United States, supposing this can only be known by the Secretary of War, the commanding general, or the commissary-general.

The above report was approved, and a copy, signed by the Chairman, ordered to be sent to the Secretary of the Commonwealth.

The Sub-Committee of Defence, having had under their consideration a letter from the Corresponding Committee for the Northern Liberties, &c. (Messrs. Duncan, Wheeler, and Lentz), wherein a request is made "that the Committee of Defence will take measures to enable the several district committees to give a pledge that the members of organized volunteer corps, whose services shall have been accepted by your Committee, shall not be held liable to militia duty," report:

That, while your Committee avail themselves of the present occasion to express their highest approbation of the patriotic spirit displayed by our fellow-citizens in forming volunteer associations for the defence of the City and County of Philadelphia, they at the same time deem it no less their duty to remove what appears to your Committee to be an erroneous impression, as to the extent of authority vested in the Committee of Defence, by laying down, in answer to the request from the Northern Liberties, the following positions:

Firstly. In the opinion of your Committee, volunteer corps can only be organized in the manner prescribed by law.

Secondly. No volunteer offer of military service to the Committee of Defence can in the least impair the obligation of those subject to militia duty to comply with all requisitions of the laws of the United States and of the State of Pennsylvania on this subject.

Thirdly. Those only who have volunteered their services for the defence of the City and County of Philadelphia, but who are not subject to militia duty, can fall under the direction of the Committee of Defence, and then only in accordance with the plans and mode of defence directed by the proper military authority.

The above report was ordered to lie on the table.

The Committee to which was referred the letter from Richard Rush to the Mayor of Philadelphia, report:

That they called at the quarters of General Bloomfield, and, as he was absent, they applied to his aid-de-camp, to know whether the general had received any communication this day from Washington, and were answered that he had not. On their return, the Committee discovered that their functions were superseded by the publication of the letter from Mr. Rush in a handbill.

The above report ordered to lie on the table.

On the representation of the Committee for the Defence of the Delaware, that the work on the carriages for the guns, &c., at Fort Mifflin, is not going on, it was

Resolved, That the Committee for the Defence of the Delaware be authorized and instructed to employ, forthwith, the necessary workmen to have Fort Mifflin put in the most perfect state of defence.

Resolved, That the Committee for the Defence of the Delaware be authorized to purchase, and have in readiness without delay, as many vessels or hulks as will be sufficient to obstruct the channel in the River Delaware, to prevent all approach by the ships of war of the enemy by means of the river.

A letter from Wm. Hess, ensign of a volunteer corps, informing that General Bloomfield had refused to accept the services of his company, being read, it was

Resolved, That Messrs. Leiper, Latimer, and Brown be a committee to wait on General Bloomfield, and inquire the reason why he has rejected the offer of services of Ensign Hess' company (Benevolent Blues); also,

Resolved, That the above Committee request of General Bloomfield to place an advance guard of infantry, agreeably to the wishes expressed in a letter received this day from Mr. J. R. C. Smith, of the videttes, which was read.

Resolved, That Messrs. Latimer, Sergeant, and Cadwalader be a committee to procure a suitable room for the sitting of this Committee.

The Committee for the Defence of the Delaware handed in a letter received from General Bloomfield, dated yesterday, which was read, and of which the following is a copy:

"FOURTH MILITARY DISTRICT.

"PHILADELPHIA, *September* 2*d*, 1814.

"The commanding general accepts the offer of this date, of the Committee of Safety of Philadelphia, to advance money to put Fort Mifflin and its guns in the best state of defence, under the direction of the Engineers and Commissaries of Ordnance of the United States, who severally will make the necessary requisitions in their respective departments, that orders be given thereon.

  (Signed)   "JOSEPH BLOOMFIELD,
        "*Brigad'r-Gen'l Commanding.*"
Adjourned.
       JNO. GOODMAN,
          Secretary.

TENTH MEETING.

PHILADELPHIA, *September 4th*, 1814.

The Committee met.

Present :—Messrs. Biddle, Goodman, Eyre, Connelly, Palmer, Reed, Sergeant, Huff, Groves, Miercken, Steel, Whitehead, Cadwalader, McFaden, Josiah, Thompson, Ferguson.

The minutes of the last meeting were read.

The Chairman stated that a copy of the report of the Committee on the letter of the Secretary of the Commonwealth had been handed to him.

The Committee for the Defence of the Delaware reported progress.

The letter received yesterday from Samuel Macferran, Chairman of the Sub-Committee for the Northern Liberties, &c., was read again, and referred to the Committee of Supplies.

A letter from A. J. Dallas, Esquire, was read, and referred, together with the resolution, moved yesterday, to request the Secretary at War to order an encampment of 2000 regulars near Philadelphia, to a committee, consisting of Messrs. Cadwalader, Miercken, Eyre, and Sergeant.

The report made yesterday by the Sub-Committee of Defence, on the letter from the Sub-Committee for the Northern Liberties, &c., concerning volunteers whose services may be accepted by the Committee, was again read, and referred to the Committee who made it, with instructions to confer with the Governor on the subject.

(The report is entered on page 75.)

The Committee who were yesterday directed to wait on General Bloomfield, reported a letter they had written to him, and his answer, on the subject of the Benevolent Blues. The following is an extract of General Bloomfield's letter (of this date), viz.:

"By orders of 29th, Second Brigade are called upon to hold themselves in readiness to take the field at a moment's warning. I will therefore now take into the service of the United States volunteer uniform companies of one hundred men, as well from the Second as the First Brigade of the First Division of the Militia of Pennsylvania."

The Committee of Correspondence were directed to inform Ensign Hess, of the Benevolent Blues, of General Bloomfield's answer.

The Committee of Correspondence were also directed to answer the letter received yesterday from Mr. J. R. C. Smith, of the videttes. See copy of answer on file.

Resolved, That the Committee of Supplies be directed to inquire into the state of the rifles at the U. S. Arsenal, offered by General Bloomfield, and, if they think proper, to have them repaired; and if the rifles are not fit for service, to inquire whether muskets can be obtained in lieu of them.

Resolved, That the Committee for the Defence of the Delaware be instructed to sound the channel opposite to

Reedy Island, and to take such persons to their aid as they may deem proper.

Resolved, That John Steel and Jas. Josiah be a committee to wait on General Swift on his arrival in the city, to confer with him concerning defence.

Resolved, That the Sub-Committee of Defence be particularly instructed to confer with the Governor of the State, and the commander of this military district, for making immediate provision for the reception of the volunteers now offering, or which may offer, in defence of our country.

Adjourned.

JNO. GOODMAN,
Secretary.

ELEVENTH MEETING.

PHILADELPHIA. *September 5th*, 1814.

The Committee met.

Present:—Messrs. Goodman, Biddle, Ronaldson, Cadwalader, Barker, Latimer, Connelly, Leib, Brown, Eyre, Miercken, Naglee, Sergeant, Josiah, Hawkins, Leiper, Steel, Thompson, Geyer, McMullin, Whitehead, Ferguson, Groves, Snyder.

The minutes of the last meeting were read.

A letter of this date, from Elisha Gordon, with an inclosure, were read, and referred to the Sub-Committee of Defence.

A letter from M. Carey, of this date, was read, and ordered to lie on the table.

A letter from Dr. Heylin, concerning the medical staff, was read, and referred to the Committee of Supplies.

A letter from Dr. S. F. Conover, offering his services in the "Department of Medicine," being read, it was

Resolved, That Dr. Conover be ordered to the medical staff.

A letter of this date, from Isaac McCauley, concerning pikes, was read, and ordered to lie on the table.

A return of the enrollment of the inhabitants of Cedar Ward, for one or more volunteer campanies, with offer of services to the Committee of Defence, was received, and ordered to lie on the table.

The above return is made by the Sub-Committee for Cedar Ward.

A report of the Committee of Enrollments for Lower Delaware Ward, was read, and ordered to lie on the table.

REPORT OF COMMITTEES.

The Committee to whom were referred the resolution offered for requesting the Secretary at War to have encamped two thousand regulars near the City of Philadelphia, and the letter from A. J. Dallas, Esquire, report:

That having considered the subject of the resolution and letter, they are of opinion that immediate application respecting them ought to be made to the Secretary at War, but that the same ought to be made through the Governor of this Commonwealth. They therefore offer the following resolution:

"*Resolved*, That a committee be appointed to wait upon the Governor, and, in the name of the Committee, to request that he will apply to the Secretary at War to have at least 2000 regulars encamped near the City of Philadelphia, with the volunteers and militia called out from Pennsylvania; and also for authority to be given to the City of Philadelphia to enlist three regiments of infantry, to be employed in the service of the United States in this military district."

The above resolution was passed, and Messrs. Cadwalader, Miercken, Sergeant, and Eyre were appointed the committee therein named.

The Committee for the Defence of the Delaware made report of the purchase of several vessels. Whereupon

Ordered, That bills of sale be made out for the vessels so purchased to Henry Hawkins and James Josiah, being the two first named on said Committee, for the use of the Corporation. Also,

Resolved, That an order be drawn on the Treasurer for four thousand six hundred and twenty-five dollars, in favor of the Chairman of the Committee for Defence of the Delaware, for the above purchases.

The Committee of Supplies, to whom was referred the offer of General Bloomfied of 1700 rifles, now in the U. S. Arsenal, to the Committee of Defence, report:

That from the information of Mr. Wickham, Inspector of Arms for the United States, the cost of repair will not exceed 75 cents for each rifle, including the expense of proving the barrel. They therefore submit the following resolution, viz.:

"*Resolved*, That the offer of General Bloomfield be accepted, it being understood that the Committee shall not be held accountable for the rifles that will not stand the proof."

The above resolution was adopted.

Resolved, That an order be drawn by the Chairman on the Treasurer for five hundred dollars in favor of Captain Ross, of the videttes, he to be accountable for the same.

Resolved, That the Commissioners of the Northern Liberties be requested to place in the hands of the Treasurer of the General Committee of Defence the sum of twenty-five thousand dollars, to be applied to the purposes for which they were appointed.

Resolved, That the Commissioners of the District of Southwark be requested to place in the hand of the Treasurer of the Committee of Defence the sum of ten thousand dollars, to be applied to the purposes for which they were appointed.

Mr. Whitehead stated that he had received the following donations in lieu of labor at the fortifications, viz.:

From Thomas Smith, No. 202 Chestnut Street.......... $20
From John Robbins, Vine near Fourth Street.......... 10
                                                    ———
                                                    $30

The above donations were ordered to be published, and Mr. Whitehead paid them over to the Treasurer.

An application being made to the General Committee of Defence for 100 tents, camp-kettles, mess-pans, and tin buckets, for the troops encamped at Kennet's Square, it was

Resolved, That the application be referred to the Committee of Supplies, with instructions to apply to the commanding general for the articles required; and if the public stores do not afford them, to apply to the general for authority to procure them; the Government of the United States to be eventually liable for the cost.

Resolved, That General Steel and Mr. Brown be excused from serving on the committee for providing for the wives and children of those in service, and that Messrs. Barker, Leiper, and Peltz be appointed on said Committee.

Resolved, That Mr. Goodman be reinstated in the Committee of Supplies, and that Mr. Reed be the Secretary *pro tempore* during Mr. Goodman's employment on said committee.

Resolved, That the Committee of Supplies be authorized to purchase a horse and chair for the convenience of the gentlemen employed to direct the works of fortifications on the west side of the Schuylkill.

Resolved, That the Committee of Supplies be authorized to procure as many wheel-barrows as may be wanted (say 25) at the fortifications erecting on the west side of the Schuylkill.

Resolved, That the Sub-Committee of Defence be authorized and required to call on the Governor of this State, and the commanding general of this military district, for such information as they may possess as to the number of volunteers, militia, and other force, that is expected to be encamped during this week for the defence of this city and district; also to continue the exertions for the reception of volunteers.
Adjourned.
FRANCIS S. COXE,
Assistant Secretary.

TWELFTH MEETING.

PHILADELPHIA, *September 6th,* 1814.
The Committee met.
Present:—Messrs. Biddle, Reed, Steel, Brown, Thompson, Groves, Whitehead, Palmer, Sergeant, Latimer, Leib, Connelly, Ronaldson, Williams, McMullin, Naglee, Ferguson, Josiah, Miercken, Cadwalader, Eyre.
The minutes of the last meeting were read.
A letter from Governor Pennington, of New Jersey, to the Committee of Correspondence, was read, and referred to said Committee.

A letter from the Secretary of War to the Chairman of the General Committee was read, and referred to the Committee of Supplies.

A letter from the Secretary at War to General Bloomfield was received from him, and read.

Ordered, That the said letter be returned to General Bloomfield, with a request that he will furnish the Committee with a copy of it.

A letter from John Goodman, dated at the U. S. Arsenal, this day, was read, and referred to the Committee of Supplies, with instructions to take such order thereon as they may think proper.

A letter from Mr. Purden was read, and referred to the Sub-Committee of Defence.

A letter from Dr. Elijah Griffith was read, and referred to the Sub-Committee of Defence.

A letter of 5th inst., from Commodore Truxtun, offering his services, was read, and the Chairman requested to return the thanks of this Committee to Commodore Truxtun, and request that he will aid the Committee for the Defence of the River Delaware.

Letters from J. R. Ingersoll, Capt. 2d Co. Washington Guards, and P. A. Brown, of Independent Blues, were read, and referred to the committee for providing for the families of those in service.

Resolved, That the names of the committee for providing for the wives and children of those who are in service be published.

Resolved, That one thousand dollars be placed at the disposal of the Committee of Supplies, to be employed for the purposes of their appointment; and that the Chairman draw an order on the Treasurer in favor of the Chairman of said Committee for the above amount.

Resolved, That the Chairman be directed to issue an order in favor of Messrs. Eyre and Cadwalader on the Treasurer, for one hundred and twenty dollars, being the amount of the expenses incurred by them on their journey to Washington.

Resolved, That Messrs. Williams, Ronaldson, and Eyre be a committee to devise and report on such methods as they may deem sufficient to deprive the enemy of every species of aid and comfort.

Resolved, That the Committee of Accounts be instructed to digest and report a plan by which all accounts shall be settled.

Resolved, That the Committee for the Defence of the Delaware be instructed to write to the proper authority to obtain the use of the revenue cutter in the Delaware.

Mr. Whitehead stated that he had received from John I. Vanderkamp a donation of ten dollars, in lieu of labor at the fortifications, which he paid over to the Treasurer.

A bill for beef, &c., from Mr. Carswell, was presented by the Committee of Supplies, and referred to the Committee of Accounts.

The Committee who were appointed to wait on the

Governor, and write to the Secretary at War, concerning the encampment of 2000 regulars, &c., *reported* that they had handed a copy of the resolution to the above effect to the Governor, who said that he would attend to it.

General Swift, from New York, attended, and, at the particular request of the Committee, consented to delay his departure for New York, for the purpose of going down the river to examine the fortifications at Fort Mifflin, and sites for fortification in that vicinity, to-morrow. Whereupon

Resolved, That Gen. Williams, Gen. Steel, and Capt. Josiah be a committee to attend General Swift in surveying the fortifications, &c., to-morrow.

Adjourned.

FRANCIS S. COXE,
Assistant Secretary.

The following is a copy of the letter from the Secretary at War to General Bloomfield mentioned in the above minutes, and taken by his permission:

"WAR DEPARTMENT, *September 4th,* 1814.
"SIR:

"By accounts from the mouth of the Patuxent, at 9 o'clock last night, the enemy's fleet, with all their troops on board, was still suspended there, waiting, as was supposed, the return of the squadron from the Potomac. Every effort which the means of the Government have permitted has been made, and is still making, to cut off their retreat, and destroy this squadron. Many gallant officers of the navy have united their exertions with those of the land forces in this undertaking, and much hope is entertained that it will not be unavailing. It is possible that the force at the mouth of the Patuxent may, in case the squadron should be put in imminent danger. attempt to relieve it. Such an attempt could only be made by an attack on our batteries, which might be approached either by land from the Patuxent to the Potomac, or by sailing up the Potomac. For either of these movements the best preparations will be made here that circumstances will permit.

"It is equally possible that the force at the mouth of the Patuxent has already moved, either against Baltimore, Philadelphia, Norfolk, or Richmond. That it will soon move against some one of those places cannot well be doubted. Desolation is its object, and the wider it is spread the more completely will that object be accomplished. It is known that the enemy promise to themselves, from the waste of our country and distress of our people, a base submission to their will. Little do they understand the true character of this virtuous and free nation. They deceived themselves by those visionary calculations in our Revolution. and the result of this contest will prove that the American people are not less faithful to their principles than the British Government is to its vindictive and barbarous policy.

"Should either of these cities be invaded, all possible

support will be given by the Government. The force already organized for the defence of each will be relied on principally, especially in the first instance, for the purpose. But as the enemy, in making either the distinct object of their vengeance, relieves the others for the moment from the pressure, a portion of the force assembled for the defence of the latter may be spared for that of a neighboring sister town. This object will be attended to by the Government in due time, and I state it that, having it in view, you may be enabled to give it the best effect which circumstances will permit.

"The City of Philadelphia, I am aware, offers by its wealth a strong inducement to the enemy to make an attempt on it. Its population, however, being great, its organized and well-trained force considerable, much confidence is entertained that it will make a defence worthy the high character which it sustains with the nation.

"To repel such danger, it will be necessary for you to have your force in the best possible preparation for action; to watch the enemy's movements in every direction, and to communicate to me, without delay, every circumstance deserving of attention.

"I have the honor to be, &c.,

(Signed) "JAMES MONROE.

"P.S.—You will have the goodness to communicate the substance of this letter to the Committee of Public Safety for the City of Philadelphia.

"BRIGAD'R-GEN'L BLOOMFIELD,
 "*Commanding District No. 4,*
  "*Philadelphia.*"

THIRTEENTH MEETING.

PHILADELPHIA, *September 7th*, 1814.

The Committee met.

Present:—Messrs. Biddle, Goodman, Reed, Connelly, Ferguson, Thompson, Leiper, Groves, Whitehead, Sergeant, Eyre, Palmer, Leib, Brown, Huff, Cadwalader, Ronaldson, Latimer, Williams, Naglee.

The minutes of the last meeting were read.

A letter of 6th inst., from Thomas Forrest, Chairman of a Committee of Safety for the Townships of Germantown, Roxbury, and Bristol (Philadelphia County), was read, and referred to the Committee of Correspondence.

A letter from George McLevin was read, and ordered to lie on the table.

A letter from Wm. Smiley, Thos. Stevenson, &c., offering to form a volunteer company for the defence of Philadelphia, was read, and referred to the Sub-Committee of Defence.

A letter from G. W. Tryon, D. Hinkles, and I. I. Henry, gunmakers, praying to be exempted from militia duty, was read, and ordered to lie on the table.

A letter of 6th inst., from Joshua Humphreys, concerning the frigate Guerriere, being read, was referred to the Committee of Correspondence, and the following resolution adopted, viz.:

Resolved, That the Committee of Correspondence be instructed to write to the Secretary of the Navy, requesting that the frigate Guerriere may be immediately fitted for service, and stationed in such position in the River Delaware as to aid in its defence, and afford support to Fort Mifflin and the fortifications in its neighborhood.

A communication from Mr. Goodman was read, and referred to the Committee of Supplies.

A letter from Kinsey Johns to the Committee of Correspondence, dated New Castle, 5th inst., was read, and ordered to lie on the table.

The Sub-Committee of Defence made the following report, viz.:

"The Sub-Committee of Defence having had under their consideration the letter signed J. G. Chambers, proposing to organize a company to act with repeating-arms, are satisfied with the efficacy of those arms. They therefore recommend the adoption of the following resolution, viz.:

"*Resolved*, That Mr. Joseph G. Chambers and his associates be, and they are hereby, authorized to form an association for the above purpose, and that the influence of this Committee will be used to exempt them from other military duty."

The above resolution was adopted.

The Sub-Committee of Defence also offered the following resolution, viz.:

"*Resolved*, That a committee be appointed to inquire. and report to this Committee, on the expediency of procuring materials for equipping in uniform the Pennsylvania militia that are or may be encamped for the defence of this military district, and the probable expense thereof."

The above resolution was adopted, and Messrs. Eyre, Groves, and McMullin were appointed the Committee therein named.

A letter from Dr. John R. Coxe, relating to the preservation of health in camps, &c., being read, it was

Resolved, That the "Observations relative to the means of preserving health in armies" be published in a pamphlet form, and that a copy be transmitted to every commanding officer of a regiment and company in the public service for the defence of this district, and that the Committee of Supplies be directed to carry this resolution into execution.

The Committee of Correspondence returned the letter of 4th inst., from Governor Pennington, of New Jersey, which was referred to them; and stated that they had shown it to General Bloomfield.

Resolved, That Mr. Sergeant be added to the Sub-Committee of Defence.

Resolved, That the sum of two thousand three hundred and twenty-two dollars and ninety cents be placed in the hands of the Committee of Supplies, and that the Chairman be authorized to issue a warrant on the Treasurer for the above amount in favor of the Chairman of said Committee.

The following resolution was read, and ordered to lie on the table, viz.:

"*Resolved,* That a committee be appointed to inquire and report what measures would be proper to secure the prisoners in the State prison, should the enemy approach and attempt the destruction of the city."

The following resolution was moved, and the consideration of it postponed until to-morrow, viz.:

"*Resolved,* That ———— be a committee to superintend and direct the immediate erection of the fortifications on the Pea Patch and Newbold Point, agreeably to the plan presented to this Committee by General Swift, with power to employ such persons as they may think proper."

Mr. Whitehead stated that he had received the following donations, several of which accompanied by letters, which are on file, viz.:

In lieu of personal labor at the fortifications—

From George Murray		$25
" Peter S. Du Ponceau		20
" Barton Field		30
" H. L. Broslasky		10
" J. J. Borie		20
" Wm. Sheepshanks		20
" Jacob Roset		10

For the relief of the wives of soldiers in service who may be in want—

From Jacob Roset		50
		$185

Amounting to one hundred and eighty-five dollars, which was paid to the Treasurer, and the list of donations directed to be published.

Adjourned.

FRANCIS S. COXE,
Assistant Secretary.

FOURTEENTH MEETING.

PHILADELPHIA, *September 8th,* 1814.

The Committee met.

Present:—Messrs. Biddle, Goodman, Latimer, Brown, Cadwalader, Miercken, McFaden, Williams, Eyre, Sergeant, Leib, Ronaldson, Palmer, McMullin, Josiah, Barker, Whitehead, Groves, Hawkins, Leiper, Geyer, Reed, Peltz.

The minutes of the last meeting were read.

A letter from Gen'l Bloomfield, requesting a further loan of $2000 for Mr. McKoy (contractor), and inclosing a letter from T. Banger for C. Irvine, Commissary-General, both of 7th instant, being read, it was

Resolved, That Messrs. Cadwalader and Eyre be a committee to whom the above letters are referred, with instructions to report thereon as soon as possible; also that said committee make inquiries of Gen'l Bloomfield concerning defective rifles said to have been furnished to certain volunteer companies.

The said Committee retired.

A letter from S. Hodgdon, and other inhabitants of North Ward, recommending to the Committee to procure uniforms for volunteers, was read, and referred to Messrs. Eyre, Groves, and McMullin, the Committee appointed yesterday to inquire into the expediency of equipping in uniform the militia for the defence of this district.

A letter from Drs. James Rush and Wm. P. C. Barton. inclosing a resolution of a number of the physicians of Philadelphia, to render gratuitously all the services in their power, in case of an attack on or a battle near Philadelphia, was read, and ordered to lie on the table.

A letter from the senior company of Kensington Guards, tendering their services to the Committee, was read, and referred to the Sub-Committee of Defence.

A letter from Charles Perry, S. B. Rawle, and Moses Kempton, Jr., a committee of the 5th Company of Washington Guards, informing that they have associated for the purpose of offering their services to the Committee for the defence of their homes, and inquiring whether arms can be procured, being read, it was

Resolved, That in answer to the above letter, the Secretary be directed to send an extract from the report of the Sub-Committee of Defence of the 3d inst., on the subject of the liability to the militia law of volunteers who may tender their services to the Committee. (See page 75.)

A letter from P. A. Brown, Captain of the Independent Blues, dated Camp Bloomfield, September 6th, requesting a supply from the Committee of 23 blankets, kettles, pans, &c., was read, and ordered to lie on the table.

A letter from James Forten, offering to *make*, gratuitously, canvas covers, or bags, for the use of the volunteers, was read, and ordered to lie on the table.

A letter from Capt. Ansley and others, of the Marine Artillery, was read, and referred to the Committee of Defence for the Delaware.

A memorial from Bucks County Infantry was read, and referred to the Committee of Supplies.

REPORTS OF COMMITTEES.

The Committee appointed to devise means of depriving the enemy of every species of aid and comfort on his approach toward Philadelphia, report:

That in the opinion of your Committee, all measures short of the authority of the Commonwealth, legally exercised, would be found ineffectual, inasmuch as the inhabitants of the part of the country through which the enemy must pass, would be proportionably injured. Recommendations, therefore, could only operate on the few who prefer the public benefit to private prosperity, and the most virtuous and patriotic citizens would consequently be the most exposed to these burdens or privations. Your Committee are therefore of opinion, that the Chairman of the General Committee, or a special committee appointed for the purpose, should, without delay, wait upon the Governor of the State, and request him to appoint proper persons to carry into effect, on the first landing of the enemy, the following indispensable measures:

1st. To cause all horses, cattle, and every species of vehicle, to be driven into the interior, out of the possible reach of the enemy, so as to deprive him of every means of transportation.

2dly. To drive off, or carry away, every animal of every description that may serve for food, and to carry away (or destroy, if there should not be time to carry away) all provisions of every kind.

3dly. To draw the lower box and take away the spear of every pump, and all the apparatus by which water may be drawn from wells.

4thly. To impede roads, as far as possible, and to stop all narrow passes by felled trees, or such other means as time and circumstances may permit.

5thly. To take an indispensable wheel from every mill, so as to prevent the possibility of its being used when in the enemy's possession.

Your Committee would not appear to dictate as to the mode of carrying these measures into the most prompt and decisive execution on the approach of the enemy, this must of course rest with the constituted authorities of the State; but they beg leave to suggest, that at least two magistrates, or other persons within each district, should be appointed, with powers to employ all necessary aid to carry the measures into full effect, and the districts determined on should not be too extensive, but fully within the exercise of this local authority, and should include all the townships in the line of approach.

Two or more districts should be under the direction of a superintendent, who should travel from point to point, and see the orders faithfully executed.

Considering the Governor of this State not only as its first civil magistrate, but also as its military commander-in-chief, and considering also that we have at our doors, as it were, a powerful and depredating foe, your Committee cannot doubt of the constitutional authority for carrying the proposed measures into effect; but if any doubts of this kind were to exist, they would surely be overcome by the law of self-preservation, which is paramount to all others.

Your Committee further report, that, in their opinion, a similar application should be made, without delay, to the Governors of the States of New Jersey and Delaware.

(Signed) JON'A WILLIAMS, ⎫
MANUEL EYRE, ⎬ *Committee.*
JAMES RONALDSON, ⎭

The above report was approved, and the Chairman directed to wait on the Governor of this State with a copy, and for the purposes therein mentioned. The Committee of Correspondence was instructed to transmit a copy of it to the Governors of the States of New Jersey and Delaware.

(Minutes of this day continued over leaf.)

The Committee for the Defence of the Delaware, report:
That they have purchased the following vessels, to

be put in readiness to be sunk in the channel near Fort Mifflin, viz.:

Brig Astrea for	$2200
Sloop Susanna for	1300
Sloop Seabrook for	1100
	$4600

Making (together with those before purchased) six vessels. Two of these vessels are at Fort Mifflin, for the accommodation of the workmen there, two are fitted and ready to be sunk, the other two are in forwardness. Six gun-carriages are to be sent down to the fort, to-morrow, completed. It was

Resolved, That a warrant be drawn on the Treasurer by the Chairman in favor of the Chairman of the Committee for the Defence of the Delaware, for four thousand six hundred dollars, to pay for the above three vessels purchased.

The Committee of Accounts, who were directed to digest a plan by which all accounts shall be settled, report as follows (this report was adopted, as amended, the 10th of September):

1*st*. No money to be drawn from the Treasurer except by a resolve of the General Committee of Defence, and an order signed for that purpose by the Chairman, and countersigned by the Secretary ("or the Assistant Secretary," ordered to be added to this article on the 9th of September).

2*dly*. That the different sub-committees appointed by

the General Committee are authorized to enter into contracts with individuals, and to make payments for purchases in all cases where they may deem it necessary, they consulting with the General Committee where they may consider it expedient.

3*dly*. Each committee must confine themselves to the purchase of the articles wanted in their department.

4*thly*. In all contracts and purchases the objects must be designated, and payments for all and every purpose must be accompanied with duplicate vouchers.

5*thly*. All applications for money by the sub-committees must be made to the General Committee by their chairman, accompanied by a resolve specifying the sum wanted.

6*thly*. The sub-committees are to exhibit accounts of their expenditures, from time to time, to the Committee of Accounts, in which it is required that they should specify particularly their object, viz.: such as in their opinion may entitle the General Committee to a claim on the United States and State of Pennsylvania, and of such as may be chargeable to the General Committee. The Committee of Accounts after examination shall report on them accordingly.

7*thly*. Any claim on this Board, which did not originate with any of the sub-committees, must be laid before the General Committee before any payment can be had.

8*thly*. A book shall be provided by the Committee of Accounts, wherein accounts shall be opened with the different sub-committees, charging them severally with all moneys placed in their hands by resolution of the General Committee of Defence, and giving them credit for their expenditures, on their examination of the accounts and their approval by the General Committee. Accounts shall also be opened against the United States, the State of Pennsylvania, and the General Committee. The vouchers for all accounts for moneys paid shall be placed in the hands of the Secretary.

The above report was ordered to lie on the table.

The Committee appointed to consider Gen'l Bloomfield's letter, &c. concerning Mr. McKoy, reported favorably. Whereupon it was

Resolved, That the sum of two thousand dollars be loaned to General Bloomfield for Mr. McKoy, taking the General's note as security for the same, and that the Chairman be instructed to issue a warrant on the Treasurer in favor of Gen'l Bloomfield for said amount.

The same Committee stated that General Bloomfield had informed them that he had issued orders to the brigade-inspector to give the volunteer companies such rifles as would answer, &c.

Resolved, That Mr. Reed be added to the Committe of Accounts.

The resolution moved yesterday, concerning the erection of fortifications on the Pea Patch and Newbold's Point, was adopted, with the following amendment, viz.: "and that the Committee report to this Board any additional works that may in their opinion be necessary." The Sub-Committee of Defence and the Committee for the Defence of the Delaware were appointed a joint committee to carry the above-mentioned resolution into effect.

Mr. Whitehead reported the following donations, amounting to one hundred and one dollars, which was paid over to the Treasurer, viz.:

From D. Charpentier, in lieu of personal labor				$10
"	Peter Lesley,	"	"	8
"	Peter Lesley, Jr.,	"	"	5
"	Wm. Smith, Minor St.,	"	"	5
"	Ed. Kelly,	"	"	10
"	Lewis Ryan,	"	"	5
"	I. H. Roberjot,	"	"	5
"	Joseph Lee,	"	"	5
"	Capt. Th. Moore,	"	"	3
"	Jno. Keating,	"	"	10
"	Aug's De Fraunce,	"	"	10
"	Jno. McCulloch,	"	"	10
"	Jno. McCulloch, for poor soldiers' wives			10
Cash (from a person who does not wish his name published)				5
				$101

Ordered to be published.

A letter of Capt. Ross, of the videttes, was read.

Adjourned.

FRANCIS S. COXE,
Assistant Secretary.

FIFTEENTH MEETING.

PHILADELPHIA, *September 9th*, 1814.

The Committee met.

Present:—Messrs. Biddle, Reed, Cadwalader, Latimer, Connelly, Eyre, Williams, Brown, Huff, Sergeant, Leib, McMullin, Ferguson, Leiper, Thompson, Miercken, Josiah, Steel, Whitehead, McFaden.

The minutes of the last meeting were read.

The Chairman stated that he had handed the report of the committee appointed to devise means for distressing the enemy to the Governor, who said that he would attend to it.

A letter from the Governor of Pennsylvania to General Williams, concerning the question of the liability of volunteer associations to militia duty, was read, and referred to the Sub-Committee of Defence.

A letter from H. McDonald, First Lieut. of Pennsylvania Guards, of this date, applying for 50 stand of arms, was read, and ordered to lie on the table.

Mr. Cadwalader stated that he had received a military appointment from the Governor, which would prevent him from devoting much of his attention to the business of the Sub-Committee of Defence. Whereupon

Resolved, That Mr. Reed be added to said committee.

The Committee of Accounts report, that they have examined the bill exhibited by John Barney, for beef purchased of him by order of the Committee of Supplies, and find it correct. They therefore offer the following resolution:

"*Resolved*, That an order be drawn by the Chairman, &c. on the Treasurer, in favor of John Barney, for five thousand one hundred and eighty-eight dollars and twenty-two cents."

The above resolution was adopted.

The Committee of Accounts also reported that they had examined the following accounts, and recommended the payment of them to the General Committee, viz.:

Joseph E. Simmons' bill for boards	$12 39
J. McGlathery, fixing stage	5 00
Thos. Shipley, 8 lb. nails	1 00
	$18 39

Whereupon

Resolved, That the Chairman, &c. draw an order on the Treasurer, in favor of James McGlathery, for the above amount of eighteen dollars and thirty-nine cents.

The Committee of Supplies, to whom was referred the application of the captain and first lieutenant of the Newtown Light Infantry Corps, report:

That, in the opinion of the Committee, the subject referred belongs to the General Committee of Defence for decision, it being in no manner within the sphere of the appointment of the Committee of Supplies. They therefore request to be discharged from the further consideration of the subject. Whereupon

Resolved. That two hundred and fifty dollars be loaned to the Newtown Light Infantry Company on the personal responsibility of the captain and first lieutenant, and that the Chairman be instructed to draw an order on the Treasurer accordingly for the said amount.

The Committee for Defence of the Delaware reported in favor of granting the request contained in the letter yesterday referred to them from Captain Ansley and others of the Marine Artillery. Whereupon

Resolved, That the Committee for the Defence of the Delaware be instructed to comply with the request contained in the above-mentioned letter from the Marine Artillery.

Resolved, That the Committee for the Defence of the Delaware be authorized and requested to call to their assistance Mr. Anthony Cuthbert and Mr. Bankson Taylor.

Resolved, That the Committee for the Defence of the Delaware be instructed to take an account of the number of ships' boats, and their situation in this harbor, and to report the same to this Committee.

The report made by the Committee of Accounts of a plan for settling accounts was taken up, and the words "or the Assistant Secretary," ordered to be added to the first article.

The report was then recommitted to said Committee for further consideration; and it was

Resolved, That Mr. Latimer be added to the Committee of Accounts for the purpose of considering the above-mentioned report.

The report of rules and regulations for this Committee was again read, and the consideration of it postponed.

The resolution adopted yesterday concerning the appointment of a committee for erecting fortifications on the Pea Patch and Newbold's Point was again taken up and considered, and the execution of it ordered to be postponed till further orders.

A letter from R. Rush to Messrs. Eyre and Cadwalader was read.

Resolved, That the Committee of Correspondence be instructed to write to the Secretary at War, requesting that General Swift be ordered to this district as soon as possible.

Resolved, That said Committee wait upon General Bloomfield, previously to writing, to know what information he may have received from Washington relative to the defence of this district.

Mr. Whitehead reported the following donations, amounting to four hundred and eighteen dollars, which was paid over to the Treasurer:

From Wm. Y. Birch, in lieu of labor	$20
" Wm. Oliver, " "	5
" Dan'l Dick & Co. " "	10
" Horatio Mann, " "	10
" John Angue, " "	10
" John Workman, " "	20
" J. G. Wachsmuth, " "	30
" R. M., " "	5
" Lewis Brown, " "	10
" Jacob Fitler, Sheriff, in lieu of labor	25
" Adolph Eringus	25
" Henry Gardiner, an alien	10
" Dr. Adam Seybert	25
" George Nugent, for general defence of the city	100
" Dan'l Braentigan, in lieu of labor	3
" " " for poor soldiers' families	5
" Francis Mitchell, " "	10
" John Angue, " "	15
" Jas. T. Spencer, " "	20
" Jos. Spencer, " "	10
" John L. Clark, in lieu of labor and for poor soldiers' families	50
	$418

Adjourned.

FRANCIS S. COXE,

Assistant Secretary.

SIXTEENTH MEETING.

PHILADELPHIA, *September* 10*th*, 1814.

Present:—Messrs. Biddle, Goodman, Eyre, Barker. Leiper, Sergeant, McMullin, Latimer, Brown, Hawkins, Josiah, McFaden, Peltz.

The minutes of the last meeting were read.

A letter from James L. Cuthbert, Lieutenant of videttes, was read, and referred to the Sub-Committee for
Defence of the Delaware.

The Committee appointed to sound the Delaware
in the neighborhood of Reedy Island made a report
in writing, which was referred to the Committee for the
Defence of the Delaware.

The Committee for the Defence of the Delaware
report:

"That they have purchased three vessels, as follows:

The sloop Two Sisters for............................	$1400 00
" schooner Ruby for...............................	1500 00
" sloop Three Sisters for..........................	1600 00
	$4500 00
They have advanced—	
Lieut. Baker for the payment of the carpenters employed in making carriages for Fort Mifflin...	564 94
	$5064 94

"Five carriages were sent to Fort Mifflin this morning, with two of the vessels prepared for sinking. The
workmen inform the Committee that eight more carriages will be ready by Tuesday next." Whereupon

Ordered, That the Chairman, &c. issue a warrant for
said sum of five thousand and sixty-four dollars and
ninety-four cents, on the Treasurer, in favor of the
Chairman of the Committee for Defence of the Delaware.

The Committee of Correspondence handed in a letter
of 6th inst. from Mr. Monroe, Acting Secretary of War,

to General Bloomfield, which was read, and ordered to be returned to General Bloomfield.

Resolved, That the Committee of Correspondence be instructed to write to the Secretary at War, requesting that the five thousand men who have been required from Pennsylvania, and have been marched in a direction toward Baltimore, may be ordered either to some position near Philadelphia, or to a position between Baltimore and Philadelphia, from which they may operate toward either, according to circumstances.

Resolved, That John Connelly, John Sergeant, and Manuel Eyre be a committee to visit Fort Mifflin to-morrow, and report to this Committee what additional labors are necessary for the immediate completion of its defences.

Resolved, That application be made to General Bloomfield for a parcel of rifles now in the U. S. Arsenal, that were originally not good or in want of repair, that the same may be put in the best order possible, and that the Committee be answerable for such only as stand proof and can be repaired.

Referred to the Committee of Supplies.

The following resolution was moved, and the consideration of it postponed, viz.:

"*Resolved*, That a committee be appointed to inquire whether guns suitable for field redoubts and other works are wanted; and if wanted, whether they can be got.

and where, and at what prices, and also what will be wanted to make them ready for service."

The letter from James Forten, received the 8th inst., was called for and read, and referred to the Committee of Supplies.

A letter from Joseph G. Chambers, of this date, to Mr. Miercken, with several inclosures, concerning repeating guns, were read, and directed to be returned to Mr. Miercken.

The report of the Committee of Accounts of a plan by which all accounts shall be settled was again read, and adopted as amended yesterday.

(See report as amended, page 104.)

Mr. Whitehead reported the following donations received this day, amounting to eighty-nine dollars, which was paid to the Treasurer, viz.:

From John Draper, Sansom St., in lieu of labor	$25
" Joseph Simons, " "	10
" a person unknown, " "	5
Inclosed in a letter, signed "A Frenchman," for poor soldiers' families	10
From Rev'd Dr. Janeway	20
" Rev'd Mr. Joyce	5
" Rev'd Mr. Skinner	5
Collected by Mrs. Oliver	9
	$89

A letter from Joseph White, Trenton, 8th inst., recommending a plan of defence, was referred to the Sub-Committee of Defence.

The Sub-Committee of Defence handed in a letter,

dated the 9th inst., which they had received from the Governor of Pennsylvania, which was read, and of which the following is a copy, viz.:

"Philadelphia, 9th September, 1814.

"To Jonathan Williams, Esquire,
 Chairman of Sub-Committee of Defence.
"Sir:

"I accord in sentiment and opinion with the Sub-Committee of Defence in their report to the General Committee of Defence, dated the 3d inst. (a copy of which has been submitted to me by Gen'l John Steele, a member of the said committee), on the subject of a communication to the Committee from the Corresponding Committee of the Northern Liberties, where they request 'that the Committee of Defence will take measures to enable the several district committees to give a pledge that the members of organized volunteer corps, whose services shall have been accepted by the Committee, shall not be liable to militia duty.' For the obvious reason that however much is to be applauded the genuine American spirit which prompts the voluntary tender of service under consideration, and (however willing to foster it) it is not competent to the constituted authorities of this or of the United States, without the express sanction of law, to employ for local purposes, and in a particular manner, any such volunteer associations.

(Signed) "SIMON SNYDER."

The Sub-Committee of Defence reported the following addition to their report of 3d inst. concerning the liability of volunteer associations to the militia duty (which see, page 79), viz.:

4*thly*. But the Committee nevertheless strongly and earnestly recommend to their fellow-citizens the formation of volunteer corps as calculated to be most useful to the country, and in every respect most advantageous to the individual, while, on the other hand, it imposes no additional duty, and subjects the volunteer to no service that might not be required of him in the militia.

This remark is made by the Committee to obviate an erroneous opinion which appears to prevail, that the volunteer corps, whether they offer or not, are liable to calls of service to which they would not be exposed in the militia. In fact, they will only be called upon as a part of the militia, and the question they have to consider is, whether, in case of emergency, they will march in the ranks of the militia, properly so called, without the preparatory exercise of drill and discipline, without an acquaintance with their officers and each other, and without a knowledge of their arms, or whether they will at once arrange themselves into companies, acquire the elements of discipline, choose their own officers and associates, become acquainted with their arms, and know when they take the field whom and what they may depend upon. The Committee think there can be no doubt of the course which prudence no less than patriotism dictates.

5*thly*. Those who are not liable to militia duty, being

above or under age, or otherwise exempt, if they mean to secure to themselves the privilege of exemption, ought to avoid associating with those who are liable to militia duty. Such corps, formed entirely of exempts, may, if they think proper, place themselves under the direction of the Committee of Defence, who will use their utmost exertions to furnish them with arms and equipments.

Resolved, That the Secretary be requested to cause one copy of the report of the Sub-Committee of Defence concerning volunteer associations (with the above addition) to be furnished to each volunteer association that has applied, or may apply, on the subject of it, and that he have it printed if he think proper.

Adjourned.

FRANCIS S. COXE,
Assistant Secretary.

SEVENTEENTH MEETING.

PHILADELPHIA, *September* 11*th*, 1814.

The Committee met.

Present:—Messrs. Biddle, Goodman, Ronaldson, Steel, Ferguson, McFaden, Miercken, Whitehead, Groves, Palmer, Leiper, Latimer, Thompson, Leib, Huff, Reed, Williams, Peltz.

The minutes of the last meeting were read.

A letter from Capt. Ross, of the videttes, Mt. Bull.

10th inst., 8h. 10m. A.M., was read; also a copy of a letter from T. B. Forman, Br.-Gen'l M. M., dated 10th inst., to Major Whann, of Elkton.

Messrs. Eyre and Cadwalader handed in a letter from the Secretary of the Navy of the 7th inst., which was read, and of which the following is a copy:

"NAVY DEPARTMENT, *September 7th*, 1814.
"GENTLEMEN :

"My incessant occupation with the preparations and measures adopted, under the hope of destroying or annoying the enemy's squadron in the Potomac, and the derangement of the department by the late disaster, may account for the delay in answering your letter of the 30th ultimo. Commodore Rodgers has returned to Baltimore with the whole of his force, and will immediately proceed to his station on the Delaware. The instructions from this department to Commodore Rodgers, in relation to the defence of your district, will be as comprehensive and discretionary as the nature of the service and due attention to the protection of neighboring districts will admit; but a powerful force of the enemy being constantly in the Chesapeake, within a few hours sail of Baltimore, which may be attacked when least expected, it is not considered expedient or safe to authorize the withdrawing of the local naval force allotted for the special protection of that place without the previous sanction of this department, where it is presumed the movements and designs of the enemy in the Chesapeake may be better known than at Philadelphia. The intricacy and hazard of the navigation of the Delaware, particularly at this season, will not admit of the approach of a formidable hostile force with such rapidity as to preclude the knowledge of this department and the execution of its orders to the force at Baltimore.

"You may, however, rest assured of the vigilant attention of this department, and the prompt application of the means it may have at command for the protection of your district, whenever the approach of the enemy shall endanger its safety.

"I am, &c.,

(Signed) "W. JONES.

"MESSRS. EYRE AND CADWALADER,
"*Sub-Committee.*"

The Committee of Supplies handed in a letter, which they had received from General Bloomfield, which was returned to them, and of which the following is a copy, viz.:

"MILITARY DISTRICT, No. 4.

"HEADQUARTERS,

"PHILADELPHIA, *9th September*, 1814.

"The General Committee of Safety for the City and Districts of Philadelphia having proposed that all the *gun-carriages* in the Arsenal of the United States, near the City of Philadelphia, shall be repaired, the *howitz, mortars*, and *field ordnance* at the same time be mounted for service, that certain *trumbills* therein be converted into traveling forges, that a quantity of ammunition for cannon and musquets be made up, under the superintendence of such person or persons as the said committee shall appoint, the expenses of doing the same to be paid by the said committee, and reimbursed by the United States—to which proposition, on behalf of the United States, the commanding general agrees, and orders that the military storekeeper of the Arsenal deliver to the order of the said committee the *gun-carriages, howitz, mortars,* and *field ordnance* and *trumbills* for the objects proposed by the said committee, and also cannon and musquet *powder,* lead, musquet bullet-moulds, and *cannon-ball* and *shot,* to be made into musquet-ball cartridges and fixed ammunition, and that the same be stored for safe keeping in the Arsenal of the State of Pennsylvania, subject only to the order of the commanding general of the fourth military district or officer of the United States commanding in Philadelphia.

"It is expected that as soon as the amount of the expenditure shall be ascertained, the same shall be exhibited for examination by an officer of the commissary-general's department, and on whose certificate the commanding general will give the proper voucher, so that the same may be charged against and paid by the United States.

   (Signed)   "JOSEPH BLOOMFIELD,
     "*Br.-Gen'l Command'g Fourth Mil. Dist.*"
Adjourned.
      FRANCIS S. COXE,
        Assistant Secretary.

EIGHTEENTH MEETING.

Philadelphia, *September* 12*th*, 1814.

The Committee met.

Present:—Messrs. Biddle, Goodman, Reed, Latimer, Leib, Palmer, Steel, Williams, McFaden, Sergeant, Leiper, Ronaldson, Miercken, Eyre, Whitehead, Ferguson, Connelly, Huff, Brown, Josiah, Hawkins, Barker.

The minutes of the last meeting were read.

A report from Patrick Lyon and Wm. Lace respecting gun-carriages, and recommending the erection of another fire-engine house at the U. S. Arsenal, was read, and referred to the Committee of Supplies.

An order from General Bloomfield to the commandant of Fort Mifflin, to deliver to Colonel Goodman a brass 9-pounder and a 6-pounder, for the purpose of being mounted, &c., was read.

The Committee for Defence of the Delaware reported a letter from the Treasury Department, authorizing them to make use of the revenue cutter in the Delaware, which was read, and returned to said committee.

The Committee for Defence of the Delaware handed in a communication from Commodore Murray, respecting the number of cannon, also gun-carriages, in the Navy Yard, which was read, and of which the following is a copy, viz.:

"Account of cannon in the Navy Yard, September 10th, 1814:

28 32-pounders.	156 9-pounders.
19 24-pounders.	32 6-pounders.
92 18-pounders.	68 4-pounders.
54 12-pounders.	1 42-pound cannonade.

"There are no gun-carriages of any description, except those made for the frigate Guerriere, 10 of which may be appropriated for the pier-battery for the 24-pounders. All the gun-boats mount one 32-pounder, of which there are 17 with a gun on board.

(Signed)   "A. MURRAY,
"*Naval Commander, Philadelphia Station.*"

The Committee appointed to visit Fort Mifflin, report:

That they, in company with Captain Josiah, Chairman of the Committee for Defence of the Delaware, yesterday performed the object of their appointment; that they, in conjunction with Captain Josiah, made arrangements for employing an additional number of carpenters and other workmen, which they deemed essential for the speedy completion of the fortifications in Fort Mifflin.

The Committee found a number of pieces of brass ordnance in the fort and at the Lazaretto, which they deem of no utility where they now are. They therefore recommend the whole to be brought up to the city and put in complete order. The list of ordnance is as follows, viz.:

In Fort Mifflin.

2 24-pounders.
2 howitzers.
1 6-pounder (requiring bushing, with carriage).
1 howitzer, with carriage.

At the Old Lazaretto.
2 brass 6-pounders, with carriages and harness.
2 caissons for carriages and harness.

They therefore recommend the following resolution, viz.:

"*Resolved*, That a committee be appointed to wait on General Bloomfield, and procure an order for all the ordnance before mentioned to be brought up to the city, and put in complete order for field service."

The above resolution was adopted, and Mr. Goodman appointed the committee therein named.

The following resolution, proposed by the committee appointed to visit Fort Mifflin, was also adopted, viz.:

Resolved, That the Committee of Correspondence be authorized to write to the Secretary at War for an officer of experience, ability, and confidence of the ordnance department, to be placed on duty in Philadelphia as early as possible.

In consequence of a communication from General Bloomfield to the Chairman, stating that fifty thousand dollars are immediately wanted to supply the contractor, commissary-general of purchases, quartermaster-general's department, &c., it was

Resolved, That this Committee loan to General Bloomfield the sum of fifty thousand dollars upon his individual responsibility, to be returned as soon as the loan now asked by the Secretary at War is obtained from the banks; that an order be drawn by the Chairman,

&c. on the Treasurer, in favor of General Bloomfield. for the said sum, and that the Chairman and Treasurer be instructed to make the necessary arrangements with General Bloomfield.

Resolved, That it be earnestly recommended to the committees appointed in the several wards of the city and in the adjoining districts to proceed immediately. by personal application, to solicit from the citizens donations of *blankets;* that this resolution be inserted in the newspapers, and a copy furnished to the person first named on each committee, with a request that such committee will immediately adopt measures to give effect to this recommendation.

Resolved, That the sum of one thousand dollars be placed in the hands of the Sub-Committee of Defence. and that an order be drawn in favor of their Chairman on the Treasurer for said amount.

Resolved, That a committee be appointed to wait upon the Governor of this Commonwealth, and inquire what means have been used to bring a competent force in men into the field, and within what time any given force may be expected to be in the field.

Messrs. Williams, Leiper, and Ronaldson were appointed said committee.

Resolved, That it is expedient to have a local force of five regiments, under the authority of the United States, for the defence of this city and its neighborhood.

and that application be made to Congress to authorize such a force.

The Committee of Correspondence were instructed to carry the above resolution into effect.

Resolved, That Mr. Reed be excused from serving on the Sub-Committee of Defence, and that Mr. Ronaldson be added to said committee.

Mr. Whitehead stated that he had received the following donations, amounting to five hundred and sixty-two dollars, which was paid over to the Treasurer, viz.:

From	Silas E. Weir, for erecting works of defence....			$100
"	Dockeray Smith,	"	"	100
"	Edward Burd, in lieu of labor, and for relief of absent soldiers' families			50
"	Henry Sheaff, for general defence			20
"	George Budd,	"	"	20
"	Thos. Moore,	"	"	17
"	John Lea, in lieu of labor			20
"	Edward Miles, in lieu of labor			10
"	Charles Pleasants, in lieu of labor			10
"	Leeson Simmons,	"	"	5
"	John Troubat,	"	"	10
"	Lewis M. Prevost,	"	"	10
"	Edward Farres,	"	"	5
"	John Perot,	"	"	10
"	C. Gobricht,	"	"	10
"	David Hogan,	"	"	5
"	Matthew Carey,	"	"	10
"	Matthew Carey, for absent soldiers' families....			10
"	Dr. John Porter,	"	"	20
"	Rev. P. F. Meyers,	"	"	10
"	Wm. Thaw,	"	"	5
"	John De la Matre.	"	"	10

Amount carried forward............... $467

Amount brought forward	$467
From the inhabitants of North Ward, in lieu of labor, viz.:	
Dr. P. Physick	10
Dr. John S. Dorsey	10
Jacob Rease	10
William Schlatter	10
John Lisle	10
Charles Massey, Jr.	10
J. R. N. Weems	5
Joseph Roberts	5
James Pleasants	1
Dr. Janney	2
Charles B. Whitlock	2
Stephen Sicard	2
George Allebeu	1
T. Benjean	5
Cash	12
	$562

Adjourned.

FRANCIS S. COXE,
Assistant Secretary.

NINETEENTH MEETING.

PHILADELPHIA, *September* 13*th*, 1814.

The Committee met.

Present:—Messrs. Biddle, Goodman, Ronaldson, Eyre, Sergeant, Connelly, Hawkins, McFaden, Miercken, Leiper, Groves, Williams, Steel, Huff, Latimer, Reed, Palmer, Leib, Whitehead, Brown.

The minutes of the last meeting were read.

A letter from J. H. Nezmos, Lieutenant of a rifle corps, at Kennet's Square, complaining of their rifles being unfit for service, was read, and referred to the Committee of Supplies.

A letter from Colonel P. L. Berry, at Kennet's Square, requesting a supply of blankets and shoes for the militia under his command, was read. Whereupon

Resolved, That said letter be referred to the Committee of Supplies, who are hereby instructed to make inquiry of General Bloomfield, whether the United States can furnish the above articles required for the militia.

An application from the Navy Yard for furloughs was read, and ordered to be sent to General Bloomfield.

A letter from Governor Rodney, of Delaware, to the Committee of Correspondence, informing of the means of defence of that State, was read, and ordered to lie on the table.

A letter from Captain Walter Sims, concerning the defence of the Delaware, &c., was read, and referred to the Committee of Defence for the Delaware.

A letter from N. B. Boileau, Secretary of the Commonwealth, in answer to the report handed to the Governor by the Chairman of this Committee, concerning the means of distressing the enemy, was read. The part of this letter relating to the removal of the shipping up the Delaware was referred to the Committee for Defence of the Delaware.

A letter from the Secretary of the Commonwealth, in answer to the Committee appointed yesterday to wait upon the Governor to know what means have been used to bring a competent force into the field, and within what time any given force may be expected to be in the field, was read; also copy of a letter from the Governor to the Secretary at War, dated 9th inst., requesting the aid of the 5000 Pennsylvania militia that rendezvoused at York, on the 5th inst., in defending the shores of the Delaware. The part of the letter from the Secretary of the Commonwealth last mentioned, which relates to the erection of fortifications, was referred to the Sub-Committee of Defence. Also

Resolved, That Messrs. Williams, Leiper, and Ronaldson be a committee to wait immediately upon General Bloomfield with the communication from the Governor of Pennsylvania (Secretary of the Commonwealth), and request from General Bloomfield an answer, in writing, as expeditiously as possible, what force he now has under his command in the field, what portion of the militia is called out into actual service under his authority, and when he expects the whole of his force encamped, and any other information he possesses relative to the preparation for defence of this district.

Resolved, That the communications that shall hereafter be received from the videttes be published.

An order from General Bloomfield, to the military storekeeper at the U. S. Arsenal, to deliver to this Committee "all the rifles called condemned rifles," was read, and referred to the Committee of Supplies.

A letter from the marshal to the Chairman of this

Committee, informing that he had "adopted the measure necessary for the removal of the prisoners confined in the new prison," was read.

The Committee of Accounts stated that they had examined a bill of Horner & Wilson, for ———, amounting to $2295.62, and a bill of Imley & Potts, for ———, amounting to $7365, both of which they find correct, and report the same for payment. Whereupon

Resolved. That warrants be drawn on the Treasurer, in favor of the Chairman of the Committee of Supplies, for the before-mentioned sums of two thousand two hundred and ninety-five dollars and sixty-two cents, and of seven thousand three hundred and sixty-five dollars.

Mr. Whitehead reported that he had received the following donations, which were paid over to the Treasurer, amounting to three hundred and eighty-two dollars and ninety-three cents, viz.:

Jno. M. Soullier,	in lieu of labor		$10 00
Robert Scott,	"	"	10 00
Richard Williams,	"	"	1 25
J. L. Bujac,	"	"	10 00
Peter Vanpelt,	"	"	5 00
Hugh Jones,	"	"	1 00
Ab. Stein,	"	"	5 00
Jos. Kebler,	"	"	1 00
Mr. Clampher,	"	"	2 00
Mr. Kunkle,	"	"	18½
C. Bartholomew,	"	"	2 00
John Bedford,	"	"	10 00
Samuel Moss,	"	"	20 00
Robert Fielding,	"	"	20 00

COMMITTEE OF DEFENCE.

Charles Brugiere, in lieu of labor		$25	00
James Ross,	" "	20	00
Dr. Mongers,	" "	10	00
Ferragus V. D. Gelore,	" "	5	00
Benj. Trott,	" "	10	00
*Daniel King,	" "	20	00
Benj. Canonge,	" "	10	00
Lewis Lay,	" "	10	00
Peter Vanpelt, for soldiers' families		5	00
James Martin,	" "	20	00
Miss Giberson,	" "	1	00
Miss Tunnel,	" "	2	00
Henry Gordon,	" "		50
W. Fest,	" "	1	00
Miss Bloer,	" "	1	00
Thos. Little,	" "	5	00
John Magoffin, at the disposal of the Committee		100	00
James Darrach, in lieu of labor and for soldiers' families		20	00
J. Ritter, Jr., in lieu of labor and for soldiers' families		20	00
		$382	93½
*Say James Ross, for labor		5	00
" for defence of citizens		15	00
		$20	00

Corrected by report sent to the press of 23d September.

Adjourned till 9 o'clock to-morrow morning.

FRANCIS S. COXE,
Assistant Secretary.

TWENTIETH MEETING.

Philadelphia, *September* 14*th*. 1814.
9 o'clock A.M.

The Committee met.

Present:—Messrs. Biddle, Goodman, Reed, Connelly, Peltz, Huff, Whitehead, Groves, Steel, Miercken, Josiah. Eyre, Williams, Ronaldson, Sergeant, Hawkins, Palmer. McFaden, Ferguson, Brown, Latimer.

The minutes of the last meeting were read.

Mr. Taylor, one of the inspectors of the prison, attended, and stated that the inspectors wished the Committee to take measures for the removal of the convicts in the prison into the interior. Whereupon

Resolved, That Mr. Connelly be requested to have a conference with the inspectors on this subject.

The Committee appointed to wait on General Bloomfield, yesterday, to know what forces he has under his command in the field, &c., reported a letter from General Bloomfield, in answer to their queries, which was read, and of which the following is a copy, viz.:

"Fourth Military District.

"Philadelphia, *September* 13*th*, 1814.
"10 at night.

"Conformably to the foregoing resolution, I have the honor to state that—

Of the first division of militia of Pennsylvania, the quota of the *first* brigade are in the field............ 1520
Five companies of the second brigade have also marched, and the residue expected to march on Friday 1686
The order of this day should bring the quota of...... 2950
                                                                                                                                                                     ─────
                                                                                                                                                                     6056

"I have not called on the distant counties of Northampton, Pike, and Lehigh, nor do I know from what counties the 5000 men, at General Winder's requisition, have been detailed. In short, I have received no return of the details made, or names of the officers designated to command the drafts which shall have been made under the requisition of the President of the United States.

"It was not until yesterday that General Cadwalader was designated, as he reported to me, when he set out to command the brigade detached from the first division.

"It is impossible to say when the men this day called for will assemble, as the militia laws of Pennsylvania are very deficient in energy. The quota of my command in New Jersey, and of which I had proposed to assemble at Billingsport, on the application of Governor Pennington to the Secretary at War, are ordered to encamp near Trenton, but subject to my orders.

They are to be... 2000
Delaware (of which half are in the field).......... 1000
Which, added to the Pennsylvania militia, give *in numbers* a force of............................. 9056
This morning's report of Fort Mifflin, delivered herewith, artillery 274

The recruits called do not exceed (under Colonel
Clemson)... 350

Total....................... 9680

"I have the honor to be, &c.,

(Signed) "JOSEPH BLOOMFIELD,
"*Brig.-Gen'l Command'g.*
"MESSRS. WILLIAMS, LEIPER, AND RONALDSON."

Resolved, That Messrs. Sergeant, Steel, Eyre, and Groves be a committee to wait upon the Governor of Pennsylvania, and inquire of him, whether arms and ammunition can be had to be placed in the hands of our fellow-citizens not liable to militia duty, or to any call, or who have not been called into service, and who are willing to organize and embody themselves for public defence.

The said committee are directed to take with them a copy of General Bloomfield's letter of yesterday to this committee. (See page 132.)

Resolved, That said committee be instructed to inquire whether any, and what measures, have been taken to bring an additional supply of arms to this city, and at what time arms may be expected here.

Resolved, That said committee be instructed to inquire whether any answer has been received to the applications made to the War Department for a force of regulars, and for authority to enlist regulars.

Resolved, That said committee be instructed to request that the Governor's answers may be in writing.

Resolved, That the said committee be instructed to inform the Governor, that it is the opinion of this Committee, that the whole body of the militia within this military district ought immediately to be called into actual service, and encamped at some distance in advance of this city.

The Committee of Supplies reported the following answer by General Bloomfield to the inquiries they were directed to make concerning blankets and shoes for Colonel Berry's men, viz.:

"It will not be prudent to take a blanket from the commissary's store. Shoes will be delivered on Governor Snyder's order, for those actually in want, and which must be deducted from their pay.

(Signed) "JOSEPH BLOOMFIELD,
Brig.-Gen'l Command'g.
"14*th September*, 1814."

Resolved, That the committee this day appointed to wait on the Governor be instructed to hand to him copies of a letter from Colonel P. L. Berry to this Committee, of their resolution to apply to General Bloomfield on the subject, and of General Bloomfield's answer.

A letter was read from B. Chew, Jr., Lieutenant Franklin Flying Artillery, with inclosures, concerning the expenses of bringing four pieces of ordnance from Baltimore, and referred to the Committee of Accounts.

A letter from Passmore & Sperry, tendering a nine-pound cannon and carriage, was read, and referred to the Committee of Supplies.

The Committee of Accounts stated that they had examined a bill for logs, amounting to $275, and a bill from Jno. Keith, doorkeeper, for $13.69, and that they found the same right, and reported them for payment. Whereupon

Ordered, That warrants be drawn on the Treasurer, in favor of the Chairman of the Committee for Defence of the Delaware, for above sum of two hundred and seventy-five dollars, and in favor of John Keith for above sum of thirteen dollars and sixty-nine cents.

Adjourned.

FRANCIS S. COXE,
Assistant Secretary.

TWENTY-FIRST MEETING.

PHILADELPHIA, *September* 14*th*, 1814.
3 o'clock P.M.

The Committee met.

Present:—Messrs. Biddle, Reed, Ronaldson, Whitehead, Sergeant, Huff, Peltz, Leib, Palmer, Steel, Eyre, Brown, Williams, Leiper, Miercken, McFaden, Ferguson, Connelly.

The minutes of the last meeting were read.

Ordered, That the doorkeeper be instructed to allow no person to come into this room, during the sittings of the Committee, except the members.

Mr. Connelly reported that he had seen the inspectors of the prison.

The committee appointed to wait opon the Governor, reported that he would give his answers in writing this evening or to-morrow morning.

Resolved, That the Committee of Correspondence be instructed to send off, immediately, an express toward Baltimore, to obtain all possible intelligence of the enemy.

Resolved, That Messrs. Ferguson and Ronaldson be a committee to have the blankets and tents at the Lazaretto and City Hospital examined.

A letter from Daniel Hinkles, offering muskets and swords for sale, and requesting furloughs for his workmen, was read, and referred to the Governor of this Commonwealth.

Resolved, That a furlough be asked of General Bloomfield for Lieutenant Westfall.

Resolved, That the Committee of Correspondence be instructed to write to the Secretary of the Navy, requesting him to give an order to Joseph G. Chambers to furnish repeating guns to a corps he has formed for the use of them, and to procure the necessary ammunition.

It having been stated to the Committee that the Secretary of the Navy had ordered some seamen now in this city to be sent to the lakes,

Resolved, That the Committee of Correspondence be instructed to write to the Secretary of the Navy, remonstrating against sending, at this time, any seamen from the city, and that Commodore Murray be requested to detain those seamen until the Secretary's answer is received.

The Committee of Accounts stated that they had examined Lieutenant Chew's account of expenses in bringing four pieces of ordnance from Baltimore, and reported the same for payment. Whereupon

Resolved, That a warrant be drawn on the Treasurer, in favor of Lieutenant B. Chew, Jr., for the above account; amount, two hundred and eighty-six dollars and thirty-nine cents.

Mr. Whitehead stated that he had received the following donations, amounting to three hundred and three dollars, which was paid over to the Treasurer, viz.:

From	Mrs. Elizabeth Powell, for relief of absent soldiers' families	$50
"	Jacob Sperry, for relief of absent soldiers' families	25
"	Samuel Wetherill, for relief of absent soldiers' families	50
"	Michael Fagan, for relief of absent soldiers' families	10
"	Passmore & Sperry, for general defence of the city	100

From John F. Dumas, for general defence of the city... $10
" Wm. Lynch, in lieu of labor.......................... 10
" Wm. White, " " 8
" Michael Fagan, " " 5
" Dr. Elijah Griffith, in lieu of labor................ 10
" Michael Fagan, in lieu of labor................... 5
" Thos. Dobson, in lieu of labor and for defence... 20

$303

Adjourned.

FRANCIS S. COXE,
Assistant Secretary.

TWENTY-SECOND MEETING.

PHILADELPHIA, *September* 15*th*, 1814,
9 o'clock A.M.

The Committee met.

Present:—Messrs. Biddle, Reed, Whitehead, Latimer, Ferguson, Huff, Peltz, Leib, Brown, Palmer, Leiper, Steel, Eyre, Groves, Miercken, Hawkins, Ronaldson, Williams, McFaden, Sergeant.

The minutes of the last meeting were read.

A letter from General Cadwalader was read.

A letter from Commodore Murray, concerning the seamen ordered for the lakes, was read.

A letter from the Secretary of the Navy to the Committee of Correspondence, dated Washington, 10th September, was read.

A general order from General Bloomfield, to have 5,000,000 musket-cartridges, was read, and referred to the Committee of Supplies, to have it carried into execution.

The marshal attended, and made a verbal communication respecting the treatment of him, by the commandant at Fort Mifflin, in pursuing an alien enemy.

Captain Hawkins obtained leave of absence for this morning.

The following address was ordered to be published in all the newspapers, viz.:

"GENERAL COMMITTEE OF DEFENCE.

"FELLOW-CITIZENS:

"We feel it our duty to make certain communications to you, but we cannot do it by public address.

"We therefore request that you will immediately appoint two respectable citizens from each ward, and the same proportion from the districts, that is to say, twelve from the Northern Liberties and Penn Township, and ten from Southwark, Moyamensing, and Passyunk, with whom we can confer, and to whom we can make known the actual state of things.

"We request our fellow-citizens, so appointed, to meet us at the District Court-room, on Saturday morning, at 10 o'clock.

(Signed) "CHARLES BIDDLE,
"*Chairman.*"

Resolved, That the Committee of Correspondence, and the chairmen of the other standing committees, be a committee to prepare a statement to be exhibited to the committees called in the above address, and that they have access to all the books and papers of this Committee for that purpose.

Resolved, That the mayor, the aldermen, and justices of the peace be required to take immediate measures to ascertain what strangers of suspicious character come into this city and its environs, to the end that the emissaries of the enemy may be detected and punished.

The mayor, aldermen, and justices of the peace are requested to meet at the mayor's court-room, to-morrow morning, at 10 o'clock.

The above resolution and notice were ordered to be published.

Resolved, That four thousand dollars be placed in the hands of the Committee of Supplies, to be invested in blankets, to be distributed to those troops in actual service who are not able to procure them at their own expense, to be issued by the order of the brigadier-general, and that a warrant be drawn on the Treasurer, for the said amount, in favor of the chairman of said committee.

Resolved, That Messrs. Brown and Huff be a committee to wait on General Bloomfield, and request him to cause the person complained of by the marshal (an alien enemy) to be immediately arrested, and brought to this city for examination.

Adjourned.

FRANCIS S. COXE,
Assistant Secretary.

TWENTY-THIRD MEETING.

PHILADELPHIA, *September* 15*th*, 1814,
3 o'clock P.M.

The Committee met.

Present:—Messrs. Biddle, Goodman, McMullin, Eyre, Connelly, Sergeant, Hawkins, Josiah, Miercken, Whitehead, Williams, Leib, Latimer, Leiper, Steel, Palmer, Geyer, Huff, Reed, Peltz, Groves.

The minutes of the last meeting were read.

A letter of this date, from N. B. Boileau, Secretary of the Commonwealth, in answer to the committee appointed yesterday to wait on the Governor, was read.

A letter from John Donnaldson, Jr., vidette, was read.

Resolved, That the Committee of Correspondence be instructed to write to the Secretary at War, and inform that, by a communication received from the Governor of this Commonwealth, it appears that there were no arms deposited at Carlisle for the use of this district, and that this Committee request his immediate attention, to place such a quantity of arms within this district as shall be adequate for its protection, which this Committee consider should be at least 10,000 stand, exclusive of those ordered to Carlisle.

Resolved, That the Committee of Supplies be instructed to procure two thousand pikes for the defence of this district.

Resolved, That the Committee of Supplies be directed to call upon the commissary-general, and procure his order upon the military storekeeper for four tons of lead, and that they be authorized to contract for the casting the same into musket-balls and buckshot, on account of the United States.

Resolved, That a warrant be drawn on the Treasurer for forty dollars, in favor of Lieutenant B. Chew, Jr., for additional expenses in bringing four pieces of ordnance from Baltimore.

A letter from Daniel Pettibone (pikemaker), requesting furloughs for John Yager and Claudius M. Cox, was read, and referred to General Bloomfield.

Mr. Whitehead stated that he had received two hundred and fifty-two dollars donations, which was handed over to the Treasurer, viz.:

From John Moss, for defence of the city..............				$50
" Christ. W. Gome (an alien), in lieu of labor......				2
" Jacob David,	"	"	......	5
" Jacob Patterson,	"	"	......	10
" A friendly alien,	"	"	......	5
" Jacob David, for relief of absent soldiers' families				5
" Matthew Roush,	"	"		10
" The Rev'd Clergy of St. Mary's, Holy Trinity, and St. Augustine, for relief of absent soldiers' families				30
" Priscella Patterson, for relief of absent soldiers' families				5
" Thos. Burke, in lieu of labor and for relief of absent soldiers' families				10
" Philip Keely, for defence of the city..............				50
" Hugh Dehaven, Jr., "		"	....	10
" Patrick McGleney, "		"	....	10

From Horore Bayol, for defence of the city...... $5
" "R.," " " 5
" J. Hughes, teacher, " " 5
" A. Vitry, " " 5
" E. Cohen, " " 5
" Sundry citizens of Lower Delaware Ward...... 20
" Priscella Patterson, for general defence...... 5

$252

Adjourned.

FRANCIS S. COXE,
Assistant Secretary.

TWENTY-FOURTH MEETING.

PHILADELPHIA, *September* 16*th*, 1814.

The Committee met.

Present:—Messrs. Biddle, Goodman, Reed, Sergeant. McMullin, Steel, Connelly, Ferguson, Ronaldson, McFaden, Hawkins, Leib, Miercken, Leiper, Williams. Whitehead, Peltz, Huff, Eyre, Latimer, Brown, Barker.

The minutes of the last meeting were read.

A letter from Captain John Uhle, of a rifle corps. requesting the Committee to pay the expense of cutting out frocks for his company, was read. Whereupon

Resolved, That the request of Captain Uhle be complied with.

Resolved, That the Committee of Supplies be instructed to furnish twelve blankets to Captain Starnes.

of the Roxborough volunteers, for the use of his company, agreeably to his application.

A statement from Major Beale, concerning the marshal's visit to Fort Mifflin, received from General Bloomfield, was read, and ordered to be returned to General Bloomfield.

A letter from a Northern Liberty rifle company, Captain Swift, requesting the Committee to furnish them with uniforms, was read and referred to a committee to report thereon, viz.: Messrs. Eyre, Reed, and Ronaldson.

An application from Captain John Annesley, of the Marine Artillery, for provision, during their absence, for their families, was read and referred to the Committee for Defence of the Delaware.

The Committee for Defence of the Delaware, report:

"That they have purchased two vessels, as follows, viz.:

The sloop Polly, for	$400 00
The sloop Adventure	1600 00
	$2000 00
Workmen's wages at the Navy Yard, at the carriages and sleepers for the platform, as per return of Mr. Samuel Humphries	321 92½
Total	$2321 92½

"That Captain Annesley, commanding the Marine Artillery, has returned 121 men under his command, has four gun-boats fitted completely, and will be ready to go to his station, at or near Fort Mifflin, whenever ordered, subject to the orders of the commanding officer of the flotilla. The works at Fort Mifflin, and the battery-pier, are progressing with as much expedition as they could expect."

Resolved, That a warrant be drawn on the Treasurer, in favor of the Chairman of the Committee for Defence of the Delaware, for the above amount, viz.: twenty-three hundred and twenty-one dollars and ninety-two and a half cents.

The Committee of Defence for the Delaware reported a letter, not signed, but supposed to be from A. McLane, concerning the revenue cutter.

The said committee was instructed to write again to Mr. McLane respecting the said letter.

A report of cannon, gun-carriages, and munitions of war between Pine and Chestnut Streets, was received.

A report of cannon, gun-carriages, and munitions of war in the southern part of Philadelphia, was received.

The Committee of Supplies reported that they had bought 720 blankets, and sent one bale to General Cadwalader.

A communication and resolution, respecting the Governor, was offered by Mr. Ronaldson, and the consideration of it postponed.

Mr. Whitehead reported the following donations received, amounting to three hundred and twenty-five dollars, which was paid over to the Treasurer, viz.:

COMMITTEE OF DEFENCE.

From	R Patterson, and the other gentlemen of the Mint, for general defence...............	$50
"	Hugh Henry, for general defence...............	5
"	A Friend, " "	10
"	Geo. Strawbridge, " "	10
"	Sam'l Carman, " "	5
"	Joshua C. Parke, " "	10
"	Dr. Gallagher, " "	20
"	D. Charpentier, for relief of absent soldiers' families...............	20
"	Hugh Ferguson, for relief of absent soldiers' families...............	10
"	Jacob S. Waln, for relief of absent soldiers' families...............	25
"	No. 189 Arch St., for relief of absent soldiers' families...............	50
"	Crooke Stevenson, in lieu of labor...............	10
"	A Citizen of North Ward, in lieu of labor......	2
"	Joseph Ball, " "	10
"	Abram Patton. " "	5
"	Jas. Black, " "	10
"	Conrad Hanse. " "	10
"	H. Huffnagle, " "	10
"	Captain Cushing, " "	3
"	Joseph Ball, for general defence...............	10
"	Jno. Cunningham, in lieu of labor and for relief of absent soldiers' families...............	20
"	Jno. Dabadie, in lieu of labor and for blankets...	20
		$325

Adjourned till 9 o'clock to-morrow morning.

FRANCIS S. COXE,
Assistant Secretary.

TWENTY-FIFTH MEETING.

PHILADELPHIA, *September* 17*th*, 1814.
9 o'clock A.M.

The Committee met.

Present:—Messrs. Biddle, Goodman, Steel, Leiper, Latimer, Eyre, Williams, Sergeant, Reed, Connelly, Ronaldson, Barker, Palmer, Groves, Whitehead, Brown, Ferguson, McFaden, Josiah, Miercken, Hawkins, Leib, Geyer, McMullin, Peltz.

The committee appointed to prepare a statement to be exhibited to the committees appointed yesterday by the wards and districts, reported a statement for that purpose, which was read and adopted.

The committees appointed in the different wards and districts to receive communications from this Committee, being notified that this Committee was ready to receive them, attended, and the above-mentioned statement, with sundry documents therein referred to, was read, whereupon the said committees retired. It was then

Resolved, That Messrs. Reed, McMullin, and Huff be a committee to wait upon their fellow-citizens from the wards and districts, and request them not to dissolve, but to adjourn to some future day, and that they may consider themselves as liable, under the authority of the town meeting, to be called upon by the Committee of Defence to aid in carrying into effect the object of their appointment. In the mean time, a committee of their body, should they deem it necessary, may have access to the documents which have been read to them, under the injunction that nothing communicated shall find its way into the public prints.

Resolved, That said committee be instructed to request their fellow-citizens from the wards and districts to furnish them with a list of their names, and the wards and districts for which they were severally appointed.

An application being received from Mr. Henry, requesting furloughs for the following persons engaged with him in making and repairing rifles, &c., viz.: Joseph Henry, Jeremiah Vandegrift, Isaac Vandegrift, James Eddy, James Coates, Abram Coster, it was

Resolved, That General Bloomfield be requested to grant furloughs to the above-named persons.

Resolved, That an order be drawn on the Treasurer, in favor of the Chairman of the Committee of Defence of the Delaware, for eleven hundred dollars.

Resolved, That a copy of the report of the Committee of Accounts, concerning the manner in which all accounts shall be settled, be given to the chairman of each standing committee.

The Committee of Accounts reported that they had examined the account of Mr. Bioren, for printing, and of Messrs. Leiper and Ronaldson, for the expenses on their journey to Harrisburg. Whereupon

Resolved, That warrants be drawn for the above accounts, in favor of Messrs. Leiper and Ronaldson, for forty-nine dollars, and in favor of Jno. Bioren, for thirty-five dollars, both on the Treasurer.

Adjourned till 5 p.m. to-morrow.

FRANCIS S. COXE,
Assistant Secretary.

TWENTY-SIXTH MEETING.

Philadelphia, *September* 18*th*, 1814.
5 o'clock p.m.

The Committee met.

Present:—Messrs. Biddle, Goodman, Latimer, Williams, McFaden, Hawkins, Sergeant, Miercken, Reed, Eyre, Connelly, Leiper, Steel, Leib, Palmer, McMullin. Brown, Peltz.

The minutes of the last meeting were read.

A copy of a report, made to the conferees appointed in the wards and districts, by a committee appointed by them for the purpose, containing the substance of the communication made to them by this Committee, together with a resolution of said conferees, of which the following is a copy, was read, viz.:

"*Resolved*, That the report of the committee just read be communicated to the Committee of Defence, and that that Committee be informed that said report has been accepted by this body, and will, as containing the substance of the communication made to them this morning by the Committee of Defence, be made known to the citizens of the different wards, townships and districts, on Tuesday evening next, under the restrictions as to publication suggested by the Committee, unless this body shall previously receive a communication from the Committee of Defence on the subject.

"Extract from the minutes.

(Signed) "JOHN HARRISON,
"*Secretary.*"

Whereupon, it was

Resolved, That the committee for the several wards and districts, who were appointed to receive the communications from the Committee of Defence, be informed that this Committee deem it inexpedient to have their communication of yesterday promulgated in the manner contemplated by these committees, the Committee of Defence having only in view, in making their communication, to exonerate themselves from any imputation of neglect of the important duties confided to them by their fellow-citizens.

Messrs. Leib, Sergeant, and Reed were appointed a committee to communicate the above resolution to the ward and district committees.

A communication from the 1st Company, 42d Regiment of Pennsylvania Militia, requesting the Committee to give a guarantee for the payment of eight dollars for each man in said company, for the purpose of procuring suitable uniforms, also a stipulation from said company to pay the said sum of eight dollars out of their first month's pay, for the above-mentioned purpose, being received and read, it was

Resolved, That the request of the above-mentioned company be granted.

Resolved, That whenever advances are made by this Committee to any persons called into actual service, as soldiers, under the requisition of the United States, or of this State, they be requested to sign receipts in the form that is usual in like cases of advance by the paymaster of the district.

General Williams and Mr. Latimer were appointed a committee to make report of the above-mentioned form.

The committee to whom was referred the application of the Northern Liberty Rifle Rangers, Captain Swift, report:

That the company consists of 90 men, of whom 50 are not of ability to procure uniforms. That these are a class of men capable of enduring hardships, and calculated to become good soldiers. The company are willing to offer their services to the United States, and to march in a few days, if they can receive from the Committee the aid they request, and without which, they allege, that they cannot continue associated, or render any service to their country.

To secure the services of so efficient a body of men,

the Committee recommended the following resolutions, viz.:

Resolved, That the sum of two hundred and fifty dollars be advanced to the company of Northern Liberty Rifle Rangers, under such regulation for reimbursement as shall be established by this Committee.

Resolved, That it be, and it hereby is, earnestly recommended by the General Committee of Defence, to the Governor of this Commonwealth, to order and direct the organization of corps of artillery engineers, pioneers, and artificers, whose services in the present emergency may be deemed essential to the public service, to be stationed in or near the City of Philadelphia, and to be employed on the manufacture and repair of arms, gun-carriages, or other implements of war, to aid and assist in fixing ammunition, and to do and perform such other services in the capacity of artificers, according to their several professions and abilities respectively, they be required to perform by the proper authority in aid of the public service.

Resolved, That it be recommended that such of the militia as already have or hereafter may obtain furloughs from the commanding general, for the purpose of aiding and assisting any person or persons engaged in business relating to the public service, be attached to this corps; and that it be the duty of the officers appointed to take charge thereof, to see that the members composing the same be constantly employed for the purposes and objects contained in these resolutions, and not otherwise.

A letter of 15th inst., from General Cadwalader, concerning the troops under his command, was read. Whereupon

Resolved, That Messrs. Williams, Latimer, and Eyre be a committee to wait on General Bloomfield, to know what portion of the United States requisition is now in the field, and what additional forces he intends sending under the command of General Cadwalader.

Adjourned.

FRANCIS S. COXE,
Assistant Secretary.

TWENTY-SEVENTH MEETING.

PHILADELPHIA, *September* 19*th*, 1814.
4 o'clock P.M.

The Committee met.

Present:—Messrs. Biddle, Goodman, Reed, Ronaldson, Connelly, McFaden, Josiah, Hawkins, Groves, Miercken, Steel, Williams, Leiper, Leib, Brown, Palmer, Whitehead, McMullin, Latimer, Sergeant, Eyre, Barker, Ferguson.

The minutes of the last meeting were read.

Messrs. Binda, Chauncey, and Hare attended, with a

copy of a resolution of the ward and district committees, appointing them a committee to confer with a committee to be appointed by this Board, and urge to them that the substance of the communication made to the said committees on the 17th inst. should be made known to the people, in ward, township, and district meetings. Whereupon

Resolved, That Messrs. Sergeant, Leib and Reed be a committee to confer with the delegates of the respective wards and districts, with instructions to urge in the conference, the opinion of the Committee of Defence, that the communication made by this Committee may not be promulgated to any meetings of the wards and districts.

A letter was received from General Cadwalader, informing that he had received the blankets forwarded to him.

The Treasurer reported that he had received $7000 from the Commissioners of the District of Southwark.

A letter of this date was received from General Bloomfield, requesting an advance of $25,000, and read. Whereupon

Resolved, That the sum of twenty-five thousand dollars be loaned to General Bloomfield on his note, to be repaid out of the loan which the banks contemplate making for the defence of this district.

The committee appointed to wait on General Bloomfield, to know what portion of the United States requisition is now in the field, and what additional forces he intends sending under the command of General Cadwalader, made a report in writing, which is on file. It was ordered to lie on the table.

A letter from Colonel John Thompson, requesting this Committee to loan to Captain Sparks' company, in the 140th Regiment, Pennsylvania Militia, four dollars for each man, they giving security for repayment of the same out of their wages, was read. Whereupon

Resolved, That Colonel Thompson's request be granted, and that the Chairman be requested to issue a warrant on the Treasurer for three hundred and sixty dollars, in favor of Captain Sparks, for the above purpose.

A letter from Jona. J. Good, Lieutenant of the Berks County Washington Blues, requesting to be supplied with nine blankets, was read. Whereupon

Resolved, That the Committee of Supplies be instructed to furnish nine blankets to said company.

Mr. Ferguson mentioned that six blankets were wanted by Captain Stevenson's company.

The Committee of Supplies were directed to furnish them.

Resolved, That the large redoubt on the hill near the "Woodlands" be called Fort Hamilton, and that General Williams be instructed to call on Mr. Hamilton and declare it to be so named.

The committee appointed to propose regulations for advances to be made to those of our fellow-citizens who have been called into the field, and who may require pecuniary aid, report:

That they have had an interview with Captain Henry Phillips, District Paymaster of the United States, and have obtained from him the annexed blank pay-roll, exhibiting the only form he can recognize in reimbursing the advances which may be made; but by complying with this form, and having duplicates in 'every case, he will repay such advances by stopping the same amount from the pay of each individual when he shall have funds for that purpose. The paymaster offers to supply all blanks that may be wanted.

Your Committee therefore recommend that, whenever advances are made, care be taken to obtain receipts in the manner and form prescribed by the district paymaster.

(Signed)   JONA. WILLIAMS,
GEO. LATIMER.

The blank pay-roll mentioned in the above report is on file.

Resolved, That the above report be adopted, and the form prescribed be followed.

Mr. Whitehead stated that he had received donations amounting to four hundred and sixty-four dollars and fifty cents, which was paid over to the Treasurer. viz.:

From Thos. Lawson, an alien, in lieu of labor....... $5 00
"   Dr. John R. Coxe, in lieu of labor........... 10 00
"   Joseph Levy.   "   " 5 00
"   Charles Billon,   "   " 12 00
"   P. Rz,   "   " 5 00
"   Jno. Lapeyre,   "   " 5 00
"   Jacob Zigler,   "   " 5 00
"   Member of Washington Benevolent Society,
         in lieu of labor................................. 5 00
"   Ganesches & Ravesies, in lieu of labor........ 25 00
       Peter Hahn,   "   " 20 00
       John Kelly,   " 10 00
"   Joseph Levy, for relief of absent soldiers'
         families 5 00
"   Alex. Wallace, for relief of absent soldiers'
         families 2 00
"   Jno. Lapeyre, for relief of absent soldiers'
         families... 5 00
"   Robt. Allen, for relief of absent soldiers'
         families... 20 00
"   A citizen of North Ward, for relief of absent
         soldiers' families............................... 20 00
"   Jas. Chalton, for relief of absent soldiers'
         families... 10 00
       Thos. Haig, for relief of absent soldiers'
         families... 5 00
"   John Kems, for relief of absent soldiers'
         families... 10 00
"   Saml. F. Conover, for relief of absent soldiers'
         families... 10 00
       Thos. Natt, for general defence............... 5 00
"   Eastern section of Walnut Ward, for general
         defence... 61 50
       Jno. Mellish, for general defence.............. 5 00
       Thos. McKee (Moyamensing), for general
         defence... 5 00
"   Alex. Wallace, for general defence............ 3 00
"   Saml. Yorke,   "   " 50 00
"   Jno. K. Graham,   "   " 20 00
"   Mark Richards,   "   " 10 00
"   Jacob J. Cohen,   "   " 10 00

From John Graff, in lieu of labor and for absent
   soldiers' families.................................... $20 00
" R. D. Duhamel, in lieu of labor and blankets... 10 00
Donations received from the Committee of South
   Mulberry Ward, viz.:
Samuel Hemple, for relief of soldiers' families...... 3 00
Mr. Schertzmeyer,   "   " 5 00
Mr. Haas,   "   " 5 00
Moses Steward.   "   " 5 00
Jno. Gullin,   "   " 5 00
Mrs. Richards,   "   " 20 00
Miss Morgan,   "   " 5 00
Lewis Fouquet,   "   " 3 00
Mrs. Buzby 5 00
Alex. McAllister... 5 00
Henry Volkman.. 5 00
Aaron Levy... 5 00

                                                         $464 50
Adjourned.

                  FRANCIS S. COXE,
                            Assistant Secretary.

TWENTY-EIGHTH MEETING.

PHILADELPHIA, *September* 20*th*, 1814.

The Committee met.

Present:—Messrs. Goodman, Biddle, Huff, Leib, Whitehead, Brown, Connelly, McFaden, Josiah, Latimer, Williams, Reed, Sergeant, Miercken, Steel, Hawkins, Eyre, Groves, Geyer, Leiper, Barker, Ronaldson.

The minutes of the last meeting were read.

A letter from James L. Cuthbert, lieutenant commanding vidette outpost, Port Penn, dated September 20th, was read, and ordered to lie on the table.

A letter from William Henderson, commanding the guard at Norristown, stating that they are out of funds, and requesting the aid of the Committee, was read, and ordered to lie on the table.

Two resolutions from the ward and district delegates, signed John Harrison, Jr., were read as follows:

"*Resolved*, That, in the opinion of this meeting, a disclosure to the people, in wards and districts, of the facts communicated by the Committee of Defence, is essential to the preservation and safety of the City of Philadelphia, and that the Committee of Defence be requested to agree that the members of this body report the same to the people in wards and districts."

"*Resolved*, That the Committee of Defence be requested to take the above resolution into immediate consideration."

(Signed) "JOHN HARRISON, Jr."

Ordered to lie on the table.

Whereupon the Committee adopted the following resolutions, viz.:

Resolved, That it is inexpedient at this time to communicate to the citizens of the wards and districts the information submitted to the delegates.

1st. Because it was not the intention of the Committee of Defence, when they made the call upon the citizens for the appointment of delegates, to make a disclosure of our state of defence to any but to the delegates; it being understood by this Committee that the communication was to be confidential, and designed to exonerate this Committee from any imputation of neglect of duty, and to excite the people, by means of the delegates, to embody all the physical force of this district, and to have it in preparation to act against the common enemy.

2*d*. Because it would be impolitic and unwise to excite dissension at this eventful moment, which would be the inevitable consequence of such a disclosure, for this Committee conceives it to be the bounden duty of every citizen interested in the safety and welfare of this section of the Union to contribute all his means to give efficacy to every measure, which has for its object the common defence and the repulsion of the common enemy.

3*d*. Because any disclosure of our weakness would be an invitation to the enemy to assail us, it being impracticable, from the nature of our institutions, to keep any communications to the people secret, and to authorize the publication of our present weakness, would justly expose the Committee of Defence to the charge of having made known our condition to the enemy, for the bare possibility of the enemy's having information of the actual state of our defence would be converted into certainty, by the authorization of this Committee to have it communicated to the citizens of the wards and districts.

4*th*. Because this Committee would rather submit to the imputation of having neglected their duty, and become the victims of public resentment, than, by any act of theirs which would exonerate them, to make known our defenceless state to the public enemy, and thereby hazard their own safety and that of their fellow-citizens.

Resolved, For the foregoing reasons, that the Committee of Defence do adhere to their determination not to permit any disclosure at this time, to the people, of their communication to the delegates from the wards and districts, and the delegates be furnished with a copy of these resolutions.

A letter, signed William Milner, relating to a supply of arms for the use of a military association, was read. Whereupon, on motion,

Resolved, That a committee be appointed to wait on the general commanding this district, and to inquire whether a quantity of arms (that may answer the purpose for drill or exercise) may be obtained at the United States Arsenal, and if so, that such arms be placed in the store-room of this Committee, subject to their order.

Messrs. Groves, Connelly, and Reed were appointed.

Resolved, That an order be drawn in favor of the Chairman of the Sub-Committee of Defence for one thousand dollars.

Resolved, That an order be drawn in favor of the Chairman of the Sub-Committee for the Defence of the Delaware for fifteen hundred dollars.

Mr. Whitehead reported that he had received donations amounting to two hundred and fifty-eight dollars, which sum was paid into the hands of the Treasurer.

From	John Cayers, for general defence	$5
"	An Alien, in lieu of labor	5
"	Jacob Idler, for relief of soldiers' families	10
"	Curtis Bolton, for general purposes	50
"	Joseph Pleasants, in lieu of one day's labor	5
"	Jeremiah Nicholas, in lieu of labor	5
"	Amos Marshall, for absent soldiers' families	5
	and in lieu of labor	5

Upper Delaware Ward.

From	Doctor Mathews, in lieu of labor	5
"	Rev. Mr. Emory, " "	2
"	Captain D. Man, in lieu of labor and general defence	10
"	George Vanderliu, in lieu of labor and general defence	4
"	John Roberts, in lieu of labor	1
"	Doctor Dyott, in lieu of labor and for absent soldiers' families	20
"	Jacob Gilbert, in lieu of labor	2
"	William Poole, " "	10
"	John Patterson, for relief of absent soldiers' families	25
"	Thomas W. Francis, for relief of the families of citizens absent on duty	50
"	Charles Francis, for relief of the families of citizens absent on duty	10
"	Charles Watson, Mr. Carrey, Mr. Franklin, and Mr. Hammell, in lieu of blankets	19
"	George Bartram, for relief of absent soldiers' families	10
		$258

Adjourned to meet on the 21st, at 4 o'clock P.M.

JNO. GOODMAN,
Secretary.

TWENTY-NINTH MEETING.

PHILADELPHIA, *September* 21*st*, 1814.
Special Meeting, 10 o'clock A.M.

The Committee met.

Present:—Messrs. Biddle, Goodman, Palmer, Whitehead, Hawkins, Steel, Ronaldson, Latimer, Brown, Sergeant, McFaden, Miercken, Josiah, Williams.

The reading of the minutes of yesterday was dispensed with.

The following resolutions were adopted, on a letter being read stating that an order had been given, by the Acting Secretary of War, to Generals Scott and Gaines, that one of them shall repair to Philadelphia, and take command there. Whereupon

Resolved, That the Committee feel highly gratified with the intelligence that one of those distinguished officers is assigned to take the command of this district, and hope that whichever it may be will repair to Philadelphia with as little delay as possible, where, this Committee can assure him, he will meet the most cordial reception.

Resolved, That the Committee of Correspondence be instructed immediately to transmit the above resolution to Generals Scott and Gaines, and to request them to inform this Committee at what time either of them may be expected to arrive at Philadelphia.

A memorial, signed Conrad Siffert, was read, stating that he had two sons in the service, and a son-in-law, and that the landlord of the latter is about to seize for rent, and requesting relief.

Ordered to lie on the table.

A letter from John Donaldson was read, stating that his three sons were in the service, and that Samuel Crugar, of the Bucks County militia, in Captain Blush's company, a hired man on his farm, is much wanted to assist him, and requests the interference of the Committee in procuring a furlough for ten or fifteen days for the said Crugar. Whereupon

Resolved, That, under the peculiar circumstances of this case, General Bloomfield be informed that this Committee recommend a compliance with the request of Mr. Donaldson.

A statement respecting blankets was read, signed by Jacob Fitler, as follows:

"The citizens composing the detachment commanded by Colonel John Thompson are in want of blankets, as follows:

Penn Township	15
Northern Liberties	36
Germantown	15
Frankford	20
Southwark	20
Moyamensing	20
Passyunk	10
Blockley and Kingsessing	15
	151

"Volunteers are not included.
"A return delivered to me by Colonel Thompson.
"JACOB FITLER.
"*September* 20*th*, 1814."

Ordered, That the number of blankets be delivered for Colonel Thompson.

The following donations were received, and paid over to the Treasurer:

From two citizens in North Ward, in lieu of labor....	$20
" Robert Whitehead, for absent soldiers' families...	5
Abram Wilt, " " ...	3
" Isaac Boyer, " " ...	5
" John R. Baker, in lieu of labor.....................	10
" Henry Riesh, " "	2
Christian Borbyshill, in lieu of labor..............	2
Jacob Thorp, in lieu of labor and for defence...	5
" Joachin Thorp, " " ...	5
" Arch. McLane, a friendly alien, in lieu of labor...	5
Edmond Bouvert, for the use of families of absent soldiers.....................................	25
" Michael Baker, N. L., in lieu of labor and absent soldiers' families...........................	10
Nicholas Biddle and James Craig, to be appropriated to the purchase of blankets, shoes, and other articles for the use of the militia at, and marching to, camp........................	500
	$597

The following resolution was moved and seconded:

Resolved, That sum of $—— be placed in the hands of the Sub-Committee of Defence, to enable them to provide the means of transportation, if necessary, for the troops at Baltimore, who are ordered toward Philadelphia by the Acting Secretary of War.

Laid on the table.

A letter or communication from Mr. Roberdeau, accompanied with a draught of the Delaware, was read.

Ordered, That Chairman report the same to the general commanding this district, and likewise to the Governor of this Commonwealth.

Whereupon adjourned.

JNO. GOODMAN,
Secretary.

THIRTIETH MEETING.

EODEM DIE, *September* 21*st,* 1814,
4 o'clock.

The Committee met.

Present:—Messrs. Biddle, Goodman, McFaden, Reed, Brown, Sergeant, Whitehead, Williams, Huff, Palmer, McMullin, Latimer, Leiper, Barker, Eyre, Connelly, Ross.

The minutes of the two preceding meetings were read. Whereupon

Resolved, That the thanks of the General Committee of Defence be presented to Colonel Fonciu for his voluntary and essential services, by the exercise of his distinguished talent as an engineer, in laying out and directing the works lately erected on the heights near the Schulykill, and that he be assured that, in returning to his native country, he carries with him the good wishes of the citizens among whom he has so long resided.

General Williams is charged with the performance of this service.

A letter from General Bloomfield, relating to arms, was read, as follows:

"Fourth Military District.

"Headquarters,

"Philadelphia, *September 21st*, 1814.

"General Order.—The General Committee of Defence having made a requisition for two thousand stand of arms, for drill and exercise, of those condemned as unfit for the field, the military storekeeper will deliver to the order of Charles Biddle, Esq., Chairman of the said Committee of Defence, from the Arsenal of the United States, two thousand guns and bayonets, of those arms said to have been manufactured in Holland from old German and British muskets, and condemned as unfit for service in the field.

"JOSEPH BLOOMFIELD,
"*Brigad'r-Gen'l Commanding.*"

A letter from Mr. Murray, referring to a letter of the 14th inst., was read.

Another letter, from Mr. Mullony, relative to defence on the Delaware, was read.

Both these letters were referred to the Committee on the Defence of the Delaware, with instructions to wait on General Bloomfield with the letters, and request a co-operation with the videttes.*

Resolved, That an order be drawn in favor of the Chairman of the Committee of Supplies for two thousand four hundred dollars.

The Committee of Supplies reported the amount of blankets on hand, and different sizes, amounting to 549; rugs, 21.

    (Signed) JAS. McGLATHERY,
            S. K. Com. of Defence.
(*September* 21st, 1814.)
Directed to D. LEIB,
    President Com. of Supplies.

Delivered per order of the Committee of Supplies 43 blankets, exclusive of the above amount.

John Harrison, Secretary of the Ward and District Delegates, appeared, and requested an answer whether their report would be returned or not. Whereupon

Resolved, That the Secretary of this body proceed to the ward and district delegates, and inform them that the paper alluded to was not in their possession, but in the hands of a member out of the city.

---

  * Letters put in hands of Captain Josiah since returned.

The Secretary performed the duties assigned him, and on his return reported the same to the Committee.

Resolved, That the Chairman of this Committee be instructed to draw an order in favor of the Chairman of the Committee of Supplies for 500 stand of the arms directed to be delivered by general order of this date, to be placed by the Committee of Supplies in the storeroom, and issued out by them to such companies as may desire their use, the said Committee taking a receipt from the commanding officer of each company who may be thus supplied for returning them when demanded.

Resolved, That the Committee of Supplies be, and they are hereby directed to inquire and report, what compensation ought to be allowed to James McGlathery for his attendance at the store of this Committee.

Resolved, That the Committee for the Defence of the Delaware be, and they are hereby instructed to inquire and report, how Fort Mifflin is supplied with provision.

Adjourned to 22d, 4 o'clock.

JNO. GOODMAN,
Secretary.

THIRTY-FIRST MEETING.

PHILADELPHIA, *September* 22*d*, 1814.

The Committee met.

Present:—Messrs. Biddle, Goodman, Latimer, McMullin, Leib, Steel, Palmer, McFaden, Brown, Hawkins, Whitehead, Miercken, Josiah, Leiper, Williams, Connelly, Ronaldson, Reed.

The minutes of the last meeting were read.

A letter from James Ronaldson, a member of this Committee, on the subject of ball proper for ordnance, was read, and referred to the Committee of Supplies.

A letter from A. Murray, inclosing a letter from C. W. Morgan, relative to lookout vessels, were read, and referred to the Committee of Defence of the Delaware.

A communication from A. C. Mitchell, on the subject of minors, was read, and ordered to lie on the table.

An invitation from James Hamilton, Esq., was read, as follows:

"James Hamilton requests the pleasure of the company of the Committee of Defence at the Woodlands, to-morrow, at 2 o'clock, to partake of some refreshments in honor of the redoubt '*Hamilton.*'"

A letter directed to General Bloomfield, signed A. McLane, informing that two frigates of the blockading squadron had put into the Capes on Sunday evening, &c.

Ordered to lie on the table.

A letter from William Jones, Secretary of the Navy, directed to the Corresponding Committee, relative to repeating-muskets, which will be delivered to the order of the Committee of Defence, to the amount of fifty, with a due proportion of ammunition for the same, upon their engagement to return the muskets when required.

Ordered to lie on the table.

The Committee of Defence of the Delaware, to whom was referred the communication of J. Mullony, report that they have taken the proposals into their serious consideration, and do not think it expedient to act on the same at present.

Ordered to lie on the table.

A letter from Colonel I. Fonciu, acknowledging "that the testimony of satisfaction which the General Committee of Defence have been pleased to give him, is, to his mind, the most flattering recompense for his services, and feeling himself happy in finding an opportunity of showing to the citizens of Philadelphia how grateful he is for the kind protection and friendship that this city hath afforded him during so many years."

Ordered to lie on the table.

Donations amounting to one hundred and ninety-one dollars and fifty cents have been received, which were paid over to the Treasurer.

From John Harned, in lieu of labor		$5 00
" D. W. Coxe,	" "	10 00
" C. Willcox & Co., in lieu of labor		5 00
	for blankets	5 00
	for general defence	5 00
	for absent soldiers' families	10 00

Inhabitants of Cedar Ward.

From Thomas McCuen, in lieu of blankets			$20 00
" John Keating,	"	"	5 00
" Daniel Daugherty,	"	"	2 00
" Wm. Pilmore,	"	"	3 00
" Augustine Bousquet,	"	"	10 00
" F. Dusar,	"	"	3 00
" Mr. Holmes,	"	"	1 00
" Edward McGee,	"	"	1 00
" Miss North,	"	"	2 50
" Mrs. Caldwell,	"	"	5 00
" Mrs. Pritchett,	"	"	5 00
" Cash,	"	"	1 00
" James Steward,	"	"	5 00
" John H. C. Baker,	"	"	5 00
" Mrs. Blair,	"	"	5 00
" John Bunting, for relief of soldiers' wives			5 00
" I. R. Malinfant, in lieu of labor and for relief of soldiers' families			5 00
" Edward Shippen Burd, for the purchase of blankets and other articles of necessity for the militia on duty			50 00
" Matthias Ronsh, for defence of city			10 00
" Thomas Crowell,	"	"	8 00
			$191 50

Resolved, That an order be drawn in favor of the chairman of the committee, to give relief to the families of absent soldiers, for five hundred dollars.

Resolved, That an order be drawn in favor of the Chairman of the Committee of Defence on the Delaware, to be appropriated for the payment of the workmen now employed on the works for the fortifications of the Delaware, for one thousand dollars.

Resolved, That a committee be appointed to confer with a committee of the conferees of the wards and districts, if they should think proper to appoint such committee, on the subject of the abstract of the communication made by this Committee, and to make such arrangements respecting that abstract as may be deemed expedient, and to report to this Committee; and the committee of conference consider the extract from our minutes as being solely the property of this Committee.

Messrs. Reed, Connelly, and Miercken were appointed.

Resolved, That the Sub-Committee of Defence be authorized to call on General Bloomfield for an organized company of artillery to be encamped at Fort Hamilton, who are to have charge of the said fort and the adjacent fortifications.

On motion.

Resolved, That the 18-pounders at the U. S. Arsenal, mounted on field-carriages, be placed in Fort Hamilton as soon as may be.

*A committee from the delegates of the wards and districts, composed of three members, including their chairman, were announced, and appeared before the Committee, requesting the delivery of their report or statement, delivered by their secretary to this body on the 18th inst., so that they may be enabled to make an

---

* This ought to be read before the resolution above named.

end to the business for which they were appointed; that they consider that paper their property.

Adjourned to 23d, 11 o'clock.

JNO. GOODMAN,
Secretary.

THIRTY-SECOND MEETING.

PHILADELPHIA, *September* 23d, 1814,
11 o'clock A.M.

The Committee met.

Present:—Messrs. Biddle, Goodman, Latimer, Leib, Whitehead, McMullin, Volmer, Brown, Sergeant, Eyre, Miercken, Hawkins, McFaden, Steel, Connelly, Reed, Leiper, Geyer.

The minutes of the last meeting were read.

An application from a number of militiamen desirous to be uniformed by the Committee of Defence, and willing to appropriate so much of their pay as will be sufficient for the attainment of the object, was presented and read. Whereupon

Resolved, That the request of Joseph Gilbert and others of Captain Fesmeyer's company of militia now in service, desirous of uniforming those who subscribe therefor, be granted on the terms and conditions adopted by this Committee. (See Minute Book No. 1, page 137.)

A committee of two members of the ward delegates

were introduced with a written resolution, which was read, as follows:

"*Resolved*, That Horace Binney and William Jackson be a committee to wait upon the Committee of Defence, and inform them that unless a further communication be received from them a report will be prepared to lay before the people in wards and districts.

"Extract from the minutes.

   (Signed) "JOHN HARRISON,
             "*Secretary.*
"*September* 23d, 1814."

Resolved, That the paper called for be returned to the delegates of the wards and districts, with an expression of the sense of this Committee that no extracts were to be made from their proceedings, and ought not in any manner to be made public, and of their wish that the paper may be destroyed.

Resolved, That furloughs be requested from General Bloomfield for John Mingle, Jr., and Patrick Lyon.

The services of John Strawbridge being wanted by the Sub-Committee of Defence as one of the officers to form and organize a corps of artillery to be employed as engineers under the direction of this Board,

Resolved, That General Bloomfield be requested to order Mr. Strawbridge, of the State Fencibles, detached for this service, and to report himself accordingly.

COMMITTEE OF DEFENCE. 177

Resolved, That an order be drawn in favor of the Committee of Supplies for two thousand dollars.

Adjourned to meet at the District Court-room, 24th, 4 o'clock P.M.

JNO. GOODMAN,
Secretary.

THIRTY-THIRD MEETING.

PHILADELPHIA, *September* 24*th,* 1814.
4 o'clock P.M.

The Committee met.

Present:—Messrs. Biddle, Goodman, Latimer, Connelly, Sergeant, McMontmollin, Williams, McFaden, Hawkins, Josiah, Steel, Leiper, Leib, Whitehead, Palmer, Huff, Reed, Peltz, Groves, Miercken, Brown.

The minutes of the last meeting were read.

A letter from Edward Clark, proposing a plan for the defence of the Delaware, was read, and ordered to lie on the table.

Resolved, That the sum of fifteen hundred dollars be placed in the hands of the Chairman of the Committee for the Defence of the Delaware for special purposes, of which a separate account is to be rendered.

Resolved, That the Committee of Defence make arrangements with the Irish citizens for further labor, and grant them permission to name a fort or fortification.

An application from Captain Grosh, for blankets for twenty men, was read, and referred to the Committee of Supplies.

The Committee for the Defence of the Delaware reported a letter addressed to them by Major Lloyd Beale, dated Fort Mifflin, 23d instant, stating that sundry articles of provision and rank, &c. were wanting. Whereupon

Ordered, That the Committee for the Defence of the Delaware supply such wants, and cause the fort to be put in such a state of defence as to them may appear requisite.

Resolved, That the sum of two thousand dollars be placed in the hands of the Chairman of the Committee for the Defence of the Delaware.

A letter from Lieutenant Cuthbert, of the videttes, Port Penn, 24th inst., 6 A.M., was read; also a letter from Captain Charles Ross, of the videttes, Mt. Bull, 20th inst., 7h. 15m. A.M.

The following donations, amounting to one hundred and twenty-one dollars and seventy cents, have been received, which were paid over to the Treasurer:

From William Shepperd, for relief of absent soldiers' families	$5	00
" Matthias Selleschart, in lieu of labor	3	00
" W. Mackensie, for relief of absent soldiers' families	10	00
From citizens of Lower Delaware Ward, as follows:		

From	Jos. White, Jr., in lieu of blankets		$3 00
"	—— Attwood, " "		5 00
"	—— Stone, " "		5 00
"	—— Vitry, " "		3 00
"	—— Ellis, " "		5 00
"	Dr. John White, " "		10 00
"	—— Bayne, " "		3 00
"	Isaac Rodrigues, " "		5 00
"	Sundry persons, " "		6 70
From	Johnson Taylor, for general purposes		20 00
From	citizens of North Mulberry Ward, viz :		
"	Jonathan Pounder, in lieu of blankets		3 00
"	John Harman, " "		5 00
"	Henry Freed, " "		5 00
"	John F. Beckman, " "		3 00
"	Oliver Evans, " "		10 00
"	Thomas Moore, Jr.. " "		3 00
"	Cash, " "		4 00
"	Saml. J. Robbins, in lieu of labor		5 00
			$121 70

Resolved, That this Committee will guarantee the payment of any sum not exceeding ninety dollars, to the militia of Captain Fesmeyer's company, for the purpose of procuring uniforms, provided the members of said company assign each man one month's pay in such manner as the Committee shall direct.

Resolved, That the Chairman of this Committee be instructed to inquire of the Governor, whether any and what answer has been received from the Department of War to the application made under a resolution of the 5th inst. to have 2000 regulars encamped near this city, and for authority to be given to the City of Philadelphia to enlist three regiments of infantry; and also to inquire whether any answer has been received to the application respecting 5000 militia that had been marched toward Baltimore.

Adjourned to meet on the 26th, at 4 o'clock P.M.

JNO. GOODMAN,
Secretary.

THIRTY-FOURTH MEETING.

PHILADELPHIA, *September 26th*, 1814.
4 o'clock P.M.

The Committee met.

Present:—Messrs. Biddle, Latimer, Leib, McFaden. Sergeant, Steel, Leiper, Whitehead, Williams, Brown. Josiah, Reed, Eyre, Connelly, McMullin, Miercken. Peltz, Ronaldson.

The minutes of the last meeting were read.

A letter from the Secretary of the Commonwealth, in reply to a resolution of the Board of the 24th inst., was read, and of which the following is a copy:

"PHILADELPHIA, *September 25th*, 1814.
"SIR:

"In answer to the inquiries contained in a resolution of the Committee of Defence, dated yesterday, and presented this morning to the Governor by their Chairman, I am instructed to say that no answer has yet been received from the Department of War relative to having two thousand regulars encamped near this city, nor with regard to the enlisting of three regiments of infantry to be employed in the defence of this district.

"The Governor received a letter from Mr. Monroe, dated 19th inst., informing him that he had ordered General Watson, with the detachment of Pennsylvania militia under his command, to march to the neighborhood of Philadelphia.

"On the evening of the 22d inst. a letter was received from General Watson, stating that a number of his men were destitute of tents, as well as the means of being sustained on their march. On the same evening the Governor sent by a confidential person $5000 to General Watson to enable him to supply his troops with provisions; and on the following morning sent from the State Arsenal 400 tents for the use of his detachment.

"By a letter from Mr. Monroe, dated 21st September, the Governor was informed that in consequence of the enemy having anchored at the mouth of the Patuxent, the former order to General Watson had been countermanded.

"With high consideration and respect,
"I am, sir, your ob't servant,
(Signed) "N. B. BOILEAU,
"*Secretary.*"

A letter from Captain Ross, of the videttes, Mt. Bull, 26th inst., 7h. 4m. A.M. Also two letters (dated Baltimore, 24th and 25th instants) from Corporal Henry Harrison, of the videttes, were read.

The Sub-Committee of Defence reported a communication from a meeting of the *natives of Ireland* resident in the city and districts of Philadelphia, declining to avail themselves of the permission of naming one of the forts granted them by a resolution of the Board of the 24th inst., and tendering their further services of labor on the fortifications.

Ordered to lie on the table.

A draft of a memorial was read, as follows:

"*To the Honorable the Senate and House of Representatives of the United States in Congress assembled:*

"The memorial of the Committee of Defence for the City of Philadelphia and the adjoining districts, respectfully showeth,

"That your memorialists are very strongly impressed, by recent occurrences, with the necessity of having a considerable regular force within each military district that offers an inducement and affords an opportunity to the enemy for annoyance, to be employed exclusively in local service.

"Militia are slowly assembled, they are still more slowly organized and equipped, and, when brought into the field, they are necessarily deficient in discipline, and in that steadiness which discipline alone can give. They ought not, therefore, your memorialists respectfully suggest, to be entirely depended upon for repelling the incursions of an active, disciplined, and experienced enemy, who has the selection of his own time and place of approach, and comes into the field with every advantage of skill derived from long habits of warfare.

"Militia, too, are more costly to the Government than regulars, not merely because a greater number of them are required for any given service, but because even the same number, it is believed, occasion a much greater expense.

"They are very costly to the nation, because they are taken from the pursuits of industry; their labor is lost for the time at all events, and there is great danger that many of them may acquire habits in camp extremely hostile to the occupations of civil life. Your memorialists cannot refrain from adding to this consideration, that the agitation and alarm which are spread through the community at a moment of danger, real or supposed, are rather aggravated than diminished by the tumult of assembling, on a sudden, large bodies of militia, and the strong personal feelings that are connected with every movement of that description of force.

"Militia, finally, are peculiarly liable to the diseases of a camp. Perhaps, indeed, they have more to fear from this cause than from the weapons of an enemy.

"For these, and many other reasons which your memorialists need not particularly state, they respectfully request that an act may be passed to authorize the enlistment of five regiments of regulars within this military district, to serve for such time as Congress in their wisdom may think fit, and be employed in local service.

(Signed) "CHARLES BIDDLE,
"*President.*
"S. FIELD,
"*Assistant Secretary.*
"*Philadelphia*, September 26th, 1814."

Which was adopted.

Ordered, That two copies of the above memorial be prepared, and signed by the Chairman and Secretary of the Board, and transmitted, without delay, to the Senate and to the House of Representatives.

That part of a letter received from William Jones, Esquire, Secretary of the Navy, dated Navy Department, 18th inst., so far as relates to repeating-muskets, was read, and referred to the Sub-Committee of Defence.

Resolved, That the Governor be requested to inform the Committee of Defence what number of volunteers are assembled in this city and its neighborhood under his authority, and whether they are armed and equipped for service.

The following donations, amounting to two hundred and thirty dollars and seventy-five cents, were received, and paid over to the Treasurer:

From citizens of Dock Ward:
" A Friend, in lieu of blankets............. $10
" Jos. McMullin, in lieu of blankets....... 3
" Hugh Harbeson, in lieu of blankets..... 5
" Joseph Hilsey, " " 2
——— $20 00
From Charles White, in lieu of work................. 6 00
" " " for relief of absent soldiers' families..................... 6 00
From citizens of Bristol Township, in lieu of labor... 10 00
" A friendly alien, " " ... 5 00
" James Gibson, military storekeeper, Fort Lafayette, Pittsburg, for general purposes... 50 00
From Charles W. Hare, to purchase blankets....... 100 00

From sundry citizens of Walnut Ward, to purchase
blankets... $33 75
                                                        ———
                                                        $230 75

Adjourned to meet the 27th inst., 4 o'clock P.M.

S. FIELD,
Assistant Secretary.

THIRTY-FIFTH MEETING.

PHILADELPHIA, *September 27th*, 1814,
4 o'clock P.M.

The Committee met.

Present:—Messrs. Biddle, Goodman, Leib, McMullin, Steel, Whitehead, Miercken, Leiper, Latimer, McFaden, Josiah, Reed, Barker, Connelly, Eyre, Brown, Peltz, Sergeant, Hawkins, Ronaldson.

The minutes of the last meeting were read.

The Chairman stated that Commodore Rodgers wished to confer with the Committee on the Defence of the Delaware, and such other subjects of defences at and near the Pea Patch, and to inquire what aid this Committee can afford him toward the erection of the defences he may deem necessary; and, on motion,

Resolved, That Messrs. Leiper, Josiah, Eyre, Latimer, and Sergeant be appointed a committee for that purpose.

A letter from General Bloomfield was read, as follows:

"HEADQUARTERS,
"PHILADELPHIA, *September 27th*, 1814.
"GENTLEMEN:

"No authority being given to call for money on the banks, I am under the necessity of representing to the General Committee of Defence of the City and Districts of Philadelphia, that the department of the commissary-general of purchases urges for $20,000 to discharge contracts made, particularly for tents and camp equipage. The troops in garrison, and at New Castle, under Colonel Clemson, have received no pay since April. They ought to be paid at least one month's pay, for which $10,000 will barely be sufficient.

"And it becomes ABSOLUTELY *necessary* to supply the quartermaster-general with funds, at least $10,000.

"I have the honor to be,
"With high respect and confidence,
"Gentlemen, your most ob't servant,
"JOSEPH BLOOMFIELD,
"*Brig.-Gen'l Commanding.*
"To CHARLES BIDDLE, ESQ.,
"*Chairman, &c.*"

On motion,

Resolved, That Messrs. Reed and Sergeant be appointed a committee to confer with General Bloomfield on the subject of his letter.

A letter from Corporal Harrison, of the videttes, Baltimore, 26th September, 3 o'clock P.M.; also a letter from

Captain Ross, of the vidcttes, Mt. Bull, 6h. 5m. A.M..
27th September, 1814, report nothing seen of the enemy.
Adjourned to meet the 28th inst., 4 o'clock P.M.

JNO. GOODMAN,
Secretary.

THIRTY-SIXTH MEETING.

PHILADELPHIA, *September 28th*, 1814,
4 o'clock P.M.

The Committee met.

Present:—Messrs. Biddle, Latimer, Sergeant, Steel. McFaden, Ronaldson, Palmer, Miercken, Josiah, Eyre. Williams, Huff, Whitehead, Reed, Brown, McMullin. Barker.

The minutes of the last meeting were read.

The proceedings of a meeting of the inhabitants of Kensington were read, as follows:

"A meeting of the inhabitants of Kensington, pursuant to public notice, was held on Friday evening. September 23d inst., at the school-house of Isaac Boileau, for the purpose of taking into consideration the situation of the wives and families of those of their fellow-citizens who have gone out in defence of our country. The meeting being organized, Mr. John Hewson, Jr., was called to the chair. It was, on motion,

"*Resolved*, That there be a committee appointed of fifteen persons to receive of the inhabitants what they may give for the wives and families of soldiers who are absent.

"The following persons were appointed as the committee, to wit: James Keen, Robert Hodgson, George Jones. Samuel Bower, Isaac Eyres, William Cornelius, John Rice, Martin Cramp, William Clark, Isaac Boileau, Isaac I. Kipp, Richard F. Bower, John Johnson, Joseph Bell, and John H. West. It was also

"*Resolved*, That there be appointed an investigating committee of five for the purpose of seeking out those families who may be in want, and to make out a regular list of their names.

"The following persons were appointed on that committee: William Clark, John Christ, John Johnson, George Jones, and John Rice. It was, on motion,

"*Resolved*, That James Keen and George Jones be a committee to present the proceedings of this meeting to the General Committee of Defence for their sanction.

"After which the meeting adjourned to meet again on Saturday evening, October 1st inst., at the same place, at 7 o'clock P.M.

"JOHN HEWSON, Jr.,
"*Chairman*.

"Jno. West,
"*Secretary*."

Resolved, That this Committee approve of the proceedings of the inhabitants of Kensington.

A letter was read from Lieutenant Cuthbert, of the videttes, dated Port Penn, September 27th, 1814, 8 A.M.. stating that a mistake had been made in Relf's paper of the 24th inst., and his intention of giving some explanation by the vidette of 28th inst.

A letter was read from Charles Ross, captain commanding videttes, Mt. Bull, 28th September, 1814. 7h. 10m. A.M.; also a letter from Corporal Henry Harrison, of videttes, dated Baltimore, 27th September. 1814, was read.

Resolved, That Messrs. Whitehead, Reed, Palmer, Ronaldson, and Biddle be appointed a committee to wait on General Scott and conduct him into the city.

On motion,

Resolved, That five hundred dollars be placed at the disposal of the Committee of Supplies for the purchase of shoes for soldiers encamped.

On motion,

Resolved, That his honor the Mayor of Philadelphia be requested to borrow twenty-five thousand dollars from the Bank of Pennsylvania, and pass the same to the credit of the General Committee of Defence.

Resolved, That Messrs. Williams, Steel, Leiper, Sergeant, Eyre, Connelly, and Hawkins be a committee to proceed immediately to New Castle, and accompany Commodore Rodgers to the Pea Patch, to view and ascertain what fortifications ought to be immediately erected on the Pea Patch and Newbold's Point, and to ascertain the propriety of sinking obstructions, and using every other means in our power for the defence of that part of the river.

Resolved, That the committee appointed to relieve soldiers' wives and families be, and are hereby instructed so to organize their distribution of money that no persons shall receive any contributions unless they produce a certificate, signed by two respectable citizens appointed in the respective wards and districts, who shall certify that the circumstances of the applicant require relief, and also the applicant to produce a certificate of her being the wife or child of a soldier now on duty in defence of this district.

Ordered, That the above resolution be copied, and signed by the Chairman of this Committee, and published.

The following letter was read, viz.:

"Sir,—A furlough was obtained for John Yager and Claudius L. Coe, of Captain Ruplis' company; these men are smiths, and were then employed by Daniel Pettibone in making pikes; for some reason they are not now so employed, and it appears to me the public interest would be benefited by their furloughs being withdrawn and they ordered to join their corps.

"I am, respectfully,
(Signed) "JAMES RONALDSON.
"Chas. Biddle, Esq.,
"*Chairman.*
"*Philadelphia,* September 27th, 1814."

Resolved, That General Bloomfield be requested to withdraw the furloughs alluded to in the above letter.

Resolved, That five hundred dollars be placed in the hands of the Chairman of the Committee of Supplies for the relief of families of absent soldiers.

Resolved, That two thousand dollars be placed in the hands of the Committee for the Defence of the Delaware.

Resolved, That the Chairman and Treasurer of this Committee be authorized to loan, for this Committee, to General Bloomfield, for ten days, upon his personal responsibility, ten thousand dollars, provided that General Bloomfield assures the Committee that this sum is to be expended in quartermaster's department.

The following donations, amounting to two hundred and seven dollars, were received, and paid over to the Treasurer:

From Citizens of Dock Ward, September 27th:				
" Dr. Monges, in lieu of blankets			$10	
" J. B. Palmer,	"	"	5	
" John Methan,	"	"	2	
" Dr. Chandler,	"	"	9	
			$26	00
Inclosed in a letter to Mr. Poulson, as the widow's mite, to relieve the distressed			15	00
From Arthur Stotesbury, in lieu of labor			5	00
From inhabitants of Abington and Cheltenham:				
" John Morrison, for general defence			10	00
" Joshua Tyson,	"	"	10	00
" Clement Shepperd,	"	"	5	00
" Robert Brooke,	"	"	5	00
" Saml. Leech, Jr.,	"	"	5	00
" Joseph Thomas,	"	"	5	00

From Dr. Stewart, for general defence			$5 00
" Wm. Webb,	"	"	5 00
" Wm. Dunlap,	"	"	3 00
" Robert Hallowell,	"	"	2 00
" Moses Highgate,	"	"	2 00
" Wm. Powell,	"	"	5 00
" Jacob Meyers,	"	"	5 00
" John Black,	"	"	5 00
" Fred. Altemus,	"	"	2 00
" John Carman,	"	"	5 00
" John Kirk,	"	"	5 00
" Lewis Woolman,	"	"	5 00
" Jeremiah Berrell,	"	"	5 00
" Benj. Roland,	"	"	5 00
" Maxwell Rowland,	"	"	5 00
" Christian Shearer,	"	"	2 50
" Joshua Wilson,	"	"	2 00
" Jacob Bisbing,	"	"	2 50
" Wm. Francis.	"	"	3 00
" Geo. Kohle,	"	"	2 50
" Alen Conrad,	"	"	2 50
" John Stephens,	"	"	5 00
" Sundry persons,	"	"	18 00
" Sundry persons, for relief of absent soldiers' families			19 00
			$207 00

Resolved, That the Committee for the Defence of the River Delaware be instructed to cause the magazine in Fort Mifflin to be made bomb-proof as soon as possible.

The Committee of Supplies, to whom was referred the letter of Mr. Ronaldson, relating to shot for heavy ordnance, on the 21st instant, was discharged from a further consideration thereof, and the Secretary directed to furnish the general commanding District No. 4 and the Governor copies thereof.

On motion,

Resolved, That the Secretary be directed to destroy the disputed paper containing the report made by the ward and district delegates on the 18th inst.

Meeting adjourned to 30th September, 4 o'clock P.M.

JNO. GOODMAN,
Secretary.

THIRTY-SEVENTH MEETING.

PHILADELPHIA, *September 30th,* 1814.

The Committee met.

Present:—Messrs. Biddle, Goodman, Latimer, Leib, Whitehead, Palmer, Miercken, Huff, Josiah, McFaden, Reed, Ronaldson, Hawkins, Peltz, McMullin.

The minutes of the last meeting were read.

A letter from Corporal Harrison, of the videttes, Baltimore, September 29th, 1814, stating that the enemy have a few vessels in the Patuxent, was read.

A letter from Lieutenant Cuthbert, of the videttes, Port Penn, September 30th, 1814, 8 A.M., was read.

A letter was read from Captain Charles Ross, of the videttes, dated Mt. Bull, 28th inst., addressed to one of the members, requesting the Committee of Defence to use their influence with General Bloomfield to obtain permission from him to consolidate the extra members of the First Troop, at that place, for the purpose of drill.

Referred to the Sub-Committee of Defence.

A letter from Hansell & Braentigam, saddlers, stating that they had work in hand for the United States, which was delayed owing to the absence of workmen on military duty, and requesting the Committee to recommend to General Bloomfield to grant furloughs to Joseph B. Kempton, of the first company Washington Guards, and Sidney Longrue, of Captain Gidders' company of militia.

Resolved, That furloughs be requested from General Bloomfield for Joseph B. Kempton and Sidney Longrue.

A letter was read from Lieutenant Cuthbert, of videttes, dated Port Penn, 29th inst., containing an explanation of the mistake in Relf's paper of the 24th instant.

Resolved, That the Chairman of the Committee be directed to write to Jonathan Smith, Cashier of the Bank of Pennsylvania, requesting him to repair to Washington, with a view to negotiate with the Secretary of the Treasury for the loan of two hundred thousand dollars, offered by the several banks of this city to the General Government, to be applied to the purposes of defence of this city.

The following donations, amounting to three hundred and thirty-one dollars and twenty-five cents, were received, and paid over to the Treasurer:

From inhabitants of High Street Ward, 29th Sept.:
" M. Lawrence, in lieu of blankets............... $5 00
" I. Wilson,   "   " 3 00
" I. Moses,   "   " 3 00

COMMITTEE OF DEFENCE. 195

From	C. Keller,	in lieu of blankets			$4 00
"	S. B. Bispham,	"	"		20 00
"	"A Yankee,"	"	"		10 00
"	G. Morris,	"	"		5 00
"	Cheeves G. Fales.	"	"		5 00
"	W. Morris,	"	"		5 00
"	Abram Link,	"	"		20 00
"	Mr. Heyl,	"	"		5 00
"	David Hall,	"	"		5 00
"	W. Hembell, Jr.,	"	"		10 00
"	Michael Baker,	"	"		20 00
"	J. Say,	"	"		5 00
"	B. Harbeson.	"	"		5 00
"	J. Carroll,	"	"		5 00
"	J. W. Sutten,	"	"		2 00
"	M. Hutchenson.	"	"		10 00
"	Isaac R. Jones.	"	"		5 00
"	Z. Collins,	"	"		20 00
"	J. G. T. Wood,	"	"		14 00
"	John Hamilton,	"	"		3 00
"	I. Hendricks,	"	"		3 00
"	J. McCulloch,	"	"		10 00
"	James Wallace,	"	"		5 00
"	John Tanguy,	"	"		5 00
"	Wallace & Ross.	"	"		2 00
"	J. W. Fraley,	"	"		10 00
"	Robert Coney.	"	"		5 00
"	Cash,	"	"		27 00
"	C. Bowlby,	"	"		5 00

From citizens of Dock Ward:

"	Thomas Shields, in lieu of blankets				10 00
"	Levi Garrett,	"	"		5 00
"	Mrs. Osborn.	"	"		3 00
"	Cash,	"	"		7 00
"	Adam Everly, in lieu of labor				10 00
"	" " for relief of absent soldiers' families				10 00

30th September, from Richard Ellis (alien), in lieu of labor.................. 3 00

From Captain George Berd, in lieu of labor and for blankets....................... 5 00

From Fred. Peper, in lieu of labor.................... $5 00
From sundry persons, between Green and Coates
Streets, the River Delaware and Ninth Street,
per Wm. Binder, in lieu of blankets............... 12 25
                                                    ———
                                                  $331 25

A letter from N. B. Boileau, Secretary of the Commonwealth, of which the following is a copy, was read:

"PHILADELPHIA, *September* 28*th*, 1814.
"SIR:
"To the inquiries contained in a resolution of the Committee of Defence, adopted the 26th instant, and presented to the Governor last evening. I am instructed to answer, that there is one regiment of volunteer infantry, consisting of 500 men, exclusive of officers; one regiment and one battalion of riflemen, consisting in the whole of 699 men, exclusive of officers, duly organized; also two troops of horse, consisting of about 60 men, exclusive of officers. The infantry would have been ready to take the field some time since were it not that the drafted militia called into service by General Bloomfield, and ordered to rendezvous at Marcus Hook, must be supplied with tents and other equipments from the State Arsenal, the United States not being able to furnish them. The volunteers having good quarters, while the ordinary militia were destitute, justice and humanity required that every possible provision should be made to furnish them with tents and equipments necessary for their comfort and defence. The Committee are already apprised that the Governor sent on to Major-General Watson 400 tents for the use of his

detachment near Baltimore, who were not provided for by the United States. The rifle volunteers came here but very partially armed. Three hundred of those rifles, drawn from the U. S. Arsenal, have been repaired by order of the Governor, and as many more rapidly repairing, and one hundred new ones have been purchased. So that in a very few days the whole of the volunteers will be armed, equipped, and ready to take the field if necessary.

"At the instance of the Governor, I ask information from the Committee, how many of the State muskets have been collected by their order, where deposited, and how many repaired, how many out of the 150 rifles put into the hands of the Committee have been repaired, and where they are? What progress has been made in preparing fixed ammunition for artillery and musketry?

"Very respectfully, Sir,
"Your ob't serv't,
(Signed) "N. B. BOILEAU,
"*Secretary.*
"Charles Biddle, Esq.,
"*Chairman Committee of Defence.*"

Referred to the Committee of Supplies.

Applications for blankets, from Captains McGlathery and Holgate, were presented and read.

Whereupon the following resolution was passed:

Resolved, That the letters just read be referred to the Committee of Supplies, and that the committee comply with the request of the applicants, if they see proper.

Resolved, That the Committee of Supplies be authorized to purchase a quantity of paper and twine for ammunition.

A report, of which the following is a copy, was presented and read by Mr. Goodman:

"Gentlemen,—Having been entrusted by this Committee, under the authority of the general commanding this district, with the superintendence of the ordnance department, I now deem it a duty to state what progress has been made toward the public defence since my appointment. In doing this I shall be as brief as possible.

"On the 6th instant I took a survey of the guns and carriages at the United States Arsenal, and found none fit for immediate service. Some of the carriages, however, on which field pieces and howitzers were mounted, did not require very much to put them in order. These are completed, properly marked, and housed in the State Arsenal, some of which have been taken in the field, under the orders of the general commanding. Six carriages, for 18-pounders, which require considerable repair, took up much of my attention; these are now finished, mounted with six handsome 18-pounders. They would have been sent to Fort Hamilton yesterday, but as there are no ammunition boxes for these guns, I directed six to be made, and also six leaden-aprons to cover the touch-holes, for which the lead is to be furnished at the Arsenal. I found it necessary also, on moving the carriages, to order drag-chains, to prevent the weight of the gun lifting the hind part of the carriage from the limber as the carriage is moved on. Chains at the Arsenal have been selected for this purpose, and a smith is directed to have them fixed.

"Gunners' belts, priming-wires, drifts, budge-barrels, and other requisites to complete them for immediate service have been ordered to be got ready. These articles can be had at the Arsenal. I thought it best to leave the guns at the Arsenal until every necessary article should be furnished for each gun before they are moved to Fort Hamilton.

"It would, however, be following a custom, heretofore too much in use, were we to move these guns and carriages to the fortification without covers for the limbers of the guns. The most that these carriages have suffered, heretofore, were from an exposure to the weather. I would therefore recommend that immediate measures be adopted to erect a proper covering for the limbers and other implements, and also for the guns when in the fortification.

"There ought also a requisition be made for spare hand-spikes, rammers and sponges, ladles and worms, hammers, pincers, priming-wires, gunners' belts, &c., for should an action take place, and any of these articles give way or be lost, the consequences may easily be calculated on. These articles may all be had at the Arsenal, except hand-spikes, of which there are a considerable number, but not fit for use. I had twelve made by a suitable person. Independent of the above, I have had the gun-carriages of the Lady Johnson's cargo overhauled, finding that the wheels (which are iron) had been put to the axles without regard to their fitting; they were all examined, properly fitted with linch-pins, and are now ready to be mounted.

"Twelve 18-pound truck-carriages have also been put in a condition fit for service; the guns may be mounted at any time.

"Ten 24-pound truck-carriages have also been completed; the greater part of the trucks of these carriages had, from long standing in one place unattended to, suffered materially. I had the worst of these trucks taken off the carriages, and supplied with iron ones found at the Arsenal. Those which were not so much damaged I retained, and had them properly repaired, and linch-pins put where wanted. These are now ready to receive the guns.

"I do not deem it necessary at this time to make a report of the work which is in hands. It will be made the subject of a future report. But, before I close, it may be proper to mention that I examined the fixed shot (which is canister) done by the men employed by the Committee. I can only say that so far their work is satisfactory. It is, however, to be regretted that we have not the necessary ball for fixing grape-shot for heavy guns.

"I ought not to omit mentioning that, in mounting the 18-pounders, besides a wheelwright and blacksmith, it required a considerable number of men. These were politely furnished by the officer commanding the Montgomery volunteers and ―――― riflemen, on my request to Major Powell, who procured them, and adding the aid of the men employed at fixing shot. The work was performed expeditiously and without accident.

"A few pounds of powder and ball will be wanted to prove a howitz, an iron 4-pounder, and a brass 3-pounder.

"A requisition ought to be made of the commanding general for the 18-pounders mentioned in this communication, because in my instructions the guns are to be at the disposal of the order of the general commanding.

(Signed) "JNO. GOODMAN."

Adjourned to meet the 1st October, at 11 o'clock in the morning.

JNO. GOODMAN,
Secretary.

THIRTY-EIGHTH MEETING.

PHILADELPHIA, *October 1st*, 1814,
4 o'clock P.M.

The Committee met.

Present: Messrs. Biddle, Goodman, Latimer, Leib. Josiah, Brown, Whitehead, Miercken, McFaden, Hawkins, Ronaldson, McMullin.

The minutes of the last meeting were read.

A letter from Jonathan Roberts, dated Washington, September 29th, 1814, addressed to Charles Biddle, Esq., acknowledging the receipt of the memorial, of the 26th ultimo, of this Committee, to the Senate and House of Representatives of the United States, was read, and from which the following is an extract:

"Your letter, inclosing the memorial of the Committee of Defence, is received, and will be presented to-morrow. I should have done it to-day, but your suggestion as to the propriety of secrecy has induced Mr. Ingersoll and me to consult the military commanders of each House, and to present them in concert."

A memorial, signed Howard & Bland, requesting leave of absence, from militia duty, for John Yager, was read, and ordered to lie on the table.

Resolved, That an order be drawn on the Treasurer, in favor of the Chairman of the Sub-Committee of Defence, for one thousand dollars.

Resolved, That the sum of one thousand dollars be placed in the hands of the Chairman of the Sub-Committee of the Delaware to pay carpenters.

Resolved, That Jonathan Smith be authorized to proceed to Washington, and to use his endeavors to make arrangements with the Treasury Department to have reimbursed to the Committee of Defence the sum of seventy-five thousand dollars, which was loaned to General Bloomfield, on condition that it should be repaid to this Committee out of a loan of two hundred thousand dollars authorized to be negotiated with the banks of this city by the Department of War.

Resolved, That the Chairman and Secretary sign and transmit a copy of the above to Jonathan Smith.

The following donations, amounting to two hundred and thirteen dollars, were received, and paid over to the Treasurer:

From William Hughes, in lieu of labor			$5
From Upper Delaware Ward:			
" Philip Barlow, in lieu of blankets			1
" Miss Hays,	"	"	1
" J. H. Jones,	"	"	5
" Dr. Dyott,	"	"	20
" H. Williams,	"	"	3
" Mrs. Bartow,	"	"	3
" Conrad Kreider,	"	"	5
" Fred. Shober,	"	"	2
" Levy & Hyneman,	"	"	5
" Miss Brown,	"	"	20
" Mr. Leibrandt,	"	"	6
" A. Wolf,	"	"	1
" Fred. Montmollin,	"	"	10
" Jos. H. Shreiner,	"	"	5
" Thos. Weltberger,	"	"	5
" Saml. P. Wakins, for relief of soldiers' families			10
" Widow Vansise,	"	"	10
" Daniel Sutter,	"	"	10
" Two female friends, for distressed left behind			10
From part of N. Liberties, extending from the Delaware to Fourth Street, and from Vine Street to Callowhill Street, in lieu of blankets			76
			$213

The Committee of Supplies reported that they had furnished forty-nine blankets to Captains McGlathery and Holt.

A letter from the Secretary of this Committee to N.

B. Boileau, in reply to his letter of 28th ultimo, was read. (See page 208.)

Reported, That the Committee of Supplies answered the Governor's inquiries of the 28th ultimo.

Two bills, for iron, &c., were presented by the Committee of Defence of the Delaware, and ordered to lie on the table.

Adjourned to meet the 3d inst., 4 o'clock P.M.

JNO. GOODMAN,
Secretary.

THIRTY-NINTH MEETING.

PHILADELPHIA, *October 3d*, 1814,
4 o'clock P.M.

The Committee met.

Present:—Messrs. Biddle, Goodman, Latimer, Ronaldson, Steel, Connelly, Eyre, Sergeant, Whitehead, McMullin, Palmer, Miercken, Ferguson, Williams, McFaden, Josiah, Hawkins, Leib.

The minutes of the last meeting were read.

A letter from Mr. Ingersoll, of which the following is a copy, was read:

"WASHINGTON, *29th September*, 1814.

"DEAR SIR:

"I received yesterday your favor of the 26th inst., inclosing the memorial from the Philadelphia Committee of Defence, which I am desired to lay before Congress. I have conferred upon the subject, this morning, with Mr. Roberts, the Chairman of the Military Committee of the House of Representatives, and the Secretary at War. From both of the latter, I understand that the views contained in the memorial respecting the expensiveness, the tardiness, and other disadvantages attending militia forces, together with the many inducements to the employment of regular troops for defensive and local, as well as distant and offensive operations, are strongly impressed on their minds, and will enter fully into the considerations to be embraced in the plan to be prepared, as soon as possible, by the War Department, and submitted to Congress, for a more extensive and effectual system of defence than has hitherto obtained. Under these impressions, both of these gentlemen thought that it would be most advisable to withhold the Philadelphia memorial from presentation to Congress. They will receive it, and pay every attention to its recommendations, in all of which they concur in opinion, without exposing Philadelphia to its unnecessary and perhaps prejudicial publication. For these reasons I have determined not to make a public presentation of the memorial, at least for the few days that will elapse while this letter goes to Philadelphia, and I wait your further instructions after receiving it. Should the Committee of Defence still believe that the memorial ought to be presented, I will do myself the honor to comply with their desire.

"Before I waited on the Chairman of the Military

Committee of the House of Representatives, or Secretary at War, I suggested to Mr. Roberts, and he agreed with me, that we should, at all events, not present the papers till to-morrow. In the mean while, I will endeavor to see him, and inform him that the Secretary at War thinks their object may be attained without being publicly presented at all.

"Very respectfully,
"Your most obedient.
"Humble servant.
(Signed) "C. J. INGERSOLL.
"CHARLES BIDDLE, ESQ."

A letter from Jonathan Roberts, of which the following is a copy, was read:

"WASHINGTON, September 30th, 1814.
"DEAR SIR:

"I wrote you yesterday, acknowledging the receipt of yours, inclosing the memorial of the Committee of Defence, and informing you that, in concert with Mr. Ingersoll, I had deferred presenting it to the Senate until we could ascertain the sentiments of the military committees respecting the manner of presentment. Mr. I. informs me he has declined offering the paper till further advised by you, which he has communicated to you. I shall also wait for further advice from you.

"I am, with much respect,
"Yours, &c.
(Signed) "JONATHAN ROBERTS.
"CHARLES BIDDLE, ESQ."

Resolved, That Jonathan Smith be, and he is hereby authorized to proceed to the City of Washington, on behalf of this Committee, to compel the negotiation of a loan of two hundred thousand dollars, proposed to be made to the United States by the several banks of this city, for the protection of the City of Philadelphia.

Resolved, That the Chairman be authorized to draw a warrant on the Treasury, in favor of the Chairman of the Sub-Committee of Defence of the Delaware, for one thousand dollars.

Resolved, That the Mayor be requested to place twenty-five thousand dollars in the hands of the Treasurer of this Committee.

Resolved, That the Committee of Correspondence be, and are hereby instructed to write to the Secretary of the Navy, and inform him of the conduct pursued by the navy agent, with respect to the charges made against the Committee for the iron-work for gun-carriages and timber for Fort Mifflin.

Resolved, That Messrs. Biddle, Williams, Latimer, and Eyre be a committee to wait upon General Scott, and know whether any arrangements can be made for his taking command of this military district.

Resolved, That the account of James McGlathery, storekeeper for the Committee of Supplies, be referred to the Committee of Supplies, and that they be authorized to make him such allowance for his services as they may deem just and reasonable.

The Committee appointed to proceed with Commodore Rodgers to the Pea Patch, report in part, and will make a final report shortly.

A representation of a machine, for the defence of the Delaware, by Captain Conners, was exhibited, and referred to the Committee for the Defence of the Delaware.

The Committee for the Defence of the Delaware *reported* that the workmen had left off, and that no work was going on at the Navy Yard.

Resolved, That the Committee of Supplies be authorized to sell to the State of Pennsylvania the blankets, purchased by the Committee, that remain on hand.

Adjourned to meet on the 4th, at 4 o'clock.

JNO. GOODMAN,
Secretary.

The following answer to the letter of Mr. Boileau, Secretary of the Commonwealth of Pennsylvania, dated 28th September, 1814, No. 2, was omitted in entering the minutes, and is inserted here, viz. (see remark. page 204):

"PHILADELPHIA, *October* 1*st*, 1814.

"SIR:

"Your letter of the 28th ult., to the General Committee of Defence, was laid before the Board yesterday. In answer to the inquiries of the Governor, 'how many of the State muskets have been collected by their order, where deposited, and how many repaired? how many out of the 150 rifles put into the hands of the Committee have been repaired, and where they are? what progress has been made in preparing ammunition for artillery and musketry?' the Committee have the following information to give: 25 rifles will to-day be completed by Shannon; 50,000 musket cartridges were to be ready last night; 107 muskets were collected by the Committee and delivered to an order of the brigade inspector. The following canister are preparing, and nearly completed: 350 24 lbs., 250 18 lbs., 300 12 lbs., 400 6 lbs.=1300; of which the following are completed: 200 24 lbs., 200 18 lbs., 200 12 lbs., 100 6 lbs. The rest are fitted, but for the want of blocks are not complete, but it is expected that the whole will be complete by Monday or Tuesday.

"I am, respectfully,
"Your obt. servant,
(Signed) "JNO. GOODMAN,
"*Secretary.*
"N. B. BOILEAU,
"*Sec'y of the Commonwealth of Pennsylvania.*"

FORTIETH MEETING.

PHILADELPHIA, *October 4th*, 1814.
11 o'clock A.M.

The Committee met.

Present:—Messrs. Biddle, Goodman, Latimer, Leib, Eyre, Sergeant, Whitehead, Williams, Steel, Leiper, Connelly, Brown, Palmer, Peltz.

The minutes of the last meeting were read.

A letter from General Scott, of which the following is a copy, was read:

"PHILADELPHIA, *October 4th*, 1814.

"GENTLEMEN:

"It is due to the Committee of Defence, to whose flattering attentions I am much indebted, to inform them that I have received a second order, of an urgent nature, to repair to Washington, which will deprive me of the honor of being associated, in the public defence, with the constituted authorities of this city.

"Accept, gentlemen, the assurance of my perfect respect.

"W. SCOTT,
"*Major-General U. S. Army.*

"MESSRS. LATIMER AND SERGEANT,
"*Corresponding Committee, &c.*"

The committee appointed to wait upon General Scott, reported that they had waited upon him agreeable to the resolution.

The following copy of a letter, from the Chairman of this Committee, was read, and the Chairman was directed to forward it:

PHILADELPHIA, *October 3d*, 1814.

SIR:

I am instructed by the Committee of Defence of this city and district to inform you, that they heard with much satisfaction that one of those distinguished officers, Generals Scott and Gaines, had been ordered to the command of this district. General Scott is now here, under the care of a very skilful surgeon, and the situation of his wound will probably require that he should remain some time longer in this city. It would, perhaps, therefore be as acceptable to him, as it would be agreeable to the Committee, if General Scott were ordered to take the command of this district. Being upon the spot, his advice and assistance could be immediately afforded; and we may truly add that his appointment would give great and universal satisfaction.

Resolved, That the sum of eight hundred dollars be placed in the hands of the chairman of the committee for the relief of soldiers' wives and families.

A letter was read from Corporal Harrison, of the videttes, dated Baltimore, 3d inst., 3 o'clock P.M., stating that Admirals Cochrane and Cockburn have sailed, the former for Bermuda, the latter for Halifax, leaving the fleet in the Potomac under the command of Admiral Malcomb, until their return with reinforcements.

An application from Captain George Schwenk, for twenty-three blankets, was read, and referred to the Committee of Supplies, to supply them if they see proper.

Ordered, That the Committee of Supplies suspend for the present the appropriations of five hundred dollars, placed in the hands of their chairman, to purchase shoes, by a resolution of the General Committee of Defence of the 28th ultimo. (See Minute Book, No. 2, page   .)

The committee appointed to view the Pea Patch, &c. presented a bill of their expenses, for ninety-seven dollars and thirty-two cents. Whereupon

Resolved, That an order be drawn upon the Treasurer, for ninety-seven dollars and thirty-two cents, in favor of Emanuel Eyre.

A bill was presented from James Givan, for uniforms furnished Captain Fesmeyer's company, and ordered to lay over for further consideration.

Adjourned to meet on the 5th, 4 o'clock P.M.

JNO. GOODMAN,
Secretary.

FORTY-FIRST MEETING.

PHILADELPHIA, *October 5th*, 1814,
4 o'clock P.M.

The Committee met.

Present:—Messrs. Biddle, Goodman, Latimer, Leib, Steel, Hawkins, McFaden, Williams, Whitehead, Josiah, Connelly, Eyre, Sergeant, Reed, Miercken.

The minutes of the last meeting were read.

The Committee of Supplies reported that they had furnished Captain Swenk with twenty-three blankets.

The following donations, amounting to one hundred and thirty-one dollars, were received, and paid over to the Treasurer, viz.:

From Thomas Wilson, in lieu of work............	$3		
absent soldiers' families....	2		
		—	$5
From Wm. I. Williams, in lieu of blankets..............		5	
" Geo. Slesman, " "		3	
" Dr. Glen, for absent soldiers' families..............		10	
From Dock Ward:			
" Miss Dempsey, in lieu of blankets............	$2		
" Cash, " "	1		
		—	3
From Joshua Byron, for families of absent soldiers.......................	$50		
" " " for defence of city...........	25		
" " " to purchase blankets.........	25		
		—	100
From W. H. Hervey, in lieu of blankets................		5	
			$131

Resolved, That the Chairman of the Committee of

Supplies be authorized to dispose of the horse and chair. the property of this Board.

Resolved, That Messrs. Leiper, Miercken, Latimer, Williams, and Connelly be a committee to wait upon General Gaines on his arrival in this city.

The committee appointed by a resolution of the 28th ultimo, to accompany Commodore Rodgers to the Pea Patch, to ascertain what fortifications may be necessary, reported as follows:

The committee appointed to examine that part of the River Delaware which runs on either side of the Pea Patch, and its adjacent shores, and, with the aid of Commodore Rodgers, to devise the best means of defence against a sudden attack by an invading force, report:

That besides the important assistance of the commodore and his officers, the committee availed themselves of the offer of Colonel Wadsworth, of the ordnance department, who obligingly accompanied them.

That considering the Pea Patch as an island but recently formed by the alluvion of the river, and perceiving that the part now visible at high tide, is only so by the reeds and other aquatic plants that grow upon it, the committee conceive that it would require much time and labor to procure a solid foundation of efficient work. It follows that a temporary fortification, hastily erected on the surface, can only be contemplated for any immediate effect. The Delaware side of the river is banked meadow, with various intersecting ditches, and soft ground. It was found impossible to rear a base in a right line on the bank, the distance between the shore and the island could not therefore be ascertained, but it is evidently equal to that between the island and the Jersey shore, which, by running a line on its sandy beach, was found to be one mile and a quarter.

For a description of the channel, on each side of the Pea Patch, the committee refer to a report made to Commodore Rodgers by the sailing-master of the frigate Guerriere, which they have subjoined as part of this report.

In the opinion of Commodore Rodgers, ample obstructions might be made in these channels by sinking about fifty hulks, many of them of a large size. The question therefore now to be considered is, whether it is practicable, by any exertions that can be made, to complete a line of defence near the Pea Patch, in time to meet an attack during the present season. The expense of it cannot very accurately be calculated, but it is presumed that the hulks, which would form the heaviest item, would probably hereafter produce as much as they cost, if circumstances should, within any reasonable time, allow them to be weighed.

The committee are not prepared to make any report on the subject of a permanent defence on the Pea Patch and the opposite shores, which require more extensive and more accurate calculation than they have been able to make.

NEW CASTLE, *October 3d,* 1814.

SIR:

In obedience to your orders of the 1st inst., I proceeded with the galley Northern Liberties, barge No. 6, and six row-boats to the Pea Patch, for the purpose of ascertaining the depth, width, &c. of the eastern and western channels in the vicinity of that island. Having completed the observations necessary for that purpose, I beg leave to report:

That on the eastern edge of the western, or ship-channel, at the distance of 400 yards from the southern point of the Pea Patch, I have placed a buoy with a flag, bearing from that point S. 22 E., and from this buoy, in a direct line across the river, I have placed another buoy, in the western edge of the channel, bearing from the above point S. 21 W., and about 400 yards below the point on the Delaware shore, contemplated for the erection of a battery. The distance, as measured between these two buoys, I find to be 1420 yards, each of them lying in three fathoms, and close to shoal water; the depth between soundings, from E. to W., as follows: 3, 3¼, 3½, 4, 4, 4¼, 4½, 4½, 4½, 4½, 4¾, 4¾, 4¼, 4, 3.

This channel, to the southward of the above line of soundings, widens gradually toward Reedy Point, while at the northward it maintains an equal width as far as the Pea Patch, from whence it again widens in its course toward New Castle. The deepest water in this channel, between the buoys, lies near the Delaware shore, as it does both to the northward and southward for some extent.

The channel to the eastward of the Pea Patch appears hitherto to have been little known, even to the oldest and most experienced pilots of this river; in it I have also placed two buoys, nearly in a direct line across the river with the others on the western side, and in a like depth of water, the soundings between them, from E. to W., as follows: 3, 3½, 4, 5, 5½, 6, 6¼, 6½, 5, 3. The buoy on the western side of the channel bears, from the southern point of the Pea Patch, S. 59½ E., and that on the eastern side bears, from the same point, S. 25 E., the measured distance between them 900 yards; to the northward and southward of this line of soundings, for some distance, there is no perceptible variation in the width or depth of this channel, and I feel confident in stating that through it vessels of the largest class may pass with safety at high water, for, although not so wide as the channel on the opposite shore, it is found to contain generally deeper water, with regular soundings, and only requiring to be better known to become an object of importance, either in the defence or navigation of the Delaware. As soon as I can obtain the necessary instruments, I shall submit to your inspection a sketch of that part of the river which I have sounded, and you will be pleased to remark that all soundings have been taken at high water.

Very respectfully,
Your obedient and very humble servant,
(Signed) JAMES RAMAGE,
Sailing-Master, U. S. frigate Guerriere.
JOHN RODGERS,
Commodore U. S. Navy.

Adjourned to meet on the 6th, 4 o'clock.

JNO. GOODMAN,
Secretary.

FORTY-SECOND MEETING.

PHILADELPHIA, *October 6th,* 1814.
4 o'clock P.M.

The Committee met.

Present:—Messrs. Biddle, Josiah, Steel, Miercken, Connelly, McFaden, Palmer, Eyre, Whitehead, Williams. Sergeant, Hawkins, Reed.

The minutes of the last meeting were read.

The following letter was read:

"PHILADELPHIA, *October 6th,* 1814.
"GENTLEMEN:

"Captain Ross, of the First Troop, requested me to inform you, that he conceives it would be more conducive to the public service, if he were to order to Mount Bull, all the members of his troop who are not in the line of videttes from *that place and Port Penn,* which would enable him to put them in a better state of discipline, and, by having sufficient men in camp, he could form *the whole line* of communication from Baltimore to Philadelphia, in twelve hours after the appearance of an enemy near the Patapsco. This arrangement would reduce the expenses of the troop, as it costs much less to maintain men in camp than on the road, and the Baltimore line, on its present establishment, being not as certain a source of information as the mail, in consequence of the uncertain movements of the Delaware troop, who form the line between Baltimore and

Elkton, where the First Troop communicates with them. As Captain Ross considers himself acting under the direction of the Committee of Defence, he submits to them this arrangement, which he hopes will meet their approbation.

"Your obedient servant,
(Signed) "R. M. LEWIS,
"*Cornet, First Troop.*
"THE COMMITTEE OF DEFENCE OF PHILADELPHIA."

Ordered to lie on the table.

An application, dated 5th inst., from Mr. Leaming, quartermaster, for means to pay the bills incurred by the First Troop of City Cavalry, on their present duty, was read, and referred to the Committee of Accounts.

A bill for expenses of an express to Baltimore, from Mr. Stockton, for fifty dollars, was presented, and referred to the Committee of Accounts.

The committee appointed to wait on General Gaines on his arrival in this city, reported that they had waited on him, agreeable to the resolution.

Resolved, That five hundred dollars be put into the hands of the Sub Committee of Defence, to be appropriated to the purchase of a carriage-rifle.

Resolved, That Messrs. Eyre, Sergeant, and Reed be a committee to call on the commanding general, to confer with him upon the subject of the videttes under Captain Ross, and ascertain at whose expense this troop has been and is to be kept in service.

The Committee for the Defence of the Delaware reported, in writing, as follows:

That they have sounded the bar, from the channel where the hulks are moored to Maiden Island, find the bottom a loose, shifting sand, unregular sounding, and full of small sand-knolls, a channel making about 300 yards below the hulks, where 17 feet may be carried over at high water.

This channel is narrow and unregular sounding; it will require some hulks to stop it. They have eight vessels moored in the main channel, over the bar, two others prepared, but at present used for the accommodation of the carpenters at work at Fort Mifflin, and carrying carriages, bricks, &c. to the fort. They may be sunk, with the eight that are moored, at a short notice, which will effectually stop the main ship-channel over the bar. The two remaining vessels are kept for the accommodation of the carpenters at the pier, and a store-vessel (this vessel will be dismantled as soon as the carpenters have finished the pier), the other as a passage-vessel, to and from Fort Mifflin, with materials and provisions, making twelve vessels they have purchased.

The committee recommended the channel now making over the bar to have hulks moored in it, sufficient to obstruct the passage, and two old vessels sunk in the channel back of the fort, which, in the opinion of your committee, will be sufficient to prevent any vessel, but of a small draft of water, getting near the fort. They contemplate mounting the guns, and hoisting the colors on the pier by Tuesday next.

Resolved, That the Committee of Defence of the River Delaware be authorized and instructed to purchase and prepare as many more vessels as they shall deem necessary for obstructing the channels and passes of the river near Fort Mifflin.

The following letter was read, and ordered to be entered in the minutes:

NEW YORK, *October* 1*st*, 1814.
BER'D HENRY, ESQ.

SIR,—I have prepared for you a torpedo, with its fulminating lock, from which any number required can be made, either for anchoring or for the various modes for attack and defence, which I have explained. But it is to be understood that I do not give to you, or to the Committee of Defence for Philadelphia, any right to draw emolument from the use of my invention. A law has been passed by Congress with a view to encourage the practice of torpedoes, that grants half of the estimated value of all vessels of an enemy that shall be destroyed by means other than vessels of the Government. Having labored for fifteen years to introduce the practice of sub-marine explosions, and being the inventor of the machinery, I cannot throw away the fruits of so many years of exertion and expense, nor will the public, who seek only for protection, require it of me. Hence, I reserve to myself, and to such persons as shall be engaged with me on those enterprises, or acting under information from me, all emoluments which shall result from torpedoes. You will please to communicate this to the Committee as the condition on which they are to be used.

I am, Sir, respectfully,
Your most obedient,
(Signed) ROBERT FULTON.

Resolved, That the Committee of Correspondence be directed to open a correspondence with similar committees in New York and Baltimore.

Adjourned to meet on the 7th, 4 o'clock.

JNO. GOODMAN,
Secretary.

FORTY-THIRD MEETING.

PHILADELPHIA, *October 7th*, 1814.
4 o'clock P.M.

The Committee met.

Present:—Messrs. Biddle, Goodman, Latimer, McMullin, Leib, Palmer, Williams, McFaden, Steel, Brown, Leiper, Hawkins, Josiah, Whitehead, Reed, Connelly, Miereken.

The minutes of the last meeting were read.

An application from Colonel Thomas Humphreys, of the first regiment volunteer riflemen, for blankets for his regiment, was read. Whereupon the following preamble and resolution was moved and resolved on:

Whereas, This Committee have been informed that the Governor has purchased blankets for the use of the militia and volunteers, and as this Committee do not think it proper to interfere with any regulation of the constituted authorities; therefore

Resolved, That Colonel Humphreys be referred to the Governor for a supply of blankets.

The following letter, from Colonel Monroe, was read:

WAR DEPARTMENT, *October 5th,* 1814.

GENTLEMEN:

In addition to the sums heretofore advanced to the several officers and agents of this department for the defence of Philadelphia, I have to request that you will pay the drafts of Mr. Robert McKoy, contractor, to the amount of fifty thousand dollars, for the supply of militia in service near your city. Until the loans offered by your banks are arranged between them and the treasury, the funds cannot be drawn by warrants through that department. I have therefore to suggest the expediency of an arrangement with the treasury, by which it may be enabled to recognize the loans, including the advances made at the request of General Bloomfield, as well as the sum referred to in this letter. When this arrangement shall have been acknowledged by the treasury, a warrant will be given to cover all advances, and the balance will be drawn through that department, in the usual way, to meet the necessary expenditures for your defence.

I have the honor to be,
Very respectfully,
Your obedient servant,
(Signed) JAS. MONROE.

THE COMMITTEE OF DEFENCE FOR THE
    CITY OF PHILADELPHIA.

Resolved, That the above letter be referred to a committee, consisting of Messrs. McMullin, Connelly, and Read.

The following letters were read:

WASHINGTON, *October 4th*, 1814.
DEAR SIR:

The Secretary informed me that the Government had no funds in any of the Philadelphia banks, but that he would write requesting them to accept my drafts.

Until some arrangement of this kind is made, you will have to endeavor to negotiate my drafts in your favor with the Committee of Defence. The annexed order, for eight thousand dollars, will keep you going until you hear from me.

Yours,
(Signed) ROBT. McKOY.
MR. ROBERT SHAW.

To-day I set out for Carlisle, to which place you will write me immediately on the receipt of this.

$8000.   PHILADELPHIA, *October 6th*, 1814.

At thirty days' sight pay to the order of Robert Shaw eight thousand dollars, on account of my contract.

(Signed)   ROBT. McKOY.
COLONEL JAMES MONROE,
   Acting Secretary of War.

THE HONORABLE PRESIDENT AND COMMITTEE OF DEFENCE:

Robert Shaw, Deputy Contractor for the City and County of Philadelphia and Delaware County, begs the favor of the honorable Committee to consider his situation now, with the number of troops at Marcus Hook and elsewhere, and being entirely out of money, begs their assistance, by advancing the money for the inclosed draft of eight thousand dollars; without it he does not know how to go on with furnishing provisions.

For ROBERT SHAW,
                              ISAAC PAINTER,
October 7th, 1814.   *Agent for Shaw.*

Resolved, That Messrs. Reed, McMullin, and Connelly be a committee to report on Captain Ross' bill for expenses of the videttes.

Resolved, That the Chairman of this Committee be instructed to write to the Secretary of War, stating their satisfaction at the appointment of General Gaines to the command of this district.

Resolved, That the sum of two thousand four hundred dollars be placed in the hands of the Chairman of the Sub-Committee for the Defence of the Delaware, for paying carpenters' and blacksmiths' bill, and for pine logs.

The Committee for the Defence of the Delaware, to whom was referred Mr. Conner's plan for the destruction of the British fleet on their arrival in the Delaware, do not think it expedient to adopt the same at this time.

Resolved, That an order be drawn in favor of William T. Stockton for fifty dollars.

Resolved, That an order be drawn in favor of the Secretary, John Goodman, for twenty-three dollars and fifty cents.

Adjourned to meet on the 10th, 4 o'clock.

JNO. GOODMAN,

Secretary.

FORTY-FOURTH MEETING.

PHILADELPHIA, *October* 10*th*, 1814.

The Committee met.

Present:—Messrs. Biddle, Goodman, Latimer, Whitehead, Sergeant, Leib, Eyre, McFaden, Peltz, Josiah Hawkins, Miercken, Leiper, Steel, Palmer, McMullin, Connelly, Ferguson, Groves.

The committee to whom was referred the letter of the

Secretary of War, of the 5th inst., and the application of Robert Shaw, reported as follows, viz.:

The committee to whom was referred the letter of the Secretary of War, of the 5th inst., and the application of Robert Shaw, deputy contractor, recommended that it would be expedient to pay the drafts of Mr. Robert McKoy, the contractor, to the amount of fifty thousand dollars, agreeably to the Secretary's request. The committee are induced to make this recommendation, on the assurance contained in the above letter, from the Secretary of War, "that as soon as the loans offered by the banks are arranged with the Treasury Department, a warrant will be given to cover all advances, including the above sum;" and also from a letter from the Secretary of War, to General Bloomfield, of the 3d inst., in which he is informed "that as soon as the arrangements above referred to are completed, he will be relieved from all personal liability incurred by him as to the former advances." The committee further report, that in order to expedite the contemplated arrangements by which the committee are to be reimbursed their advance, they offer the following resolution:

Resolved, That the Committee of Correspondence be instructed to address a letter to the Secretary of War and Treasury on the subject.

The committee offer the following resolution:

Resolved, That eight thousand dollars be paid to Robert Shaw, on Robert McKoy's draft for that sum, dated the

6th inst., on the Secretary of War, in part of the fifty thousand dollars agreed to be advanced to Mr. McKoy.

Adopted.

Resolved, That the Committee for the Defence of the Delaware cause an experiment to be made with the torpedo purchased by this Committee.

The committee appointed to confer with the commanding general of this district, upon the subject of the videttes, report:

That they had a satisfactory interview with General Gaines, who stated to your committee that he should consider the videttes in the service of the United States from the time of their being first called out, and that he wished the Committee to make any necessary advances, and give such directions as shall appear proper. The General stated, also, that instead of calling home the videttes, he wished a line extended from this city to Egg Harbor, and that the expense would be borne by the United States, and the proper accountant would settle the accounts as soon as he could make the necessary arrangements.

Resolved, That the Chairman be requested to inform Captain Ross of the substance of this report, and that he will consider himself and troop under the orders of General Gaines, and in the service of the United States.

Resolved, That the sum of one thousand dollars be advanced to Mr. Thomas F. Leaming, for the expenses of the videttes under Captain Ross, to be settled and accounted for hereafter.

Resolved, That the Corporations of Southwark and Township of the Northern Liberties, pay over further sums of money, agreeably to the resolution of the 9th September.

Adjourned until Thursday the 12th inst.

S. FIELD,
Assistant Secretary.

FORTY-FIFTH MEETING.

PHILADELPHIA, *October* 12*th*, 1814.

The Committee met.

Present:—Messrs. Biddle, Latimer, Leib, Whitehead McFaden, Hawkins, Josiah, Groves, Ferguson, Palmer.

The minutes of the last meeting were read.

A letter from the Secretary of the Commonwealth, of which the following is a copy, was read:

PHILADELPHIA, *October* 11*th*, 1814.

SIR:

I am directed by the Governor to give to the Committee of Defence the following extract of a letter from the Department of War, dated 4th October, inst., and received on the evening of the 8th, viz.: "The Congress have under consideration a plan for the protection and defence of the sea-board of the United States (including Pennsylvania), by organizing local and permanent corps, after the organization of which corps, the views of the citizens of Philadelphia, alluded to in the resolves of their Committee of Defence, will be met." I have also to state, that the Governor, this day, made out a requisition for two hundred rifles from the U. S. Arsenal, in favor of a gunsmith, who had engaged to repair them immediately for the use of the State. The military storekeeper informed the Governor that the last rifle had been drawn out by the Committee of Defence. I am instructed to ask how many have been drawn by that committee, and where they are, and how many are repaired, and how long before the residue will be in a state of repair ready to be delivered into the hands of the men now in service?

Very respectfully,
Sir, your obedient servant,
N. B. BOILEAU,
Secretary.

CHARLES BIDDLE, ESQ.,
Chairman of the Committee of Defence.

Referred to the Committee of Supplies.

The Chairman stated that he had been applied to, by Colonel Humphreys, for three hundred blankets. Whereupon

Resolved, That the Chairman of the Committee of Supplies be directed to inform Colonel Humphreys that his application be referred to the Governor, it being the opinion of this Committee that he is authorized by law to supply them.

The Committee of Accounts reported that they had examined the accounts of money expended by the Sub-Committee of Defence, amounting to seventeen hundred and three dollars and eleven cents. Whereupon

Ordered, That the same be credited on the books of the Committee of Defence.

Resolved, That the sum of eight hundred and fifty dollars be placed in the hands of the Chairman of the Committee for the Defence of the Delaware, for blacksmiths, and plank.

The following letters were read:

QUARTERMASTER-GENERAL'S OFFICE,
PHILADELPHIA, *October* 12*th*, 1814.

SIR:

You will perceive, by the inclosed extract of a letter from the accountant of the War Department, that I am directed by the Secretary of War to receive my funds from the Committee of Defence.

I don't know what arrangements have been made with respect to the $200,000 to be loaned by the banks, but presume it is to be at the disposal of the Committee; if it is, or any other money in your hands that can be disposed of in that way, I will thank you to inform me, as my funds are entirely exhausted, and very heavy demands are daily made on me, not only from the militia in the service of the United States, but for the works at Fort Mifflin.

Be pleased to inform me, as soon as convenient, the result of your deliberation on this subject.

With sentiments of high respect,

I am, Sir, your obedient servant,

WM. LINNARD,
Quartermaster-General.

CHARLES BIDDLE, ESQ.,
Chairman of the Committee of Defence.

Extract of a letter from Tobias Lear, Esq., accountant, Department of War, dated Washington, October 6th, 1814:

SIR,—I duly received your letter of the 1st inst., and that part which alludes to a supply of funds being more properly within the province of the Secretary of War, to him your letter was submitted, and on its return to this office, the following indorsement was made:

"Colonel Linnard must get his money of the Committee of Safety at Philadelphia."

Respectfully,

Your obedient servant,

(Signed)   TOBIAS LEAR.

COLONEL WILLIAM LINNARD,
Quartermaster-General, Philadelphia.

The Chairman was directed to inform Mr. Linnard that the Committee have no funds which they can at present appropriate to his use.

Resolved, That the Chairman of the Sub-Committee of Defence be instructed to pay the Chairman of the General Committee of Defence eleven dollars, being the amount of two bills paid by him, viz.:

Shebel's bill, for wine for patriotic young ladies.......... $5
Cook's bill, for cutting out frocks for rifle corps.......... 6
_____
$11

Adjourned to meet on the 14th October inst., four o'clock in the afternoon.

S. FIELD,
Assistant Secretary.

FORTY-SIXTH MEETING.

PHILADELPHIA, *October* 14*th*, 1814,
4 o'clock P.M.

The Committee met.

Present:—Messrs. Biddle, Latimer, Leib, Connelly, Eyre, Huff, Hawkins, Whitehead, Palmer, McFaden, Groves, Ferguson, Leiper, Josiah, Steel, Reed.

The minutes of the preceding meeting were read.

A letter from the Secretary of the Commonwealth, of which the following is a copy, was read:

PHILADELPHIA, *October* 14*th*, 1814.
SIR:

By direction of the Governor, I addressed a note to you, as Chairman of the Committee of Defence, on the

11th inst., asking information as to the number of rifles drawn out by the Committee from the United States Arsenal, and how many were repaired, fit for use, and how long before the residue would be ready to put into the hands of the men. I am urged to renew the inquiry, as the officers are continually applying to me on the subject of rifles. Those put in the hands of gunsmiths by me, have very nearly all been repaired and delivered. And I could get repaired, in the course of one week, two or three hundred more, had I possession of them.

Very respectfully, Sir,
Your obedient servant,
N. B. BOILEAU,
Secretary.

CHARLES BIDDLE, ESQ.,
Chairman of Committee of Defence.

The Chairman was instructed to inform Mr. Boileau that Mr. Ronaldson has the rifles under his charge, and is out of town.

The following donations, amounting to one hundred and ten dollars and sixty-two and a half cents, were received, and paid over to the Treasurer:

From Moses Levy, in lieu of personal labor.......	$10 00
" Samuel Leech, Montgomery County, in lieu of personal labor.............................	5 00
" Wm. Smith, Minor Street, for absent soldiers' families.................................	10 00
" R. W., for absent soldiers' families..........	5 00
From inhabitants of the District of Spring Garden :	
Geo. Laudenslayer, in lieu of blankets.......	5 00

From Peter Hater, in lieu of blankets			$5 00
" Jacob Zell,	"	"	4 00
" Rudolph Neff,	"	"	3 00
" Jacob Hoff,	"	"	5 00
" Henry Barcap,	"	"	3 00
" John Moon,	"	"	5 00
" Henry Crum,	"	"	3 00
" Sundry persons, "		"	37 62½
" Christian Lawrence, for absent soldiers' families			10 00
			$110 62½

Resolved, That the sum of five thousand dollars be placed in the hands of the Chairman of the Committee for the Defence of the Delaware, for the purchase of vessels, and paying carpenters.

Resolved, That a committee be appointed to confer with the commander of the district, General Gaines, and Commodore Rodgers, on the best and cheapest mode of defence of the forts and obstructions at the Pea Patch and Newbold's Point, and report at our next meeting.

Resolved, That Messrs. Williams, Steel, Leiper, Sergeant, Eyre, Connelly, and Hawkins be a committee for that purpose.

Adjourned to meet at 4 o'clock in the afternoon, Monday, October 17th inst.

S. FIELD,
Assistant Secretary.

FORTY-SEVENTH MEETING.

PHILADELPHIA, *October* 17*th*, 1814,
4 o'clock P.M.

The Committee met.

Present:—Messrs. Biddle, Latimer, Leib, Sergeant, Steel, Palmer, Connelly, Miercken, Leiper, Eyre, Hawkins, Whitehead, McFaden, Ferguson.

The minutes of the last meeting were read.

The following extract from the journal of the Board of Commissioners of the Northern Liberties was read:

"The Board of Commissioners, Northern Liberties, having received from the Chairman of the Committee of Defence a request for a further payment of moneys, appointed the President and Mr. Adolph a committee to inform the Committee of Defence that it is impossible, at the present time, for this board to obtain the moneys requested of them, and to inquire in what manner the moneys already advanced have been appropriated, and what expectations are entertained of said moneys being refunded.

"Extract from journal.

(Signed) "THOS. TIMINGS,
"*Clerk.*
"*N. L.*, October 14th, 1814."

Whereupon

Resolved, That Messrs. Leib and Whitehead be a committee to confer with the committee of the Board of Commissioners for the Northern Liberties.

The Committee of Correspondence reported that they had received a letter from the Committee of Vigilance and Safety of Baltimore, dated 15th inst., of which the following is a copy:

BALTIMORE, *October 15th*, 1814.

GENTLEMEN:

The Committee of Vigilance and Safety for this city received your communication of the 11th instant, this day, and highly approving of the proposed interchange of early and authentic information of the movements of the enemy, or any other matter that may be deemed important to the general welfare, they have appointed us, their chairman and secretary, to correspond with you for that purpose.

The latest authentic intelligence we have received of the movements of the enemy, is from the masters of two bay craft, which arrived here yesterday evening. They state that on Thursday last four British ships and one schooner were in the mouth of the Patuxent, and that two schooners and two barges were seen above Sharp's Island. We have every reason to believe that there were then no British vessels above those points, but, as to any which may be below, we have no late and correct information.

We are, respectfully,
Your obedient servants,
(Signed)   EDWARD JOHNSON,
Chairman.
THEODORICK BLAND,
Secretary.

To MESSRS. GEO. LATIMER AND JOS. REED,
Com. of Correspondence, Philadelphia.

Resolved, That an order be drawn in favor of the chairman of the committee for the relief of soldiers' families for twelve hundred and fifty dollars.

Resolved, That an order be drawn in favor of Jonathan Smith for forty dollars, being for his expenses on a journey to Washington.

Resolved, That the Mayor of this city be requested to place twenty-five thousand dollars in the hands of the Treasurer of this Committee.

The following invitation was presented and read:

The Committee for the Defence of the Delaware beg leave to inform the General Committee of Defence, that the battery on Davis' Pier is nearly completed, the guns are mounted, and the flag-staff erected. They therefore request the company of the General Committee, to-morrow morning, precisely at half-past eight o'clock, on Christian Street wharf, to proceed down in their sloop, and partake of some refreshments usual on such occasions.

By order of the Chairman.

JAMES JOSIAH.

October 17*th*, 1814.

Whereupon

Resolved, That the above invitation be accepted, and that Commodores Rodgers and Murray, and Commodore Porter, if in town, be invited to go down to the fort with the Committee.

COMMITTEE OF DEFENCE. 239

Resolved, That General Gaines also be invited to accompany the Committee to the fort.

A letter from Major-General Gaines was presented and read, of which the following is a copy:

FOURTH MILITARY DISTRICT.

HEADQUARTERS,
PHILADELPHIA, *October* 17*th*, 1814.

SIR:

I take the liberty, through you, to state to the Committee of Defence of this city, that I have received the report of Colonel Linnard, my quartermaster-general, informing me that he is in want of funds to meet the current expenses of this department, and that he has reason to believe the Committee are disposed to advance a sum sufficient for present use, on receiving satisfactory assurances, on the part of the United States, that the money shall be speedily returned.

Although I have received no authority or advice on this subject from the Department of War, I feel it to be my duty to observe, that much injury to the service might result from the delay that would probably take place in obtaining funds through the regular channel, and I feel persuaded that the money will be thankfully received and promptly returned with the proper interest. I therefore request that the Committee will be pleased to furnish Colonel Linnard, quartermaster-general, on account of the United States, a sum not exceeding ten thousand dollars.

Accept, Sir, and tender to the Committee of Defence, assurance of my high consideration and respect.

(Signed)   EDMUND PENDLETON GAINES,
Major-General Commanding.

CHARLES BIDDLE, ESQ.,
Chairman of the Committee of Defence.

Whereupon

Resolved, That Messrs. Leiper, Latimer, and Leib be a committee to wait, immediately, upon General Gaines.

The committee appointed to wait on General Gaines returned, and reported:

That they had had an interview with him, and that he requested a loan of ten thousand dollars, upon his personal responsibility, from this Committee. They also reported, that General Gaines accepted the invitation of the General Committee to accompany them to the fort.

Whereupon

Resolved, That the sum of ten thousand dollars be lent to Major-General Gaines upon the terms proposed in his letter of this day to the Committee.

Adjourned to meet the 19th instant, at 4 o'clock in the afternoon.

S. FIELD,
Assistant Secretary.

FORTY-EIGHTH MEETING.

PHILADELPHIA, *October* 19*th*, 1814,
4 o'clock P.M.

The Committee met.

Present:—Messrs. Biddle, Goodman, Leib, Leiper, Sergeant, Hawkins, Whitehead, Palmer, Huff, Connelly, McFaden, Reed, Miercken, Josiah, Eyre.

The minutes of the last meeting were read.

A letter from Robert Hare, of which the following is a copy, was read:

DEAR SIR,—Mr. Clymer requests me to state, in writing his desire, that the Committee of Safety would allow him a conference on the subject of his projects for the annoyance of the enemy.

I am, Sir, respectfully,
Your obedient servant,
(Signed) ROBERT HARE.

CHARLES BIDDLE, ESQ.
October 19*th*, 1814.

Referred to the Sub-Committee of Defence.

The Chairman of the Committee of Supplies, report:

That they had sold three bales of blankets, for two thousand one hundred and fifty-one dollars and twelve cents, and that one bale was sent to General Cadwalader's camp. Whereupon

Ordered, That the above two thousand one hundred and fifty-one dollars and twelve cents be placed in the hands of the Treasurer of this Committee.

Resolved, That the Committee of Correspondence be, and are hereby instructed to write again to the Secretary of the Treasury, and request his immediate attention to the reimbursement of the moneys advanced to the commanding general, &c. for the defence of this district.

The committee appointed to confer with the commanding general of this district and Commodore Rodgers, reported as follows:

The committee appointed to confer with the commanding general of this district and Commodore Rodgers, report:

That they had an interview with the general and commodore this morning. They both agreed upon the propriety and necessity of immediately commencing the fortifications on the Pea Patch, Newbold's Point, and the Jersey shore opposite. They both agreed that the safety of Philadelphia in a great measure depends upon the erection of those fortifications and the placing of obstructions. They stated, upon the commencement of those works, they would place a force there which they hoped and expected would prove sufficient to protect the prosecution of the works.

The estimate of General Gaines for the land fortifications would not, in his opinion, exceed fifty or sixty thousand dollars. The expense for the obstruction of the river, in advance of the Pea Patch, will not, in the opinion of Commodore Rodgers, exceed thirty thousand dollars. Upon these estimates, the whole would not amount to one hundred thousand dollars, which is the opinion of both the general and commodore, jointly and separately. They also agreed that, with these works completed, and manned with fifteen hundred to two thousand men, the whole force of the enemy could not force a passage through that avenue to this city. That, in their opinion, the whole contemplated works could be completed within six weeks or two months from this time, provided the General Committee will furnish the adequate funds, and appoint a sub-committee to act in co-operation with them, and such officers as may be designated to superintend the erection of these works.

Resolved, That in case the commanding general of this military district, or the Department of War, shall deem it expedient to erect suitable fortifications on the Pea Patch, Newbold's Point, and Jersey shore, and for making and sinking obstructions in the River Delaware, this Committee will advance the sum of fifty thousand dollars, and any further sum requisite for completing said works and obstructions, provided the whole sum shall not exceed one hundred thousand dollars, to be reimbursed by the United States, in the manner heretofore agreed by the late Secretary of the War Department in his correspondence with the Councils of the City of Philadelphia.

Resolved, That Messrs. Williams, Josiah, Eyre, McFaden, and Leiper be a committee to superintend the erection of fortifications on the Pea Patch, Newbold's Point, and the Jersey shore, and for making and sinking obstructions in the River Delaware, in advance of the Pea Patch, and that they shall act in co-operation with the commanding general, Commodore Rodgers, and such officers as may be appointed to superintend the erection of those works, and that the Chairman and Secretary of this Committee be authorized to draw orders upon the Treasurer of the General Committee, in favor of the said committee, at such times and for such sums of money as may be requisite for the objects before stated, provided the whole sums so drawn shall not exceed one hundred thousand dollars.

The following letter was presented and read, viz.:

PHILADELPHIA, *October* 19*th*, 1814.

To THE COMMITTEE OF DEFENCE.

GENTLEMEN.—Owing to my present situation, I am induced to lay before you some facts; they are as follows, to wit: I voluntered my services in Captain P. A. Brown's Company of Independent Blues, and marched to camp, at Kennet's Square, where I was taken sick, and brought home. Since that my physician has despaired of my life. After I was able to walk out I was called on to return to camp. My physician gave me a certificate, stating that I could not endure service from my delicate state of health. I am now employed by

Edward Kinsey in making knapsacks for the use of the State of Pennsylvania, and, as I have been informed that I must go to camp, request your interference, as I can be of no use there. I therefore ask the favor of you to recommend me to Major-General Gaines for a discharge from the above company, at least for the present.

I am, Gentlemen, with much respect,

Yours, &c.,

(Signed) JOHN B. WEIR.

The facts above stated I know to be correct.

(Signed) EDWD. KINSEY.

Whereupon

Resolved, That Major-General Gaines be requested to grant a furlough to John B. Weir.

Adjourned until the 21st instant, at 4 o'clock P.M.

S. FIELD,

Assistant Secretary.

FORTY-NINTH MEETING.

PHILADELPHIA, *October 22d*, 1814,
4 o'clock P.M.

The Committee met.

Present:—Messrs. Biddle, Goodman, Latimer, Leib, Sergeant, Whitehead, Josiah, Hawkins, Williams, Connelly, McMullin, Eyre, Miercken, Palmer, Reed, Groves.

The minutes of the last meeting were read.

A letter from Captain Ross, of the videttes, was read, as follows:

VIDETTE OUTPOST,
Mount Bull, 7h. 55, 21st October, 1814.

SIR:

Report says the enemy (a sail of the line) are as high as Alexandria. What seems confirmatory, the bay craft have stopped; none having been seen from this since the night before last. Our view this morning extends to Poole's Island. No vessel to be seen.

CHARLES ROSS,
Captain Commanding Videttes.

CHARLES BIDDLE, ESQ.

A letter from Robert Shaw, deputy contractor, was read. Whereupon the following resolution was passed:

Resolved, That a warrant be drawn in favor of Robert Shaw, deputy contractor, for eight thousand dollars, and that the Chairman and Secretary be, and they are hereby authorized to draw on the Treasurer of this Committee, in favor of Robert McKoy, the contractor, drafts for the further sum of thirty-four thousand dollars, as his orders may be presented, being the balance of fifty thousand dollars agreed to be advanced him by a resolution of this Committee of the 10th instant. (See Minute Book No. 2, page 56.)

The Chairman of the Committee of Supplies reported that they had sold the chair (agreeably to a resolution of this Committee of the 5th inst.) for the sum of one hundred and ten dollars, which was paid into the hands of the Treasurer, and that the horse was dead.

Resolved, That a warrant be drawn on the Treasurer of this Committee, in favor of the Chairman of the Committee for the Defence of the Delaware, for fifteen hundred dollars.

Resolved, That in directing an experiment to be made of a carriage-rifle, at the expense of the Committee of Defence, according to the proposition of Mr. Lukens, it was not intended to hold him liable to damages in case of failure of the experiment, provided there be no neglect on the part of the proposer.

Resolved, That the Committee of Supplies be instructed to sell all the bread and one-half the salt provisions, some time ago purchased by this Committee, if a fair price can be had for the same. The remaining half of the salt provisions to be retained for the use of the men to be employed on the Pea Patch.

The following donations, amounting to sixty dollars, were received, and paid over to the Treasurer:

From Jonathan Smith, cashier of bank. $10
" Wm. Tilghman, Esq., for general purposes....... 50
$60

Resolved, That the thanks of this Committee be presented to the Volunteer Association of Engineers, for the activity, zeal, and ability with which they have directed, superintended, and assisted in the erection of works of defence on the heights west of Schuylkill, and for the valuable service they have rendered to this Committee, and to their fellow-citizens generally, by exploring the roads and marking the military positions connected with the defence of the city.

Resolved, That the names of all the citizens composing the Volunteer Association of Engineers be entered at large upon the minutes of this Committee.

Adjourned to meet on the 25th inst., at half-past three o'clock P.M.

JNO. GOODMAN,
Secretary.

October 25th, drew an order in favor of Robert Shaw for $8000, agreeably to a resolution—preceding page.

October 27th, copy of a draft handed to Mr. Biddle, Chairman of the Committee, by the Secretary, viz.:

PHILADELPHIA, *October 25th,* 1814.
$34,000.

Pay to the order of Charles Biddle, Esq., Chairman of the Committee of Defence of the City of Philadelphia, thirty-four thousand dollars.

(Signed) ROBERT McKOY.
COLONEL MONROE,
Secretary of War.

October 31st, drew an order in favor of Robert McKoy, contractor, for $10,000, agreeably to resolution, page

November 3d, drew an order in favor of Robert McKoy for sixteen thousand dollars, agreeably to resolution, page .

FIFTIETH MEETING.

PHILADELPHIA, *October 25th*, 1814.
3½ o'clock P.M.

The Committee met.

Present:—Messrs. Biddle, Goodman, Latimer, Whitehead, Hawkins, Leib, Leiper, Josiah, McFaden, Palmer, McMullin, Eyre, Sergeant, Connelly, Williams, Naglee.

The minutes of the last meeting were read.

The following letter, from Brigadier-General Cadwalader, was read:

CAMP DUPONT, *October 22d*, 1814.
SIR:

A number of men under my command being destitute of great-coats, stockings, and mittens, and the weather being already so cold as to endanger their lives, unless properly clad, I trust that the Committee, with its usual liberality, will appropriate a sum for the purchase of 50 blanket great-coats, 100 pairs of stockings, and 100 pairs of mittens.

I have the honor to be, with great respect,
Sir, your obedient humble servant,
THOS. CADWALADER,
Brig.-General Commanding Light Brigade.

CHARLES BIDDLE, ESQ.,
Chairman of the Committee of Defence.

Referred to the Committee of Supplies, with instructions to furnish the articles.

A letter, of which the following is a copy, was read:

THE COMMITTEE OF DEFENCE FOR THE CITY AND COUNTY
OF PHILADELPHIA.
GENTLEMEN:

I am directed by Captain Charles Ross to inform you that it is necessary that he should be furnished with some money, and that it would be prudent to forward it immediately. That it is probable an attempt will be made on Baltimore by the enemy, and in that case his orders are to extend the line of videttes from Elk to Baltimore.
     With high consideration,
      From your obedient servant,
       (Signed) J. Y. BRYANT.
Philadelphia, October 25th, 1814.

Ordered to lie on the table.

Resolved, That Messrs. Goodman and Ferguson be a committee to inquire about what quantity of clothing there is at the United States Arsenal which is intended to be disposed of, the condition such clothing may be in, and the probable expense of repairing the same, and to make report.

Resolved, That the chairman of the committee for the relief of soldiers receive an order of the Treasurer for eight hundred dollars.

Resolved, That an order be drawn in favor of the Chairman of the Sub-Committee of Defence for five hundred dollars.

Resolved, That the Committee of Correspondence be instructed to write immediately to the Secretary of War, and request that a warrant may be drawn in favor of the Chairman of this Committee for the amount they have advanced, and have, at his request, engaged to advance to the officers of the United States, that is to say, for the sum of one hundred and forty-five thousand dollars.

Resolved, That Mr. Whitehead be a committee to examine and report what amount of money has been paid into the treasury of this Committee for the purpose of purchasing blankets, clothing, and other necessary articles for the comfort of the militia and volunteers, and what part of the same has been already expended.

Resolved, That the committee appointed to superintend the erection of works on the Pea Patch be instructed to ascertain the expense of making a chevaux-de-frise.

Mr. Goodman reported that the following fixed shot hath been made up by the persons employed by the Committee of Supplies, to wit: 300, 24-pounders; 323, 18-pounders; 897, 12-pounders; 1300, 6-pounders—total, 2820; and further stated that there is no shot fit for bag or grape-shot, which are much wanted for 18-

pounders; nor are there any more canisters for 18-pounders: that tin is scarce, and suggested the propriety of using light sheet-iron, painted, for that purpose.

Ordered to lie on the table.

Mr. Ferguson presented a bill from Bunting & Watson, for planks and boards furnished the Arsenal, amounting to one hundred and fourteen dollars and fifteen cents.

Ordered to lie on the table.

Mr. Ferguson reported cartridges done up and delivered at the United States Arsenal by the Committee of Supplies, to wit: 287,728.

Mr. Leib reported, verbally, that the committee appointed by a resolution of the 10th instant, to confer with the committee of the Commissioners of the Northren Liberties, have had a conference with them, and that it was the opinion of the committee on the part of the Commissioners that arrangements ought to be made for the payment of the twenty-five thousand dollars which the Committee of Defence required of that Board.

Adjourned to meet on the 27th inst., at 3½ o'clock P.M.

JNO. GOODMAN,
Secretary.

FIFTY-FIRST MEETING.

PHILADELPHIA, *October 27th*, 1814,
3½ o'clock P.M.

The Committee met.

Present:—Messrs. Biddle, Goodman, Latimer, Leib, Miercken, Whitehead, McFaden, Sergeant, Eyre, Josiah, Connelly, Ferguson, Palmer, Reed.

The minutes of the last meeting were read.

The following letters were presented and read:

WAR DEPARTMENT, *October 24th*, 1814.

SIR:

Conformably to the request of the Committee of Correspondence of Philadelphia, I have ordered one hundred and forty-five thousand dollars remitted to you for adjusting the advances of eighty-five thousand dollars made through General Bloomfield, ten thousand to Colonel Linnard, through General Gaines, and fifty thousand dollars advanced by the General Committee of Defence to Robert McKoy, Esquire, contractor. You will be charged with the amount on the books of the accountant of this department, to be passed to your credit when you shall forward the proper vouchers to charge the several agents on whose account the advances have been made.

The balance of the loan made by the several banks in

Philadelphia will be drawn in the usual way, and expended for the defence of that city.

I am, Sir, with great respect,
Your obedient servant,
(Signed)   JAS. MONROE.

CHARLES BIDDLE, ESQ., Philadelphia.

DEPARTMENT OF WAR,
Accountants' Office, October 24th, 1814.

SIR:

The Treasurer of the United States will transmit you one hundred and forty-five thousand dollars, being amount of warrant, No. 1578, issued by the Secretary of War on account of the following appropriations, viz.:

Pay	$15,000
Subsistence	70,000
Clothing	40,000
Quartermaster's department	20,000
	$145,000

For which you are held accountable. You will accordingly be pleased to forward a receipt to the office.

I am, Sir,
Your most obedient servant,
(Signed   TOBIAS LEAR.

CHARLES BIDDLE, ESQ., Philadelphia.

Ordered to lie on the table.

The committee appointed by a resolution of this Committee of the 25th instant, to examine what amount has been paid into the treasury of this Committee for the purpose of purchasing blankets and other necessary articles for the militia and volunteers, and what part of the same has been already expended, reported donations received until the 27th instant, viz.:

For soldiers' families...............................	$1275 00
" labor..	1339 43½
" blankets and other articles of necessity for militia on duty..................................	550 00
" blankets..	961 32
" erecting works of defence.....................	200 00
" general defence...................................	1238 50
	$5564 25½

Resolved, That the committee appointed to aid in the erection of works of defence at and near the Pea Patch, be instructed to have a direct and immediate communication with the Secretary of War, urging to the propriety of proceeding to the immediate erection of works for the further defence of the Delaware, at such points as may be deemed expedient by the commanding general of this military district, and that the committee be authorized to assure the Secretary of War that any sum not exceeding one hundred thousand dollars will be advanced for the purpose, on condition that the War Department will guarantee the reimbursement of the sums advanced at some convenient period, and allow interest until reimbursement shall be made.

Resolved, That the salary of the Assistant Secretary be forty dollars per month, and that a warrant for twenty-five dollars in his favor, on the Treasurer (being the balance due him on the 23d instant) be drawn.

Resolved, That the letter of Mr. Monroe, the Secretary of State, just read, be referred to the Committee of Correspondence, with directions to procure the proper vouchers.

Adjourned to meet the 29th instant, at 3½ o'clock in the afternoon.

JNO. GOODMAN,
Secretary.

FIFTY-SECOND MEETING.

PHILADELPHIA, *October* 29*th,* 1814,
3½ o'clock P.M.

The Committee met.

Present:—Messrs. Biddle, Latimer, Leib, Sergeant, Connelly, McFaden, Whitehead, Palmer, Eyre, Hawkins, Josiah, Williams, Reed, Ferguson.

The minutes of the last meeting were read.

The committee to whom was referred the letter from Mr. George Harrison to the Chairman of the Sub-Committee for the Defence of the Delaware, with two accounts for plank from the Navy Yard, reported:

That they have had an interview with Mr. Harrison, and the master-carpenters at the Navy Yard, who have agreed to deduct from one account of eight hundred and eighty-eight dollars the sum of three hundred and twenty dollars, making that account five hundred and sixty-eight dollars. The other account, of eleven hundred and seventy-three dollars and seven cents, the committee agree to be correct, and request orders to be taken to settle it. Whereupon

Resolved, That a warrant be drawn in favor of the Chairman of the Committee for the Defence of the Delaware, to pay the above-mentioned accounts, for seventeen hundred and forty-one dollars and seven cents.

A letter from J. Y. Bryant, containing an application on behalf of Captain Ross for money for expenses of the videttes, was read.

Resolved, That Messrs. Reed and Eyre be a committee to wait on General Gaines with the above letter, and confer with him on the subject.

Resolved, That a warrant be drawn (on Wednesday next, the 2d November instant), in favor of the chairman of the committee for the relief of soldiers' families for seven hundred dollars.

Resolved, That a warrant be drawn in favor of the Chairman of the Committee for the Defence of the Delaware for five hundred dollars.

The Chairman of the Sub-Committee of Defence was instructed to write to the Secretary at War.

Adjourned to meet on Friday, November 4th, at $3\frac{1}{2}$ o'clock in the afternoon.

S. FIELD,
Assistant Secretary.

FIFTY-THIRD MEETING.

PHILADELPHIA, *November 4th*, 1814.
3½ o'clock P.M.

The Committee met.

Present:—Messrs. Biddle, Goodman, Latimer, Raguet, Leib. Miercken, Connelly, Whitehead, Reed, Ferguson, McMullin, Steel, Hawkins, Leiper, McFaden, Williams, Sergeant.

The following letter from General Gaines was read:

FOURTH MILITARY DISTRICT.

HEADQUARTERS,
CHESTER, *October 30th*, 1814.

SIR:

I beg leave, through you, to state to the Committee of Defence, that my paymaster and quartermaster-general not having received a supply of cash to meet the current disbursements of their respective departments, the consequent demands of the service compel me to request of the Committee a further sum of twenty thousand dollars, on account of the United States, for pay, camp-equipage, and contingent expenses of the troops under my command, which sum shall be duly accounted for.

I have the honor to be,
    Most respectfully, Sir,
        Your obedient servant,
          (Signed)   EDMUND P. GAINES.

CHARLES BIDDLE, ESQ.,
    Chairman of Committee.

Resolved, That Messrs. Latimer, Connelly, Leib, Reed, and Sergeant be a committee to wait on General Gaines.

Resolved, That an order be drawn in favor of the Chairman of the Committee of Defence for the Delaware for eighteen hundred and fifty dollars, to pay for logs. planks, carpenters, &c.

The following letter was read:

CAMP GAINES, *October 30th*, 1814.

THE COMMITTEE OF SAFETY OF THE CITY OF PHILADELPHIA.

GENTLEMEN:

The undersigned, commanding officer of the Second Brigade, Pennsylvania Volunteers and Militia, now in service, respectfully solicits the Committee to furnish, for the use of the soldiers now under his command, blankets and stockings, in conformity, if possible, to the inclosed requisition. The liberality of the Committee will afford to me a strong expectation of procuring in part or entirely the amount of the requested supplies.

I have the honor to be, very respectfully,
Your most obedient servant,
(Signed)   THOMAS SNYDER,
Brig.-General Commanding.

Resolved, That the Chairman of the Committee of Supplies be authorized to purchase, for the use of the brigade of militia commanded by General Thomas Snyder, two hundred pairs of stockings; and also that an order be given for one hundred blankets, for the purpose of converting them into watch-coats, to be delivered on the same terms that the blankets heretofore have been, viz.: to be returned to the Committee of Defence by the quartermaster on the return of the troops from duty.

Mr. Whitehead reported that he sent the one hundred and fifty blankets, received per order from the Committee of Supplies, to the troops at Camp Gaines, on the 2d instant, directed to the care of General Snyder, to be by him delivered to such men under his command as are in want of them, on condition that such soldiers should give a written obligation to deliver the same at the store of the Committee on his return to the city, otherwise the value to be deducted out of their pay.

Ordered that the above report be entered on the minutes.

Resolved, That the Committee approve of the order furnished Mr. Whitehead, by the Chairman of the Committee of Supplies, for one hundred and fifty blankets for the use of the brigade of militia now at camp under the command of General Snyder.

The committee appointed to wait on General Gaines returned, and reported that they had had an interview with him. Whereupon

Resolved, That twenty thousand dollars be loaned to General Gaines, on his guarantee to reimburse the loan out of the sum of fifty-five thousand dollars remaining to the credit of the War Department in the Bank of Pennsylvania.

The following letter was read:

"THE COMMITTEE OF DEFENCE FOR THE CITY AND COUNTY OF PHILADELPHIA.

"GENTLEMEN:

"I had the honor of presenting to you, some time since, an application, in the name of Captain Charles Ross, for some money for the purpose of paying for supplies for his troop on vidette service, called into that service by and acting under the orders of your Committee. I have now the honor to inform you, that Captain Ross has ordered a regular account of the expenses of this establishment to be made out, and as soon as the proper vouchers can be obtained, which will be in a few days laid before you, together with such documents as will show to you, satisfactorily, that these expenses have been incurred in consequence of your orders, and with a view to the furtherance of objects under your direction.

"I have also to inform you, that Captain Ross is now entirely without funds; that he has had, and now has, between sixty and seventy men and horses to provide for. I therefore, in his name, and by his orders, solicit you to appropriate, immediately, for the present necessities of his corps, a few hundred dollars, say *five hundred*.

"With high consideration,
"I am, &c.,
"For CAPTAIN CHARLES ROSS,
"J. Y. BRYANT.

"*Philadelphia*, November 4th, 1814."

Referred to a committee.

Resolved, That Messrs. Reed, Sergeant, and Leib be a committee to write to Captain Ross in reply to the above letter.

The following letter from the Volunteer Association of Engineers was read:

PHILADELPHIA, *October* 31*st*, 1814.

TO THE GENERAL COMMITTEE OF DEFENCE FOR THE CITY OF PHILADELPHIA AND THE DISTRICTS ADJOINING.

GENTLEMEN:

The citizens composing the Volunteer Association, acting as field engineers in the erection of the works on the Schuylkill, have received, in full meeting, the minutes of your resolution of the 20th instant, and have directed us to return you their thanks for this gratifying communication, and to renew to you the tender of their services should they be wanted on any future occasion.

We are likewise directed by the Association, as private citizens, to make you the offer of one day's labor, to complete the sodding of the embrasures of Fort Hamilton, in order to prevent their being destroyed by the approaching winter.

By order of the meeting.

  (Signed) JOS. CLOUD,
        R. M. PATTERSON,
        THOMAS M. SOUDER,
          Special Committee.

LIST OF THE CITIZENS ACTING UNDER THE ORDERS OF THE COMMITTEE OF DEFENCE AS FIELD ENGINEERS IN THE ERECTION OF WORKS ON THE SCHUYLKILL.

Chief of Engineers.
General Jonathan Williams.

Topographical Department.
Dr. R. M. Patterson, William Strickland, Robert Brooks, William Kneass, Jonathan Jones, Esq.

For Superintending the Works.
Thomas M. Souder, Joseph Cloud, Adam Eckfeldt, Isaac Forsyth, Nicholas Essling, Saml. Richards, Spencer Sergeant, Jno. Cox, Chandler Price, Fredk. Sheble, Geo. W. Morgan, Fredk. Gaul, Jos. Watson, Thos. McKean, Jacob S. Otto, Alex. Ramsey, Wm. Davis, Saml. Nicholas, Jacob Clements, Wm. Spohn, Wm. Whitehead, Fredk. Eckstine, Conrad C. Wesener, James J. Rush, Thos. Hart, Aaron Denman, Joseph P. Zebley.

Commissary Department.
Stephen Kingston, Peter Wager, Thomas P. Roberts, Anthony Groves.

Topographical Engineers in the service of the United States.
Major Roberdeau and Captain Clarke, assisted by Robert Frazer, Esq.

Resolved, That an order be drawn on the Treasurer, in favor of the chairman of the committee for the relief

of soldiers' families, for nine hundred dollars, and that
Mr. McFaden be added to the committee.

A letter from George Clymer, relative to defence of
the Delaware by steam vessels of war, was read, and
directed to be placed on the files.

The committee appointed on the 25th ultimo, to
inquire what quantity of clothing there is at the United
States Arsenal intended to be disposed of, the condition
the clothing may be in, and the probable expense of
repairing the same, report:

That they have attended to the duty assigned them,
and, on inquiry, find that there are some hundreds of
suits of military clothing, such as coats, vests, and panta-
loons, numbers of which are in good condition, and made
up of excellent cloth, the colors and facings various, and
those which are not in the best order are somewhat
moth-eaten.

Your Committee were informed that the reason why
these uniforms are not used for the army is that they
differ from the patterns or customs now in use. There
is also a large number of leathern caps in the Arsenal,
that do not altogether accord with those in use at this
time, which are likewise laid aside, and may perhaps
be had if application is made to the proper department.
Your Committee were referred for further particulars
to the Commissary-General's Department.

Resolved, That Messrs. Goodman and Ferguson be a
committee to purchase, at public sale, at the Arsenal,
five hundred suits of soldiers' uniforms, provided the

purchase can be made without bidding against the Commonwealth of Pennsylvania.

The following letter was read:

PHILADELPHIA, *November 4th*, 1814.

SIR:

A quantity of boxes is necessary to be furnished for the packing up of the canisters now charged with grape-shot at the U. S. Arsenal, the property of the Committee of Defence, for the 24-pounders, 18-pounders, and 12-pounders, of such size as may be most convenient for carriage.

N.B.—It is supposed that there may be sufficient number of the old grape boxes for to pack the 6-pounders canisters in.

    (Signed) WILLIAM POWELL.

JNO. GOODMAN, ESQ.

And referred to the Secretary of this Committee to act discretionary; also with respect to the six 18-pound guns at the U. S. Arsenal, to house them or to send them to Fort Hamilton, and place them in a safe condition against the weather.

Resolved, That Captain Robertson be continued in the service of this Committee during the winter, at a salary of fifty dollars a month, and two rations.

Adjourned to meet on Friday afternoon, at 3½ o'clock, November 11th instant.

          JNO. GOODMAN,
            Secretary.

FIFTY-FOURTH MEETING.

PHILADELPHIA, *November* 11*th*, 1814,
3½ o'clock P.M.

The Committee met.

Present:—Messrs. Biddle, Latimer, Goodman, Reed, McFaden, Connelly, McMullin, Leib, Ferguson, Palmer, Huff, Leiper, Hawkins, Steel, Josiah, Miercken, Peltz, Williams, Whitehead, Sergeant.

The minutes of the last meeting were read.

SIR:

NAVY DEPARTMENT, *November* 8*th*, 1814.

The annexed is a copy of my letter of this day, to the Committee of Vigilance and Safety of the City of Baltimore, in answer to an earnest application from that committee for a steam floating-battery, such as the one just launched at New York, to be constructed and equipped at Baltimore.

My earnest solicitude for the security of the shores of the Delaware, and of the City of Philadelphia in particular, prompts me to offer the same means of protection to the wealth, industry, and population of that flourishing city, provided the conditions are speedily adopted. There is not a moment to be lost, and as the sum appropriated will cover only one more such battery, you will make the overture through such channels as you may deem expedient, and let me know the result without delay. Having examined the subject maturely, divested of its theoretic attractions, I am most perfectly satisfied of the substantial advantages it has over every other species of force for harbor defence, and particularly in the economy in seamen, of all others the most important to us. A single vessel of this kind, together with the defences and obstructions now, I understand, in operation at the Pea Patch, would render the Delaware perfectly secure, and supersede the immense expenditure, loss, and anxiety which the inhabitants of its shores must otherwise sustain.

I am, respectfully,
Your obedient servant,
(Signed) W. JONES.

GEORGE HARRISON, ESQ.,
Navy Agent, Philadelphia.

SIR:
NAVY DEPARTMENT, *November 8th*, 1814.

Messrs. Smith, Moore, and McKim did me the favor to present your letter of yesterday, with the sentiments and objects of which I most perfectly accord. Indeed, the work would have now been in operation, but for the embarrassments of the Treasury by the interruption in the transmission of public moneys through the agency of the banks and the suspension of specie payments. I am now enabled to say, that if one hundred and fifty thousand dollars (the estimate cost of the floating-battery) shall be placed at the credit of the United States, in any bank of the City of Baltimore, the same shall be applied to the building and equipping of a steam floating-battery, such as the United States vessel, "The Fulton," at New York. The individuals or body loaning the said sum, will be entitled to receive, for the reimbursement of said loan, six per cent. stock of the United States, to be created under existing or future authorities, to raise money by loan, either at a rate to be now agreed upon between the Treasury and the lenders, respectively, or to be fixed by the rate of any general loan hereafter to be obtained, and to bear interest from the day the said loan shall be placed to the credit of the Treasurer of the United States.

I am, &c.,

(Signed) W. JONES.

EDWARD JOHNSON, ESQ.,
Chairman of the Com. of Vigilance and Safety, Baltimore.

Resolved, That a warrant be drawn in favor of the Chairman of the Committee for the Defence of the Delaware, to make an experiment on a chain for defence of the Delaware.

The following donations, amounting to thirty-one dollars, were received, and paid over to the Treasurer:

> Donations collected and paid to the Committee of Defence, by Henry Probasco, Esquire, from District of Northern Liberties, commencing north side Coates Street to south side Poplar Lane, and from Delaware to Sixth Street, for the purchase of blankets for the use of volunteers and militia at camp.................. $26
> From Doctor Neal, Southwark, for soldiers' families... 5
> $31

Resolved, That the Committee of Supplies be instructed to sell all the whisky in their possession.

Resolved, That an order be drawn in favor of the Chairman of the Committee of Supplies for fifteen hundred dollars.

Resolved, That a warrant be drawn on the Treasurer, in favor of the Chairman of the Sub-Committee of Defence, for eight hundred dollars.

Resolved, That an order be drawn on the Treasurer, in favor of the Chairman of the Committee for the Defence of the Delaware, for sixteen hundred dollars.

Resolved, That a warrant be drawn on the Treasurer, in favor of the chairman of the committee for the relief of soldiers' families, for eight hundred dollars; also that Mr. McFaden be excused from said committee, and Mr. Brown be added thereto.

Resolved, That Messrs. Whitehead and Ferguson be a committee to inquire whether this Committee can give any assistance to forward the works at Marcus Hook, and be authorized to give such assistance, provided the expense shall not exceed two hundred and fifty dollars.

A letter from Geo. Clymer, relative to the defence of the Delaware, was read, and referred to a committee, to consist of General Williams and the Committee for the Defence of the Delaware.

A letter from J. Y. Bryant, with documents, relating to a further advance of money to Captain Ross' troop of videttes, was read, and referred to the committee appointed by a resolution of the 4th instant, to write to Captain Ross, viz., Messrs. Reed, Sergeant, and Leib.

The committee appointed to purchase a quantity of clothing disposed of by the United States, reported that they attended the sale, but finding that the Secretary of the Commonwealth and adjutant-general had orders to purchase them, your Committee did not interfere, and therefore offer the following resolution:

Resolved, That the said committee be discharged.

Which resolution was adopted.

Resolved, That the Committee of Supplies be authorized to sue N. Dilhorn for having deceived them in the quality of bread which they purchased from him.

FIFTY-FIFTH MEETING.

PHILADELPHIA, *November* 18*th*, 1814,
3½ o'clock P.M.

The Committee met.

Present:—Messrs. Biddle, Goodman, Latimer, Eyre, Reed, Sergeant, Leib, Connelly, Huff, Whitehead, Steel, Miercken, Palmer, Williams, McMullin, Ferguson, Hawkins, Josiah.

The minutes of the last meeting were read.

A letter from Daniel Pettibone, requesting payment for certain pikes made by him and not delivered agreeably to contract, was read, and ordered to lie on the table.

The committee appointed by a resolution of the Board of the 11th instant, to inquire whether this Committee can give any assistance to forward the works at Marcus Hook, and be authorized to give such assistance, provided the expense shall not exceed two hundred and fifty dollars, reported:

That from information obtained from General Gaines on the subject, as well as from Major Roberdeau, who is superintending the works, and contained in his letters of the 14th instant, that a supply of whisky would be of very great importance in forwarding the works, your Committee purchased, and sent to the Hook, to the care of Samuel Blair, Jr., who was authorized to take charge of, and attend daily to the troops during fatigue duty, two hogsheads and three barrels of whisky, amounting to two hundred and seventy dollars and sixty-three cents. The Committee also report that, in consequence of a requisition from Major Roberdeau, they sent down for the same objects, fifteen buckets, seven tin-cups, thirty-seven pounders and rammers, and thirty-two hand-barrows; these articles are a part of those formerly purchased and used at the fortifications near the Schuylkill. Such of which as are not lost or destroyed are to be returned to the Committee so soon as the works are completed. The Committee request that the Committee of Supplies be authorized to pay the bills for the whisky.

The following letters were read:

CAMP GAINES, *November* 14*th*, 1814.
MY DEAR SIR:

The many good deeds rendered the soldiers now in field by the Committee of Defence may, at this inclement season, be very humanely increased by ordering to this camp a supply of good shoes. A number of my regiment are in great want. The effects, I fear, will be serious as respects their health; the severity of the weather, and the appearance of the men this morning, urges me to this mode, as the only one I know to rely on to obtain a supply. If they cannot be donated, I will have the price secured out of their pay. Three hundred pairs will supply my regiment. If they can be ready, the bearer, Mr. Sutton's receipt for them, and if it be charged, give me the price at which they can be issued. As you love your country, do not send the wagon back to camp without. Our guards, this morning, have a good, comfortable appearance in the fine watchcoats sent on by the Committee. They arrived very seasonable. Receive their and my hearty thanks for the favor.

In haste, very respectfully,
Your obedient servant,
(Signed)   JOHN THOMPSON,
Col. 2d Brig. 1st Div. Penn. Militia.

CHARLES BIDDLE,
Chairman of the Committee of Defence.

To the Com. of Safety of the City of Philadelphia.

Gentlemen:

The Second Brigade, now in service, have experienced the most important service from the very liberal supply of blankets, watch-coats, and stockings received from you, which were distributed in such a way as was supposed would meet your approbation. Those most in want were first supplied. Orders have been issued that the blankets and coats be restored to the quartermasters, when the campaign closes, to be carefully returned to the Committee. At the present time nothing would prove more acceptable than a donation of shoes. Most of the men are greatly in want of them, as they have been in service upwards of two months. An immediate supply would undoubtedly save many lives. It is hoped the Committee will terminate their praiseworthy exertions by a compliance with this last appeal to their feeling and patriotism.

I have the honor to be,
Very respectfully,
Your obedient servant,
(Signed) JACOB S. OTTO,
Aid-de-Camp to Gen. Snyder.

Resolved, That an order be drawn in favor of James Whitehead for two hundred and seventy dollars and sixty-three cents, amount of bills for whisky purchased for the use of the troops doing fatigue duty at the work at Marcus Hook; and also an order in his favor for two hundred and twenty dollars and fifty cents, amount of bills for two hundred pairs of shoes purchased for the use of such militia and volunteers belonging to the brigade under the command of General Snyder, now on duty at Camp Gaines, as are in want of them.

A letter, of which the following is a copy, was read:

FOURTH MILITARY DISTRICT.

HEADQUARTERS,

PHILADELPHIA, *November* 18*th*, 1814.

GENTLEMEN:

Since the date of the last communication which I had the honor to address to the Committee of Defence, through their Chairman, I have received from Brigadier-General Bloomfield, my predecessor, copies of letters from the Secretary of War to him, in relation to the two hundred thousand dollars loan, obtained from the Bank of Pennsylvania, for defraying the expenses incident to the defence of this district.

From these letters, I find it was the intention of the Department of War that the amount of the loan should be placed under the control of the commanding general, and be drawn as he should require it. But I am told by the President of the Bank of Pennsylvania that the remaining balance of the loan cannot be drawn without a Treasury warrant for that purpose. The proper warrant will probably be forwarded to me shortly. In the mean while, however, much injury to the service is likely to result from the want of funds. My Quartermaster-General's Department being entirely without, and unable to purchase even STRAW or *fuel* for the troops.

Under these circumstances, I take the liberty to ask of you the further sum of fifteen thousand dollars, to be replaced out of the remaining balance of the before-mentioned loan. I avail myself of this occasion to apprise the Committee of Defence that my surveys and plans are so far completed as to enable me to set about the construction of our defences at the Pea Patch; and have to request the Committee to point out to me the mode of obtaining the funds which they have been pleased to appropriate for that purpose. A suitable person will be appointed to make all the purchases and disbursements, under the immediate direction of the general commanding.

I have the honor to be, with much respect,

Gentlemen, your obedient humble servant,

(Signed) EDMUND P. GAINES.

The Committee of Defence for the
    City of Philadelphia.

Whereupon

Resolved, That a warrant be drawn in favor of General Gaines for fifteen thousand dollars, and that so much of the preceding letter as relates to the Pea Patch be referred to the committee on Pea Patch.

The following donations, amounting to twenty-five dollars, were received, and paid to the Treasurer.

From Jesse Laverty,			in lieu of labor.	$5
"	"	"	for defence	5
"	"	"	for blankets	5
"	"	"	for absent soldiers' families	10
				$25

Resolved, That the Chairman of the Committee of Defence be instructed to inform the Secretary of War that the Committee have appropriated one hundred thousand dollars, to carry into effect the plans of defence of the commanding general of this military district, for the defence of the River Delaware, at and near the Pea Patch, and that the Committee are ready to advance the whole, or any part of this sum, to the commanding general, on the terms offered by the corporations of the city, and accepted by the late Secretary of War.

The committee appointed on the letter from the Secretary of the Navy to the Navy Agent, dated 8th November instant, and by letter communicated to the General Committee of Defence, report:

That, in their opinion, the offer of the Secretary of the Navy, causing the sum of one hundred and fifty thousand dollars to be appropriated for building a steam-frigate for the defence of the River Delaware, on conditions of raising the money on the credit of the United States, ought to be accepted, and measures ought to be taken to build and equip the said frigate with all possible dispatch. The committee, in consequence of the urgent request of the Secretary to have an immediate answer, wrote to him on the 12th instant, a copy of which letter is here annexed:

PHILADELPHIA, *November 12th*, 1814.

SIR:

Your letter to the Navy Agent, of the 8th instant, having been communicated to the General Committee of

Defence, last evening, it was referred to us to make report thereon at the next meeting, which will be on the 18th inst.

As you have had the goodness to offer the aid of your department in procuring a steam-battery similar to the one lately constructed in New York, and are pleased to add, "There is not a moment to be lost, and the sum appropriated will cover only one more such battery," we are induced to inform you, that our determination is to report in favor of the proposition, and the General Committee will, no doubt, exert themselves to obtain the means, so that there may be no delay in carrying the plan into execution.

We have the honor to be, &c.,

(Signed) JAMES JOSIAH,
HENRY HAWKINS,
JONA. WILLIAMS,
Committee.

THE HONORABLE WM. JONES,
Secretary of the Navy.

The committee to whom was referred the letter of Mr. George Clymer, relative to the defence of the Delaware, reported:

That they are not able to comprehend Mr. Clymer's mode of warfare for want of accurate description. In the opinion of your Committee, every inventor is bound to exhibit either a demonstration of his invention, on known principles, or the result of actual experiment, attested by competent judges, before he can expect the reliance of the General Committee on the success or usefulness of his project.

Resolved, That the Committee of Defence of the Delaware and General Williams be a committee to inquire at what place, and in what time, a steam-frigate can be built, and on what terms, and report.

Resolved, That this Committee accept the offer of the Secretary of the Navy, communicated to them by Mr. George Harrison, and will advance such sum of money, not exceeding one hundred and fifty thousand dollars, as may be necessary for the purpose of constructing a steam floating-battery, to be employed in the defence of the shores of the Delaware and of the City of Philadelphia, the moneys to be reimbursed in such manner as may be agreed between the Secretary of the Navy and this Committee.

Resolved, That the Committee of Correspondence be a committee to communicate to the Secretary of the Navy the above resolution, and to arrange with him the manner and terms of reimbursement.

Resolved, That the Committee of Supplies be authorized to purchase one hundred pairs of shoes for the use of the brigade of militia, under the command of General Snyder, now on duty.

The committee appointed on the application of Mr. Bryant, on behalf of the corps of videttes, report the following resolution:

Resolved, That the sum of five hundred dollars be advanced to Captain Ross, of videttes, for the use of the corps of videttes, for which he shall be accountable; and that he be requested to furnish the accounts of the expenses of the establishment, distinguishing the amount incurred before and since the 10th day of October last.

Which resolution was adopted.

Resolved, That a warrant be drawn on the Treasurer, in favor of the chairman of the committee for the relief of soldiers' families, for twelve hundred dollars.

Resolved, That a warrant be drawn in favor of Job Scott, for logs, for six hundred and two dollars and fifty cents.

The Committee of Accounts reported that they had examined the account of the Committee of Supplies, and that, from the vouchers exhibited therewith, they are entitled to a credit of nineteen thousand and twenty-six dollars and fifteen and a half cents; also that they had examined the account of the Sub-Committee of Defence, and find, from their vouchers, that they are entitled to a credit of three thousand two hundred and thirty dollars and forty-eight cents from the General Committee.

FIFTY-SIXTH MEETING.

PHILADELPHIA, *November 25th*, 1814,
3½ o'clock P.M.

The Committee met.

Present:—Messrs. Biddle, Goodman, Latimer, Leib, Whitehead, Peltz, Connelly, Miercken, Josiah. Eyre, Hawkins, Williams, McFaden, Groves, Leiper, Reed. Steel.

The minutes of the last meeting were read.
The following letter was read.

WAR DEPARTMENT, *November 22d*, 1814.
SIR:

I have had the honor to receive your letter of the 19th instant, inclosing the resolution of the Committee of Defence of Philadelphia, offering to loan to the Government one hundred thousand dollars, for the purpose of fortifying the Delaware at and near the Pea Patch.

In accepting this loan, I cannot refrain from expressing the satisfaction which the Government feels for this additional proof of the patriotism of the City of Philadelphia. In order to conform to the established rules of the Treasury, the loan must be deposited in some bank in Philadelphia, to the credit of the Treasurer of the United States; to be drawn from the Treasury by warrants in favor of such staff-officers, engineers, and other authorized agents as the commanding general of the

Fourth Military District shall designate, and when thus drawn, to be expended under his control, solely for the purpose of the defence of the Delaware at and near the Pea Patch.

When the receipt of the cashier shall have been received, acknowledging the amount of the loan to the credit of the Treasurer, a certificate will be issued by the Treasury Department, in favor of the Committee of Defence for the amount, bearing an interest of six per cent. per annum, the principal to be reimbursed at the termination of the present war, in conformity with the terms offered by the Corporation of the City of Philadelphia, and accepted by this department on the 1st of July, 1814.

I have the honor to be, Sir,
Your obedient servant,
(Signed)   JAS. MONROE.

CHARLES BIDDLE, ESQ.,
Chairman of the Committee of Defence.

Ordered to lie on the table.

A letter from J. Y. Bryant, in behalf of Captain Ross' corps of videttes, was read, and referred to the committee appointed on the 4th instant, on the subject of his letter of that date.

A letter from Danl. Pettibone, relative to pikes made by him for the Committee of Supplies, was read, and ordered to lie on the table until the return of Mr. Ronaldson.

The Committee of Supplies reported that they had

sent thirty blankets to Captain Raguet, which was approved of by the Committee.

The committee appointed to communicate with the Secretary of the Navy, relative to the building of a steam-battery, reported the following letter (see page).

NAVY DEPARTMENT, *November* 23d, 1814.

SIRS:

Last evening I received your letter of the 19th inst., covering copies of two resolutions of the Committee of Defence, on the subject of steam floating-battery.

I am authorized by the Secretary of the Treasury to say, that he will accept the proposed loan on the best terms for the lender, which he may allow for the three million loan now advertised.

Should this proposition meet the approbation of the Committee, you will be pleased to place one hundred and fifty thousand dollars to the credit of the Treasurer of the United States, for the purposes of this agreement, in order that I may, without loss of time, give the necessary instructions for the commencement of the work.

I am, respectfully,

Your obedient servant,

(Signed) W. JONES.

MESSRS. GEO. LATIMER AND JOHN SERGEANT.

Mr. Whitehead reported that he paid the following bills, as directed by a resolution of the Committee on the 18th instant. The vouchers for which have been placed in the care of the Secretary, viz.:

John & Wm. Whitehead, 2 hhds. whisky	$190	23
Jacob Culp & Co., 3 bbls. whisky	80	40
Fred. Foering, 100 pairs shoes	120	00
Wainright & Thomas, 100 pairs shoes	100	50
	$491	13

The Committee of Accounts reported that they had examined the accounts of the committee of relief, and have passed to the credit of their chairman, for expenditures for the relief of absent soldiers' families, the following sums, viz.:

20th October, expended	$705
26th " "	726
2d November, "	766
9th " "	947
16th " "	782
	$4126

Resolved, That a warrant be drawn in favor of the Chairman of the Sub-Committee of Defence for five hundred dollars.

Resolved, That a warrant be drawn in favor of the Chairman of the Committee for the Defence of the Delaware for sixteen hundred and fifty dollars.

Resolved, That the Treasurer of this Committee be instructed to place the sum of one hundred and fifty thousand dollars in the Bank of Pennsylvania, to the credit of the Treasurer of the United States, upon the terms and for the purposes mentioned in the letter this day received from the Secretary of the Navy.

Resolved, That the Committee of Correspondence be instructed to forward a copy of the above resolution to the Secretary of the Navy, and inform him that the money will be forthwith deposited in bank.

Resolved, That the Committee of Correspondence and Mr. Leiper be a committee to call upon the Corporations of New Castle and Wilmington, and the inhabitants of those towns and the adjacent country, to contribute toward the expense of establishing defence at and near the Pea Patch, and building a steam floating-battery.

Resolved, That Messrs. Goodman, Leib, and Whitehead be a committee to digest and report a plan for raising, by subscription or otherwise, the sum of ——— dollars, for defraying the expense of building a steambattery for the defence of the Delaware.

The committee appointed to communicate with the Secretary of the Navy on the subject of a steam-battery, reported that they had written a letter, of which the following is a copy (see page   ).

PHILADELPHIA, *November* 19*th*, 1814.
SIR:

We have the honor to inclose to you copies of two resolutions of the Committee of Defence on the subject of a steam floating-battery. You will perceive that the Committee have agreed to advance the sum that may be necessary for this object as soon as the terms of reimbursement shall be arranged, and have authorized us to make the arrangement. You will be good enough to inform us whether the arrangement is to be made with the Navy Department or with the Treasury, and if with the former, which of the modes proposed in your letter to the committee at Baltimore will be most acceptable.

We are desirous to have the matter arranged as soon as may be convenient, that there may be no delay in commencing the work, which the Committee concur with you in considering to be of very great importance.

We are, respectfully,
Sir, your most obedient,
(Signed) GEORGE LATIMER,
JOHN SERGEANT,
Committee of Correspondence.

HON. WM. JONES,
Secretary of the Navy.

Resolved, That there be a special meeting of the General Committee of Defence, on Saturday, the 3d of December instant, and that notice thereof be given in the newspapers.

Resolved, That a warrant be drawn in favor of the Assistant Secretary for forty dollars.

Resolved, That the Mayor of this city be requested to place in the hands of the Treasurer of this Committee the sum of one hundred thousand dollars, being part of a loan appropriated by the City Councils for defence of the City of Philadelphia and districts adjoining.

Resolved, That the Treasurer be instructed to make a deposit in the Bank of Pennsylvania, to the credit of the Treasurer of the United States, to be applied to the purpose of fortifying the Pea Patch, agreeably to the instructions contained in a letter from the Secretary of War of the 23d instant, for fifty thousand dollars.

Resolved, That an order be drawn in favor of the chairman of the committee for the relief of soldiers' families for eight hundred dollars.

Resolved, That the chairman be instructed to inform General Gaines that the fort is finished, and ready to be delivered up to him.

The Committee of Supplies were discharged from further duty in mounting guns and fixing ammunition.

The committee appointed to aid in the erection of works of defence on the Pea Patch, by a resolution of the 14th October, 1814, were discharged from further duty.

The committee to whom was referred the resolution of the Select and Common Councils of the City of Philadelphia, report:

That they have had two conferences with the committees of the Select and Common Councils on the subject of the said resolution.

At the first, which was on the 14th instant, your Committee exhibited, and delivered to the committees of Councils, a statement, of which a copy is here annexed, marked A, and informed them that the ten thousand dollars received from the Northern Liberties were in part of a sum of twenty-five thousand dollars which had been called for by the Committee of Defence, and the seven thousand dollars from Southwark were in part of a sum of ten thousand dollars that had been in like manner called for.

At the second, on the 23d instant, your Committee exhibited, and delivered, a supplemental statement, intended to show the changes in the state of the funds of the Committee of Defence since the former conference, of which also a copy is hereto annexed, marked B, and, at the same time, informed the committees of Councils, that the Committee of Defence had accepted the offer of the Secretary of the Navy mentioned in the former statement, and that nothing remained to be done on that subject but to settle the terms and manner of reimbursement.

The committees of Councils expressed a wish that, in obtaining advances of money, the Committee of Defence would, as far as practicable, preserve a just proportion between the different corporations.

They also expressed a wish that the Committee of Defence would call upon the Corporation of Penn Township, and the Township of Moyamensing, to aid in the common defence, by contributing in proportion to their means.

Both these suggestions appear to your Committee to be perfectly just. Indeed, the first of them has been, as nearly as was in their power at the time, observed by the Committee of Defence in their calls for money.

The other suggestion is manifestly equitable, not only because the townships mentioned are interested in the common defence, but also because they are represented in the Committee. Your Committee therefore submit the following resolutions:

Resolved, That a committee be appointed to call upon the Corporation of the Northern Liberties, and request that they will, as soon as may be convenient, pay the balance of the twenty-five thousand dollars heretofore called for.

Resolved, That a committee be appointed to call upon the Corporation of Penn Township, and the Township of Moyamensing, and request that they will, respectively, contribute for the common defence.

Resolved, That copies of this report, and the papers annexed to it, be presented to the Select and Common Councils of the City of Philadelphia, the Corporations of the Northern Liberties, Penn Township, the District of Southwark, and the Township of Moyamensing, respectively.

A.

The City Councils appropriated $300,000, of which the Committee received........................	$175,000 00
The Corporation of Northern Liberties appropriated $41,000, of which the Committee received...	10,000 00
The Corporation of Southwark, $20,000, of which the Committee received........................	7,000 00
Donations received...	5,711 00
	$197,711 00
Deduct expended by Committee............	106,563 00
Balance cash in Treasury...................	$91,148 00

Balance due from United States, for money loaned to General Gaines...............	$20,000	00
Amount due for provisions sold...............	10,000	00
Value of provisions on hand...............	11,486	66
Difference to be accounted for, being expended for sundry purposes, the greater part of which will be chargeable to the United States...............	65,076	34
	$197,711	00

The probable further expenditures will require, viz.:

For the payment of accounts not rendered......	5,000	00
For an advance to the United States, a sum not exceeding $100,000, toward establishing defences at the Pea Patch, to be reimbursed after the war, and in the mean time interest to be paid...............	100,000	00
The Committee have now before them a proposition from the Navy Department to the following effect, that is to say, that there shall be a steam-frigate built in, and for, the port of Philadelphia. The money to be advanced by the Committee, and to be repaid, as advanced, by stock of the United States, to be taken at the rate and upon the same terms of the loan...............	150,000	00
	$255,000	00

NOTE.—The above statements are not to be considered as perfectly accurate. They are as nearly right as in the present state of the accounts they can be made.

B.

Balance of cash in Treasury, per statement delivered the Committee from Councils.........	$91,148	00
Cash since received from Corporation of Southwark...............	3,000	00
	$94,148	00

Advanced to General Gaines....... $15,000 00
Sundry orders on Treasurer, and
paid.................................... 2,191 13
————— $17,191 13

Balance in Treasury.................... $76,956 87
Loan to General Gaines............................ 35,000 00
Due from McKoy, for provisions................. 10,000 00
Value of provisions on hand...................... 11,486 66
Balance to be accounted for, the principal of
which, it is expected, will be repaid by the
United States.. 64.267 43

$197,710 96

November 22d, 1814.

Resolved, That Messrs. Leib and Whitehead be a committee to wait on the Commissioners of the Northern Liberties with a copy of the above report and resolution. And

Resolved, That Messrs. Peltz and Groves be a committee to wait on the Corporation of Penn Township with a copy of the same.

Adjourned to meet on Friday afternoon, at 3½ o'clock, December 2d inst.

FIFTY-SEVENTH MEETING.

PHILADELPHIA, *December* 2d, 1814.
3½ o'clock P.M.

The Committee met.

Present:—Messrs. Biddle, Goodman, Latimer, Leib. Whitehead, Williams, Reed, Groves, Steel, Josiah, Hawkins, Ferguson, Miercken, McFaden, Leiper.

The minutes of the last meeting were read.

A letter from J. Y. Bryant, in behalf of Captain Ross' corps of vidcttes, dated December 2d, 1814, was read.

The committee appointed to call upon the Corporations of New Castle and Wilmington, and the inhabitants of those towns and the adjacent country, to contribute toward the expense of establishing defences at and near the Pea Patch, and of building a steam floating-battery, report:

That on Tuesday, the 29th ultimo, they proceeded to the Borough of Wilmington, and in the evening of that day had a conference with the council of the borough in their chamber, and afterward a conversation with such of the gentlemen as had met in councils at our quarters, and we have the pleasure to say, that assurances, quite satisfactory to the minds of your Committee, were given that they would come forward with such sum or sums of money, toward the expense of a work so highly desirable as establishing defences at and near the Pea Patch, as would be fully satisfactory to the Committee of Defence, and quite as much as could be expected them to come forward with.

Your Committee, the next day, went to New Castle, and there had a conference with Chief Justice Johns, George Read, Esq., and Nicholas Van Dyke, Esq., part of a delegation appointed to meet your Committee (the others being hindered partly by absence and partly by sickness), and have the satisfaction to say that their assurances, on the part of New Castle, were equally pleasing with those of the Council of Wilmington.

Your Committee beg leave to add, that it appeared clearly to be necessary that arrangements should be made so as that the Council of Wilmington may be authorized to place what money it may come forward with in a bank in Wilmington, and that what may be furnished in New Castle may be placed in the bank of that town. This appears to your Committee necessary, because the money, or the greater part of it, is expected to be borrowed from those institutions, and also that they may respectively correspond with the Secretary at War on that subject. This your Committee were induced to suggest at the conferences before mentioned, because the resolution of the ———, 1813, state their advances of money are to be made through the Councils of this city; for the purposes your Committee recommend that a committee be appointed to *word* the necessary correspondence on these subjects.

The committee appointed to digest and report a plan for raising by subscription, or otherwise, the sum of ——— dollars, for defraying the expense of building a steam-battery for the defence of the Delaware, report:

That as, in the present state of public and private

embarrassment, it may not be practicable to obtain by subscription a sum sufficient to build and equip a steam-frigate, and as it is nevertheless desirable that the advance of funds for this object may not be wholly confined to this city and the adjacent districts, they submit to the Committee of Defence, whether it would not be expedient to apply to the Legislature of the Commonwealth to obtain a grant of the duties arising from sales at auction for this and other objects of defence. It will not be expected from your Committee that they are to produce a train of argument to illustrate the propriety of the application, and the well-founded claim which this section of the State has upon this fund. It is too self-evident to need any illustration from us, and if it could be obtained, would be competent to the special object of building a steam-frigate and the supply of arms and munitions of war for future exigences. The moment is peculiarly favorable for such an application to the General Assembly; for, as they have on many occasions expressed great zeal for the maintenance of the war, and an earnest determination to risk their lives, their fortunes, and their sacred honor in defence of those rights for which the war was undertaken, the committee must believe that there can be no hesitancy in appropriating this fund for this great common object. They therefore submit the following resolution:

Resolved, That an application be made to the State Government to appropriate the duties arising upon sales at auction for the purpose of building a steam-frigate, other means of defence, and supplying arms and munitions of war, and that the committee who brought in the report be appointed to draft a memorial.

Resolved, That the Committee of Correspondence be instructed to inform the Secretary of War, that it is the wish of the Committee of Defence that the certificate of stock for the money loaned to the Government of the United States, for defence at the Pea Patch, be issued in the names of the following gentlemen, viz.: Thomas Leiper, James Whitehead, and Robert McMullin, and that the certificate so issued be forwarded to George Latimer, Esq., Treasurer of this Committee.

Resolved, That the Committee for the Defence of the Delaware and General Williams be a committee to inquire and report on the propriety of placing a chain across the Delaware.

Resolved, That a fire-engine be purchased for Fort Mifflin.

Resolved, That the Committee of Supplies be instructed to sell all the provisions remaining on hand.

Resolved, That a warrant be drawn in favor of the Chairman of the Committee of Supplies for five hundred dollars.

Resolved, That a warrant be drawn in favor of the Chairman of the Committee of Defence of the Delaware for five hundred dollars.

Resolved, That copies of the letters from the Secretary of War, and the answers thereto, relative to the loan for erecting fortifications on the Pea Patch, be handed to General Gaines.

Resolved, That the future meetings of this Committee be held on Tuesdays and Fridays.

Resolved, That on Tuesday, 6th instant, at half-past 3 o'clock, a special meeting be held, and that notice thereof be given in the public papers.

Resolved, That a warrant be drawn in favor of George Latimer for twenty-five dollars and thirty cents, for expenses of the committee at Wilmington.

Adjourned to meet December 6th instant, at 3½ o'clock in the afternoon.

FIFTY-EIGHTH MEETING.

PHILADELPHIA, *December 6th*, 1814,
3½ o'clock.

The Committee met.

Present:—Messrs. Biddle, Goodman, Latimer, Ronaldson, Williams, Reed, Leib, McMullin, McFaden, Leiper, Eyre, Brown, Groves, Hawkins, Josiah, Miercken, Whitehead, Connelly.

The minutes of the last meeting were read.

The Committee of Correspondence, appointed to communicate with the Secretary of War on the subject of a floating-battery, reported the following letters:

NAVY DEPARTMENT, *November* 30th, 1814.
SIRS:

I have received your letter of the 26th inst., covering two resolutions of the Committee of Defence for the City of Philadelphia, directing the Treasurer of the Committee to place the sum of one hundred and fifty thousand dollars in the Bank of Pennsylvania to the credit of the Treasurer of the United States, upon the terms and for the purposes mentioned in my letter to you, dated the 23d instant, and have now the honor to inclose a copy of my instructions of this day to George Harrison, Esq., Navy Agent, in conformity with the agreement entered into with the Committee for the purposes stated in the aforesaid letter.

I have the honor to be, very respectfully,
Your obedient servant,
(Signed) W. JONES.
GEO. LATIMER, JOHN SERGEANT, JOS. REED, ESQS.,
Com. of Cor. for the Com. of Defence, Philadelphia.

(COPY.)

NAVY DEPARTMENT, *November* 30th, 1814.
SIR:

The Committee of Defence for the City of Philadelphia have agreed with this department to loan to the United States one hundred and fifty thousand dollars, to be applied to the construction and equipment of a steam floating-battery for the defence of the River Delaware, similar to that which has been recently constructed for the United States at the City of New York.

You will therefore advise this department, as soon as the sum aforesaid shall have been so placed in any bank in the City of Philadelphia, in order that a warrant may be drawn in your favor for the amount and for the purposes aforesaid, and inviting to your aid Manuel Eyre, Henry Hawkins, and James Josiah, Esquires, you will immediately enter into the necessary contracts and engagements for materials and equipments, and for the building of a steam floating-battery in all respects similar to that in New York called "Fulton the First," built by Messrs. Browns, and designed and superintended by Mr. Fulton, and with whom it will be proper to enter into a correspondence in order to procure the necessary draughts, plans, and instructions, as well for constructing the vessel as the steam-engine and machinery. As everything depends upon the correct construction and apportionment of the power to the body to be propelled, Mr. Fulton's aid in this branch of the business will be indispensable.

The vessel may be built either in the Navy Yard, by the builders of the Franklin (whose salary in that case must be paid out of the special fund), or elsewhere, as yourself and your colleagues shall deem most advantageous. In respect to this object time is very precious, and particularly as it respects the construction of the engine and machinery.

One of the builders should proceed with a letter from you to New York, in order to procure the draughts, plans, and estimates for materials, and to examine critically the entire construction of "Fulton the First."

The best economy and management will be indispensable, otherwise the fund and appropriation will fall short.

I am, respectfully,

Your obedient servant,

(Signed) W. JONES.

Geo. Harrison. Esq.,

Navy Agent, Philadelphia.

The Committee of Correspondence reported the following letter:

Department of War, *December 2d*, 1814.

Gentlemen:

Your letter of the 26th ultimo, inclosing the receipt of the Bank of Pennsylvania for fifty thousand dollars in favor of the Treasurer of the United States, has been received. I inclose to you a copy of a communication from the Secretary of the Treasury to this department, explaining the mode which must be pursued to enable the Committee of Defence to obtain certificates of the loan made for the erection of works at the Pea Patch. Whenever these works are commenced, and money is wanted for their prosecution, the warrants of this department will be issued for such sums and in favor of such persons as the commanding general shall designate.

I have the honor to be,

Respectfully, Gentlemen,

Your most obedient servant,

(Signed) JAS. MONROE.

Messrs. Geo. Latimer, John Sergeant, Jos. Reed,

Com. of Cor. of the Com. of Defence of Philadelphia.

Copy of a communication from the Secretary of the Treasury to the Secretary of War, relative to the loan from the Committee of Defence of Philadelphia to the Department of War for the purpose of fortifying the Pea Patch:

"The contract of the Secretary of War will be carried into effect at the Treasury for the amount specified, as a part of the appropriation for the War Department. But it is in the nature of a special contract, and it would be inconvenient, on several accounts, to complete a new kind of stock for it. On stating, specifically, the terms and objects of the contract, and on the requisition of the Secretary at War, the debt will be assumed at the Treasury in the regular form of a temporary loan."

Referred again to Committee of Correspondence.

A letter from Major-General Gaines, requesting a loan of ten thousand dollars. Whereupon

Resolved, That a loan of ten thousand dollars be made to General Gaines, to be repaid when the fifty thousand dollars loaned to the United States by the Committee for the purpose of fortifying the Pea Patch shall have been received by him.

Resolved, That the Committee of Supplies be directed to pay the accounts presented to them for uniform, as far as such payments have been assumed or guaranteed by this Committee, on receiving from the captains the pay-rolls and muster-rolls of their several companies, agreeably to the resolution of the 18th September last.

Resolved, That a warrant be drawn in favor of the chairman of the committee for the relief of soldiers' families for five hundred dollars.

Resolved, That a warrant be drawn in favor of the Chairman of the Committee of Supplies for one thousand and three hundred dollars.

Adjourned to meet on Friday afternoon, at 3½ o'clock, December the 9th instant.

FIFTY-NINTH MEETING.

PHILADELPHIA, *December 9th,* 1814,
3½ o'clock P.M.

The Committee met.

Present:—Messrs. Biddle, Goodman, Latimer, Leib. Sergeant, McFaden, McMullin, Williams, Miercken, Eyre, Reed, Whitehead, Ronaldson, Connelly.

The minutes of the last meeting were read.

Mr. Biddle retired, and Mr. Goodman was called to the Chair.

The following letter was read:

WILMINGTON, *December 7th,* 1814.
GENTLEMEN:

Your letter of the 4th instant, covering one from the Secretary of War, is received, and on Monday was laid before the Council, and I am directed to inform you that the Council of the Borough of Wilmington have appropriated fifteen thousand dollars for the purposes mentioned in your letter, and as soon as the first five thousand dollars is placed in one of our banks you shall be notified.

  I am, Gentlemen,
   With great respect,
    Your obedient servant,
     JAS. BROBSON,
      First Burgess.

COMMITTEE OF CORRESPONDENCE.

The committee appointed to confer with the Board of Commissioners of the Northern Liberties, and urge the expediency of paying to the Committee of Defence the balance of twenty-five thousand dollars, which was required by a resolution of the Committee of Defence, report:

That your Committee addressed a note to the President of the Board of Commissioners, requesting an interview with the Board on the subject of their appointments; that your Committee were informed by the President that a committee had been appointed by the Board of Commissioners to negotiate a loan to answer the requisition, which rendered unnecessary the interview requested.

Resolved, That Messrs. Sergeant, Williams, Leib, Reed, Eyre, Whitehead, Latimer, and Josiah be a committee to consider and report what objects require the attention of the Committee which will call for an expenditure of money, what amount of money will be requisite, and how the same can be raised.

Resolved, That a warrant be drawn in favor of the Chairman of the Committee for the Defence of the Delaware for five thousand five hundred dollars.

The Committee of Correspondence reported a letter from them to the Secretary of the Navy, of which the following is a copy:

PHILADELPHIA, *November* 26*th*, 1814.

SIR:

We have the honor to inclose to you copies of two resolutions adopted yesterday by the Committee of Defence. The money will be deposited in the Bank of Pennsylvania, in the course of a few days, to the credit of the Treasurer of the United States, when we shall take care to advise you, and to transmit the proper voucher to the Secretary of the Treasury.

We are, very respectfully,

Sir, your most obedient,

(Signed) GEORGE LATIMER,
JOHN SERGEANT,
JOS. REED.

HON. WM. JONES,
Secretary of the Navy.

Resolved, That the Committee of Supplies be authorized to receive from the contractors two hundred pikes that were not ready for delivery by the time limited in the contracts, provided the pikes are of the specified quality.

A verbal application was made by General Williams for General Cadwalader, on the authority of General Gaines, for a loan of fourteen thousand dollars, for the use of his brigade, which was referred to a committee, consisting of Messrs. Williams and Reed.

Adjourned to meet on Tuesday afternoon, at 3½ o'clock, December 13th.

SIXTIETH MEETING.

PHILADELPHIA, *December* 13*th*, 1814,
3½ o'clock P.M.

The Committee met.

Present:—Messrs. Biddle, Goodman, Leib, Reed, McMullin, McFaden, Williams, Whitehead, Josiah, Huff, Ferguson, Eyre, Hawkins, Ronaldson, Groves.

The minutes of the last meeting were read.

The following letters were read:

FOURTH MILITARY DISTRICT.

HEADQUARTERS,
PHILADELPHIA, *December* 13*th*, 1814.

SIR:

I have the honor to inclose a letter just received from Captain Clark, of the topographical engineers, and beg to know whether he can have the use of the hulks, purchased by the Committee, for the purposes mentioned in his letter.

I have the honor to be, &c.,

(Signed) THOS. CADWALADER,
Br.-Gen. Commanding Fourth Mil. Dist.

To the Chairman of the Committee of
Defence, Philadelphia.

Philadelphia, *December* 13*th*, 1814.

Sir:

According to my orders, I intend, as soon as the necessary arrangements can be made, to proceed to the Pea Patch, with the intention of constructing a landing, and preparing the ground for the tower, now building in the Northern Liberties. For the temporary accommodation of the soldiers and workmen three vessels will be required. The hulks purchased by the Committee of Safety would answer well for this purpose. I entreat you, sir, to have the goodness to mention this circumstance to the Committee.

I am, Sir, &c..

(Signed) THOS. CLARK,
Of Top. Engineers.

To Brig.-Gen. Cadwalader.

Referred to the Committee of Defence of the Delaware.

The Committee of Correspondence reported the following letters:

Sir: *December 8th*, 1814.

We have the honor to acknowledge the receipt of your letter of the 2d instant, covering a communication from the Secretary of the Treasury to the Department of War. In this communication it appears to us, that the Secretary of the Treasury asks of you to "state specifically the terms and object of the contract under which we have placed fifty thousand dollars to the credit of the Treasurer of the United States." He will, no doubt, be informed by you, that the object is the defence of the Delaware, by works to be erected at and near the Pea Patch, and the terms of the loan for the necessary fortifications are those agreed upon by the late Secretary of War with the Corporation of this city on the 1st of July last, and recognized in your letter to us of 23d ultimo. It was on the terms then agreed upon that the fifty thousand dollars were paid by the Committee of Defence into the Bank of Pennsylvania to the credit of the United States, for which you have received the receipt of the cashier. But it appears by the communication of the Secretary of the Treasury, that it would be inconvenient on several accounts to *complete* a new kind of stock for this loan. On this subject we have no hesitation to say, that if, on any account, it would be for the convenience of the Treasury to give certificate of stock for our loan on such terms as the three million loan now advertised for may be negotiated at, it would be acceptable and agreed to, or perhaps

Treasury notes might be received. This alteration of the terms, you will be pleased to observe, is mentioned in consequence only of the communication of the Secretary of the Treasury, forwarded to us in your letter of the 2d instant. Permit us to observe, that as the sum offered by us to the War Department, for the defence of the Delaware, has been borrowed by the corporation of the city from the Bank of Pennsylvania, it is all-important. and, indeed, indispensably necessary, that we should have transferable stock, or other negotiable security. without which we apprehend a total failure of our means to procure the necessary funds to complete the works on the Delaware, deemed so essentially necessary for the safety of the city. The loan was negotiated on the assurance contained in your letter of the 23d ultimo. that a certificate would issue, &c., and without it, or other negotiable security, we cannot expect the bank will comply with the terms of the contract and complete the loan.

  We have the honor to be,
   Very respectfully,
    Your obedient servants,
     (Signed)   GEO. LATIMER,
             JNO. SERGEANT,
             JOS. REED,
         Committee of Correspondence.

THE HONORABLE JAS. MONROE,
 Secretary of War.

PHILADELPHIA, *December 9th,* 1814.
SIR:

We have the honor to inclose copies of a correspondence between the War Department and the Committee of Defence of this city, to which we beg to call your attention. In consequence of the Secretary's letter of the 22d November, the sum of fifty thousand dollars has been paid into the Bank of Pennsylvania to the credit of the United States, in part of the loan of one hundred thousand dollars for the defence of the Delaware at or near the Pea Patch. The corporation of the city having borrowed the money from the Bank of Pennsylvania, and the Committee having paid fifty thousand dollars on an assurance that a certificate of stock would be issued according to the terms of Colonel Monroe's letter above referred to, it has become important, and, indeed, indispensably necessary, that we should have transferable stock, or other negotiable security, without which we apprehend a total failure of our means to procure the necessary funds to complete the works on the Delaware, so important to the safety of the city. If (as is intimated in the communication from the Treasury Department received from the Secretary of War) stock cannot be created for the purpose, as we had supposed, to be reimbursed at the end of the war, we are authorized to say that we will receive Treasury notes for the amount, or certificates of stock, on the same terms the three million loan now advertised may be negotiated at. In either case the difficulty suggested at the Treasury will be obviated, and the time of payment extended, to meet the views and convenience of the Government.

We have the honor, &c.,

  (Signed) GEO. LATIMER,
        JOHN SERGEANT,
        JOS. REED,
      Committee of Correspondence.

HONORABLE A. J. DALLAS.
 Secretary of the Treasury.

    Papers inclosed.

One letter, November 22d, Secretary of War to the Committee.

One letter, November 26th, Committee of Correspondence to Secretary.

One letter, December 8th, same to same.

Proceedings of Committee relating to Pea Patch.

    WAR DEPARTMENT, *December* 10*th*, 1814.

GENTLEMEN:

I herewith have the honor to transmit articles of agreement for the loan of one hundred thousand dollars, intended for the fortifications of the Pea Patch, which articles have been drawn by the Secretary of the Treasury. Messrs. Leiper, McMullin, and Whitehead will sign these articles, after which you will transmit them to the Secretary of the Treasury for his signature. One of these articles will be forwarded these gentlemen, the other retained at the Treasury Department.

I have the honor to be, respectfully,

    (Signed) JAS. MONROE.

GEO. LATIMER, JNO. SERGEANT, JOS. REED,
 Committee of Correspondence.

Articles of Agreement between Alexander James Dallas, Secretary of the Treasury of the United States, of the one part, and ——— on the other part, made and concluded the ——— day of ———, one thousand eight hundred and fourteen.

WHEREAS, by an Act of Congress, passed on the twenty-fourth day of March, one thousand eight hundred and fourteen, the President of the United States is authorized to borrow, on the credit of the United States, a sum not exceeding twenty-five millions of dollars; and whereas, the President of the United States did, by an act or commission under his hand, dated the twenty-ninth day of March, one thousand eight hundred and fourteen, authorize and empower the Secretary of the Treasury to borrow the said sum on the credit of the United States, pursuant to the aforesaid act.

NOW THESE PRESENTS WITNESS, That it hath been and is hereby agreed between the parties of the first and second part, that the said parties of the second part shall advance and lend to the United States one hundred thousand dollars, of which sum fifty thousand dollars has been already paid at the Bank of Pennsylvania, on the twenty-sixth day of November last, and the remaining sum of fifty thousand dollars shall be paid at the said bank on the ——— day of ———.

2. The sum thus loaned shall bear interest at the rate of six per cent. per annum, payable quarter-yearly at the Treasury of the United States—the first payment of said interest being demandable on the first day of January next.

3. The United States shall reimburse or repay to the said party of the second part the aforesaid sum of one hundred thousand dollars, at or on the expiration of one year from and after the ratification by the Senate of the United States of a treaty by which the existing war between Great Britain and the United States shall be terminated.

In testimony whereof, the said Secretary of the Treasury hath hereunto subscribed his hand, and caused the seal of the Treasury to be affixed, and the said

subscribed these presents, and affixed ——— seal, ——— day and year first above written.

The committee appointed to digest and report a plan for raising the sum of ——— dollars for defraying the expense of building a steam-battery for the defence of the Delaware, reported the following

MEMORIAL.

To the Senate and House of Representatives of the Commonwealth of Pennsylvania, in General Assembly met:

The petition of the subscribers, citizens of the City and County of Philadelphia, respectfully showeth, That your petitioners are sensibly impressed with the necessity of affording to this city and vicinity a prompt and a competent defence against the approach and ravages of the common enemy, and look to the General Assembly, as the common guardian of the Commonwealth, to bestow its care and attention upon the metropolis of this great and powerful State.

During the last autumn great alarm was excited among the people of this quarter in consequence of the menaces of the enemy in the Chesapeake, the barbarous mode of his warfare, and the unprovided means of our military means to repel an invading foe; and in the then existing state of danger and alarm, it became essential to the safety and protection of this section of the Commonwealth that the resources and energies within the sphere of your petitioners should be promptly employed, to afford such means of resistance as the occasion demanded. The corporations of the city and the adjacent districts, with a zeal and a patriotism highly honorable to them, appropriated three hundred and ——— thousand dollars for the purposes of defence, under the direction and management of a committee selected by the people. By means of these appropriations fortifications were erected and repaired, implements of war were supplied, and provision made for the comfort and subsistence of the troops. By the aid of our patriotic militia, and the resources afforded by the corporations, this great and important metropolis was preserved from pillage and the fate of Washington. Should, however, the war be continued, greater and more efficient efforts will be required to guard this city against the approaches of the enemy. His naval superiority, and the facilities thereby afforded him of assailing our maritime frontier, exposes this city to his attacks, and to the execution of the denunciation of Admiral Cochrane against all available places; it becomes essentially necessary therefore that the River

Delaware should be guarded, not only by suitable fortifications, but that we should be provided with naval armaments in aid of those on shore. Competent and able naval commanders have ascribed great efficiency to the steam-frigate lately built in our sister city, New York, and your petitioners are anxiously solicitous to possess such a means of defence and annoyance in the River Delaware. They therefore approach the General Assembly with a confident hope that, as it is in their power to afford it to them, it will be freely and patriotically granted.

Your petitioners take the liberty to point to the source from which this necessary defence can be derived; and it is a source which springs exclusively from this section of the Commonwealth. The State generally is excepted from the contribution derived from sales at auction, and while the citizens of almost every other part of the Commonwealth can make sale of their real and personal property without any tax being demanded from them by the Government, the people of this section are subject to the payment of duties for every article disposed of at auction, thus introducing an inequality in the system of taxation, which warrants the assertion of your petitioners, that this source of revenue is exclusively derived from them. It cannot be urged in this case, as in others, that the consumers buy or pay the tax; for it is an indisputable fact that the duty in this instance falls upon the vender, who, in general, resorts to this expedient of disposing of his property, either from necessity, or some motive of speculation.

The duties, then, arising from sales at auction, would provide an adequate fund for this object, and perhaps for other objects of no small importance, a permanent supply of arms and munitions of war, and in the appropriation of this fund for those great and beneficial ends, the General Assembly will have the proud satisfaction of redeeming the pledge, which has been often given by the State, to support the war by all its resources and energies, and thus aid in hastening it to an honorable issue. Your petitioners therefore pray that the duties arising upon sales at auction may be appropriated toward building a steam-frigate for the defence of the River Delaware, and to the permanent supply of arms and munitions of war for the militia.

Resolved, That the committee who reported the above memorial be instructed to cause one hundred copies of the same to be printed, and also to inquire and report the names of persons in the different wards and districts suitable to form committees for obtaining signatures.

Resolved, That the letter from the Secretary of War and the draught of an agreement inclosed in it, be referred to the Committee of Correspondence, with authority to correspond with the Secretary of the Treasury on the subject, and to relinquish the condition of payment immediately after the termination of the war, if by so doing negotiable stock or other transferable evidence of public debt can thereby be obtained on the terms of the loan of twenty-five millions.

The committee to whom was referred the application

of General Cadwalader for a loan to the United States for the use of his brigade, report:

That the money wanted, they find upon inquiry, to be to pay debts contracted by the brigade for the supply of fuel and other articles of consumption while in the field. That the Government has no money remaining in hand resulting from the two hundred thousand dollars which had been loaned by the banks in Philadelphia for the defence of this district.

That if the General Committee think proper to loan the money in question, there appears no special fund appropriated for its reimbursement, unless a reimbursement in Treasury notes can be so called.

To try the question respecting the application, the committee would propose the following resolution:

Resolved, That the sum of fourteen thousand dollars be advanced to the Government of the United States, for the use of General Cadwalader's brigade, on a deposit of an equal sum in Treasury notes, or any part thereof, from time to time, as said notes to an equal amount may be deposited.

Which was postponed.

Resolved, That the Sub-Committee of Defence be authorized to sell the tools purchased by them for the purpose of making fortifications.

Adjourned to meet on Friday, 16th instant, at 3½ o'clock in the afternoon.

SIXTY-FIRST MEETING.

PHILADELPHIA, *December* 16*th*, 1814,
3½ o'clock P.M.

The Committee met.

Present:—Messrs. Biddle, Goodman, Latimer, Leib, Miercken, Eyre, Connelly, Groves, Huff, Reed, Whitehead, Williams, McFaden, Josiah.

The minutes of the last meeting were read.

An estimate of the cost of chevaux-de-frise by Mr. Joseph Grice, was read, and ordered to lie on the table.

The Committee of Correspondence reported the following letters:

PHILADELPHIA, *December* 15*th*, 1814.

SIR:

We have received from the Department of War a letter of the 10th December, covering articles of agreement proposed to be executed for securing reimbursements of moneys advanced for fortifications at and near the Pea Patch. They have been submitted to the Committee of Defence, and we have now the honor to inclose to you a copy of the resolution they have adopted on the subject. You will perceive, from the resolution, that the Committee are very desirous to have stock or other transferable evidence of public debt; and supposing that the time of reimbursement was the only circumstances which distinguished this from other contracts of the Government, and obliged the Treasurer to adopt the form of a special agreement, they have authorized us to relinquish that condition upon the terms stated in the resolution.

The reasons of the Committee we will take the liberty briefly to explain. The money advanced for the fortifications has been or is to be contributed, in different proportions, by no less than five public bodies, to whom, in the same proportions, the Committee are to account, and deliver the evidences they may receive from the Government as soon as it shall be in their power. What their respective proportions will be cannot now be ascertained. The agreement, you will perceive, will not enable us, when necessary, to make this distribution.

We would further suggest, referring for fuller explanation to the last letter we had the honor to address to you, that the possession of the stock would very much aid in raising the funds that may be necessary for other objects connected with the public defence.

We therefore request that you will take into consideration the subject of the resolution, and inform us, as soon as your convenience will permit, whether the wishes of the Committee can be complied with.

We have the honor to be,
Your obedient servants,
(Signed) GEO. LATIMER,
JOHN SERGEANT,
JOSEPH REED,
Committee of Correspondence.

HONORABLE A. J. DALLAS,
Secretary of the Treasury.

TREASURY DEPARTMENT, *December* 13*th*, 1814.
GENTLEMEN:

Your letter of the 9th instant has been received, relating to the loan for fortifying the Pea Patch in the River Delaware. The contract on this subject can only be recognized at the Treasury through the War Department; but I have no objections to state my views of it, unofficially, for your information.

It appears from General Armstrong's letter of the 1st July, 1814, that a plan for fortifying the Pea Patch, which had been approved in April preceding, was to be immediately commenced, and that the funds for accomplishing the object were to be advanced by the Corporation of Philadelphia, *to be refunded by the War Department within one year after the termination of the present war, with interest at the rate of six per cent. per annum.*

This is the whole contract between the War Department and the Corporation of the City of Philadelphia. It is recognized as such in the minutes of the proceedings of the Committee of Defence, dated the 19th October and the 18th of November, 1814, and it is a special contract to loan 100,000 dollars, at six per cent. interest, for a specific object and for a given period.

It is true, that the Secretary of War, in his letter of the 22d November, mentions that, under certain circumstances, a certificate will be given by the Treasury Department in favor of the Committee of Defence for the amount of the loan, bearing an interest of six per cent. per annum, but he acts expressly on the terms of the contract with General Armstrong of the 1st July, which was a special contract, and not a subscription to a public loan calling for a certificate of stock. Such special contracts are not unusual, and the form proposed at the Treasury for giving it effect is the general official form. It only remains to add, that this department will execute, in good faith, the contract of the War Department upon the requisition of the Secretary of War. But it must be distinctly understood, that to issue a certificate of stock in a case like the present would be a novelty at the Treasury; and that to change a temporary loan at six per cent. into a loan for stock to be issued at any rate less than par, would be inconsistent with my views of official propriety. The reimbursement of the special loan by Treasury notes would constitute a new contract in every respect, and of course it does not lie with me to adopt the proposition.

I am, very respectfully,

Gentlemen, your obedient servant,

(Signed) A. J. DALLAS.

Messrs. Latimer, Sergeant, and Reed,

A Committee, &c., Philadelphia.

The Committee of Accounts report that they have examined the vouchers (being duplicates) delivered to them by the Committee for the Defence of the Delaware for disbursements, in repairs of Fort Mifflin, Fort Gaines, &c., and that the following is the result, viz.:

Expended for repairs of Fort Mifflin, making carriages for guns, &c. $20,427 06
Expended for repairs of Fort Gaines, making carriages for guns, &c. 9,132 21

Repairs to gun-boats	$617 84
For purchase of hulks, &c.	21,470 64
For torpedo to B. Henry	130 00
For experiments of a floating-chain	111 47
	$51,889 22

Resolved, That the above sum of fifty-one thousand eight hundred and eighty-nine dollars and twenty-two cents be placed to the credit of the Committee for the Defence of the Delaware in the books of accounts of the General Committee of Defence, and that the duplicate vouchers for the same be placed in charge of the Secretary to this Board.

Resolved, That an order be drawn in favor of the Chairman of the Committee for the Defence of the Delaware for eight hundred dollars.

Adjourned to meet on Tuesday, December the 20th, at 3 o'clock in the afternoon.

SIXTY-SECOND MEETING.

PHILADELPHIA, *December 20th*, 1814,
3 o'clock P.M.

The Committee met.

Present:—Messrs. Goodman, Biddle, Latimer, Leib, McFaden, Peltz, Ronaldson, Williams, Hawkins, Connelly, Josiah, Miercken, Whitehead, Sergeant, Eyre.

The minutes of the last meeting were read.

The committee appointed by a resolution of the 13th instant, to cause a memorial to the Legislature of Pennsylvania to be printed, reported that one hundred copies (the number resolved on) had been printed and delivered into their possession. Whereupon

Resolved, That an order be drawn in favor of Mr. Goodman to pay the amount of the printer's bill for printing said memorial, that is to say, for five dollars.

The Committee of Accounts report they have examined the accounts of the Sub-Committee of Defence presented to them, with duplicate vouchers, and that it appears they have expended for the following purposes, viz.:

Fortifications west side of Schuylkill...............	$519 40
For expense account.................................	76 81
	$596 21

Resolved. That the above sum of five hundred and ninety-six dollars and twenty-one cents be placed to the credit of the Sub-Committee of Defence on the books of the General Committee, and that the vouchers for which be placed in charge of the Secretary to the Board.

Adopted.

Resolved, That an order be drawn on the Treasurer, in favor of the commanding general of this military district, for five thousand dollars, to enable him to make an advance of pay to General Spering's Brigade of Pennsylvania Militia, whose necessities require it to prosecute

COMMITTEE OF DEFENCE. 321

their march to their own homes, on condition that sufficient security be obtained for the reimbursement of this sum to this Committee out of the pay of troops of this brigade.

Resolved, That an order be drawn on the Treasurer, in favor of the Chairman of the Committee of Supplies, for two thousand dollars.

Adjourned.

SIXTY-THIRD MEETING.

PHILADELPHIA, *December* 23d, 1814.
3 o'clock P.M.

The Committee met.

Present:—Messrs. Biddle, Latimer, General Cadwalader, Messrs. Leib, McFaden, Whitehead, Ronaldson. Reed, Williams, Eyre, Ferguson, McMullin, Naglee.

The minutes of the last meeting were read.

The following letters and receipt from General Cadwalader, relative to the appropriation of money for General Spering's brigade, were read:

HEADQUARTERS,
PHILADELPHIA, *December* 23d, 1814.
GENTLEMEN:

On the 19th instant I was furnished by your order with the sum of $5000, for the purpose of supplying the soldiers belonging to Brigadier-General Spering's brigade with means of returning to their homes.

21

I accordingly placed in the hands of Captain Philips, district paymaster, the sum of $4000, on the terms stated in his receipt inclosed, and have this day paid out to the Treasurer of your Board the balance, $1000 —total, $5000.

I also inclose copies of a letter I thought it expedient to write to Mr. Bussier, the State paymaster, and of his answer of this date.

I have the honor to be, with great respect.

Gentlemen, your most obedient servant,

(Signed) THOS. CADWALADER,

Brig.-Gen. Commanding Fourth Mil. Dis.

To the Committee of Defence, Philadelphia.

(Copy.)

Fourth Military District.

Headquarters,

Philadelphia, *December* 20*th*, 1814.

Sir:

The soldiers of Brigadier-General Spering's brigade of militia, now in quarters at the new prison, being discharged from the service of the United States, and the men being generally destitute of funds to enable them to return to their homes, the Committee of Defence has supplied me with a sum of money, out of which I have furnished the district paymaster with $4000, to be distributed to the brigade on account of the pay due from the United States, the paymaster engaging to refund the amount out of the first moneys placed in his hands for the payment of those men.

As it may possibly happen that funds may be advanced by this State for the payment of its troops, and the moneys may pass through your hands instead of Captain Philips', the United States paymaster, I request from you a few lines, stating that the sum before mentioned be refunded by you for the payment of General Spering's brigade, the pay-rolls and receipts being regularly made out and delivered over to you.

I am, &c.,
(Signed) THOS. CADWALADER,
Brig.-Gen. 1st Brig. Div. P. M., Com'g 4th Mil. Dis.
To DANIEL BUSSIER, ESQ.,
Paymaster of the State of Pennsylvania.

(COPY.)

PHILADELPHIA, *December* 23*d*, 1814.
SIR:

I have the honor to acknowledge the receipt of your letter of the 20th instant. As no payments of the nature alluded to can be made by me without instructions from his Excellency the Governor, I do not see how I can give a promise, or even enter into any conditional stipulations on the subject. I may, however, add that it will give me great pleasure to act agreeably to your wishes.

I remain, very respectfully,
Your most obedient humble servant,
DANIEL BUSSIER,
Paymaster-General.
GENERAL CADWALADER.

Received from Brigadier-General Cadwalader four thousand dollars, for the payment of Brigadier-General Spering's Brigade of Pennsylvania Militia, which I promise to refund out of the first money I shall receive for the payment of that brigade.

(Signed)   HENRY PHILIPS,
(Duplicates.)   *Division Paymaster.*
$4000.

Philadelphia, December 20th, 1814.

Ordered to be entered on the minutes.

The Treasurer stated that General Cadwalader had returned him one thousand dollars, of the five thousand dollars appropriated by a resolve of the Committee of the 20th instant, for General Spering's brigade, and that he had deposited it in the Bank of Pennsylvania to the credit of the Committee of Defence.

A letter from the Secretary of the Treasury, of which the following is a copy, was read:

TREASURY DEPARTMENT, *December* 17*th*, 1814.

GENTLEMEN:

I have received your letter of the 15th instant. It is only necessary to observe that my communication to you, dated the 13th instant, contains an answer to all the points of your inquiry. If, however, it can accommodate you, I will agree, on the request of the Secretary of War, to issue a certificate of six per cent. stock, in the usual form, for the amount of the city advance on account of the fortifications at the Pea Patch, instead of entering into a contract, as is usual in the case of a temporary loan. But you will be pleased to recollect that I have no power on this occasion to change the terms of the original contract unfavorably to the Government, or, in other words, to issue a certificate for any greater sum than the actual amount of the advance.

I am, very respectfully, gentlemen,
Your most obedient servant,
(Signed)   A. J. DALLAS.
MESSRS. LATIMER, SERGEANT, AND REED,
Committee of Correspondence.

Resolved, That the Committee of Correspondence be instructed to write an answer to the above letter to the Secretary of the Treasury.

Resolved, That an order be drawn in favor of the Assistant Secretary for one month's salary, ending this day, for forty dollars.

Adjourned to meet on Tuesday, December 27th, 1814, at 3½ o'clock in the afternoon.

SIXTY-FOURTH MEETING.

PHILADELPHIA, *December 27th*, 1814,
3½ o'clock P.M.

The Committee met.
Present:—Messrs. Biddle, Goodman, Latimer, Huff, Whitehead, Naglee, Miercken, Josiah, Reed, Leib, Williams, Hawkins, McMullin, McFaden.

The minutes of the last meeting were read.

The Committee appointed by a resolution of the 13th instant (page   ), to inquire and report the names of persons in the different wards and districts suitable to form committees for obtaining signatures to the memorial to the Senate and House of Representatives of the Commonwealth of Pennsylvania, agreed to by resolution of the same date, reported the following list of names for the different wards and districts, which being read and amended, was adopted, and ordered to be entered on the minutes.

NORTHERN LIBERTIES AND PENN TOWNSHIP.

Henry A. Beck, William Binder, Cornelius Trimmel, Fredk. Wolbert, Edward D. Corfield, Daniel Bickley, C. Bartling, John Whitehead, Conrad Hester, Daniel Brentigam, Frederick Hockley, Joseph Staure, Jacob Clemens, Frederick Fricke, William Fitler, Samuel McFarran, Henry Graba, Jacob Belsterling, Henry Probasco, William Smith, Sebastian Zimmerman, Andrew Barclay, Lawrence Cauffman, Jacob Walters, Enoch Wheeler, Isaac Johnson, Jesse Shelmire, Philip Justice, Frederick Sheble, William West, T. Wagoner, Jacob Juvenal, Joseph Grice, Saml. Bowers, George Eyre, John Harrison, Isaac Boileau, George Houser, David Shuster, Geo. Meyers, Frederick Staal, Joseph Watkins, (Falls.)

CITY.

Upper Delaware.—John Miller, Alexander McCaraher, William Rush, Peter Wager, Lewis Rush, Isaac Boyer.

Lower Delaware.—Conrad Wile, Geo. Slesman, Andrew Leinau, Thomas Pratt, Joseph Clark, Joseph Hertzog.

North Mulberry.—Adam Eckfeldt, Alex. Cook, Alex. Ramsay, J. Clawges, Peter Fritz, John Shibley.

South Mulberry.—Joseph Morris, Robert Imley, Jacob Keigler, Dr. Alberti, Saml. Richards, Valentine Borer.

North Ward.—Paul Beck, Joseph Cloud, Jacob Leibrandt, Charles Massey, Stephen Phipps, Aaron Denman.

High Street.—James H. Cole, Joseph Price, C. W. Morris, Lawrence Seckel, Hugh Cooper, Jacob Chrystler.

Chestnut.—Samuel S. Meeker, David Lapsley, Wm. Bell, John Willis, William Smith, Richard Tybout.

Walnut.—Geo. Bartram, James Queen, Thomas Biddle, Peter Lohra, James Kitchen, John L. Baker.

Dock.—Levi Garret, Joseph S. Lewis, John McMullin, Levi Hollingsworth, Paul Cox, Joseph McCalla.

New Market.—John W. Thompson, Daniel Smith, Anthony Stoddart, John Coulter, Anthony Cuthbert, John Y. Bryant.

Middle.—James Vanuxem, Reuben Etting, Simon Gratz, William Guier, Jacob Strembeck, Robert Elpray.

South.—John S. Leib, Isaac Forsyth, John Welsh, William Newbold, Wm. J. Duane, Benj. Tilghman.

Cedar.—George Summers, Alphonso C. Ireland, John Douglass, Reading Howell, George Beck, David C. Claypole.

Locust.—Geo. Sheaff, B. Newcomb, Andrew Pettit, William Willig, Walter Kerr, Wm. Grimmel.

SOUTHWARK.

Richard Renshaw, Esq., Charles Penrose, George Weaver, Benjamin Morton, Jesse Williamson, James Engle, Garret Beckhorn, John Curtis, Phineus Eldridge, John Thum, John R. McMullin, Henry Engles, James Ellis, Joseph P. McCorkle, George Rees, Cornelius Stevenson, George Spangler, James Fulton, Thomas Lake, George Rehn, Alex. Steel, Esq., James Linnard.

MOYAMENSING.

John Hunter, Esq., Michael Freytag, Thomas Dixey, Daniel Guirey, Michael Cooper.

PASSYUNK.

John Lentz, Andrew Hannus, Israel Israel, Esq.

Resolved, That the memorial above mentioned be published in the several papers of this city.

Resolved, That the Committee of Correspondence be instructed to inform the Secretary of the Treasury that this Committee will accept the certificate of stock on the terms contained in his letter of the 17th instant, and that the Committee of Correspondence be also instructed to request the Secretary of War to take the necessary measures to procure the certificate.

Resolved, That a warrant be drawn in favor of the Chairman of the Committee for the Defence of the Delaware for one thousand dollars.

Resolved, That the Secretary be requested to cause to be published in three of the papers, calling upon all persons who have claims against the Committee of Defence to present them forthwith for settlement, to James Josiah, No. 23 Dock Street, Chairman of Committee for Defence of the Delaware; Michael Leib, Chairman of Committee of Supplies; Jonathan Williams, Chairman of Sub-Committee of Defence, or James Whitehead, Chairman of Committee of Accounts.

SIXTY-FIFTH MEETING.

PHILADELPHIA, *January* 3*d*, 1815,
3½ o'clock P.M.

The Committee met.

Present:—Messrs. Biddle, Goodman, Huff, Connelly, Eyre, Josiah, Reed, Williams, Groves, Leiper, Brown, McMullin, Ronaldson, Leib, Sergeant, Whitehead, Hawkins.

The minutes of the last meeting were read.

The Committee of Defence reported, in writing, as follows:

The Committee for the Defence of the Delaware, report:

That they have laid up secure from the ice, at the piers at Gloucester Point, seven of the hulks. Four at Fort Mifflin, under the care of Major Beale, for the accommodation of some of the garrison. Three they have delivered up to Captain Clark, engineer at the Pea Patch, who has had them hauled up there in safety, for the accommodation of the men employed. The packet that went down with the hulks was caught in the ice on her return, and the captain obliged to make a harbor at the Lazaretto, where she has been dismantled, and laid up for the winter. Captain Clark wrote the committee that he was in want of another vessel for a packet, the three he had being only sufficient to accommodate his men, and requested that the committee would furnish him one immediately, as he was left only with an open boat. As the General Committee would not meet for three days after they received the letter, and it being necessary that no time should be lost in sending one down, owing to the uncertainty of the navigation being stopped by the ice, they have taken on themselves to have another vessel fitted and sent down to Captain Clark, trusting that the General Committee, when they meet, would sanction it. They therefore offer the following resolution:

Resolved, That the Committee on the Delaware be requested to let Captain Clark have another of the hulks for his accommodation at the Pea Patch, he paying the expense of fitting her, and that they let him have as much stone-ballast as will be sufficient to sink the wharf to be erected there, he replacing it when the navigation opens.

Adopted, and report approved.

Resolved, That an order be drawn in favor of the Chairman of the Committee for the Defence of the Delaware for fourteen hundred dollars.

The following letter was read:

PORT OF PHILADELPHIA, *December* 31*st*, 1814.
SIR:

Being called on by Captain McFaden, on Sunday, the 18th September last, to render what assistance I could to my son Francis, then at Fort Mifflin, superintending the affairs of the fort with the carpenters taken off the frigate Guerriere, to get more people and send down to him immediately, and to go myself and assist him; I inquired if it was at the request of the Committee, and was informed it was, and that he had called on me for that express purpose. To which I immediately attended; set about getting the people, and sent down a gang that afternoon, and continued to assist until the 26th of the present month, on which day I received verbal orders from Mr. Miercken to break the people off and do no more. My son Francis having left Philadelphia on urgent business for the southward on the 20th, for which attendance, from your notice in the paper, I have taken the liberty to make the inclosed demand of one hundred and thirty-five dollars.

With respect and esteem,
Your obedient servant,
(Signed) JOSEPH GRICE.

To CAPTAIN JAMES JOSIAH,
Chairman of Com. of Def. for Bay and River Delaware.

Referred to the Committee for the Defence of the Delaware.

Resolved. That the committees appointed in the several wards and districts be earnestly requested to use all possible diligence in procuring the signatures of the citizens within their precincts to the petitions to the General Assembly, and as soon as completed to deliver the petitions to the Chairman of this Committee, in order that they may be forwarded to the Legislature.

Resolved, That the Committee of Correspondence be instructed to write to the representatives in Congress from the City and County of Philadelphia, requesting them to use their endeavors to have the money which has been deposited in bank to the credit of the Treasury of the United States, for erecting fortifications at the Pea Patch, immediately applied to that object.

Resolved, That a committee be appointed to wait on the commanding general to know what preparations are making for sinking the obstruction in the Delaware near the Pea Patch, and that said committee consist of Messrs. Williams, Connelly, and Josiah.

On motion of General Williams,

Resolved, That a committee be appointed to form a digest of all the proceedings of this Committee, from its first appointment to the end of January, eighteen hundred and fifteen, stating the money it has received, its several appropriations and expenditures under each appropriation, and, generally, every matter that may in their opinion be proper to be submitted to our constituents.

Resolved, That Messrs. Williams, Connelly, Leib, Reed, Josiah, and Sergeant be said committee.

SIXTY-SIXTH MEETING.

PHILADELPHIA, *January 6th*, 1815.

The Committee met.

Present:—Messrs. Biddle, Latimer, Williams, Leib, Cadwalader, Leiper, Josiah, Ferguson, Reed, Hawkins, Connelly, Ronaldson, Whitehead, McFaden, Naglee.

The minutes of the last meeting were read.

The Chairman of the Committee of Supplies reported an account of sales at auction of damaged bread, viz.: one hundred and thirty-five barrels (part of a quantity purchased by the committee from N. Dilhom), for one hundred and sixty-one dollars and ninety-six cents, which sum was received and paid to the Treasurer of this Committee.

The Committee of Correspondence reported a letter from the Secretary of the Treasury, of which the following is a copy:

TREASURY DEPARTMENT, *January 2d*, 1815.
GENTLEMEN:

I have received your letter of the 27th ultimo, and have requested the Controller of the Treasury to direct the Commissioner of Loans, at Philadelphia, to issue a certificate or certificates of six per cent. stock of 1812, in the names stated in your letter, for the sum of fifty thousand dollars placed to the credit of the Treasurer of the United States in the Bank of Pennsylvania, by your direction, on the 26th day of November last.

I have the honor to be, gentlemen,
Your most obedient servant,
(Signed) A. J. DALLAS.

MESSRS. LATIMER, SERGEANT, AND REED,
Committee, &c., Philadelphia.

PHILADELPHIA, January 3d, 1815.
GENTLEMEN:

We inclose to you a resolution of the Committee of Defence, on a subject of very great importance to the City and County of Philadelphia. The Committee have agreed with the Secretary of War to advance the money that may be necessary for establishing defences at the Pea Patch, not exceeding the sum of one hundred thousand dollars. On the 26th of November last, they deposited fifty thousand dollars, part of that sum, in the Bank of Pennsylvania, to the credit of the Treasury of the United States, and immediately advised the Secretary of War of the deposit. The season for doing the work is passing away, and the work, we are very sorry to perceive, progresses very slowly, so that we are apprehensive that it will not be finished before the commencement of the next compaign. The delay is said to be owing to the want of money, by which we understand to be meant that the War Department has not placed the money deposited in bank at the disposal of those who have the superintendence of the work. The inclosed copies of letters from General Cadwalader, to which no answers have been received, are communicated for your information.

The object of the inclosed resolution is to request you to call upon the Secretary of War, and, if necessary, upon the Secretary of the Treasury, and endeavor to have the necessary arrangement made for immediately applying the money, which we are informed remains in bank, to the object for which it was inteded.

We beg you will write to us as soon as may be convenient.

(Signed) GEORGE LATIMER,
JOHN SERGEANT,
JOSEPH REED,
Committee of Correspondence.

P. S.—Permit us also to request your aid in procuring a certificate for the amount of the loan, as far as the money has been paid, on the terms proposed by the Secretary of the Treasury in his correspondence with us, to which we have acceded.

THE HONORABLE MESSRS. A. SEYBERT, C. J. INGERSOLL, AND CONRAD, AND WILLIAM ANDERSON,
The Representatives in Congress from the City and County of Philadelphia.

HEADQUARTERS,
PHILADELPHIA, *December* 23*d*, 1814.

SIR:

On the 20th of November, the Committee of Defence of this city deposited in the Bank of Pennsylvania, to the credit of the Treasurer of the United States. $50,000, on account of a loan of $100,000, for the purpose of fortifying the Pea Patch on the River Delaware. Your letter to the Sub-Committee of Correspondence, under date of 2d instant, acknowledges the receipt of the certificate of that deposit, and states that "whenever these works are commenced, and money is wanted for their prosecution, the warrants of your department will be issued for such sums, and in favor of such persons as the commanding general shall designate." In anticipation of the receipt of such warrant, the Committee advanced to General Gaines $10,000 to meet the immediate demands for labor and materials, the general engaging to refund that sum to the Committee as soon as he should be supplied with the means of so doing from the War Department, and at his departure he placed in my hands the unexpended balance of the $10,000, amounting to $3837.48, to be applied to the payment of the workmen, &c. Of that balance I have expended nearly the whole, having but a few hundred dollars remaining. The Committee having this day requested me to repay the advance made to General Gaines, and the expenses of the works now in operation requiring a further supply of funds, immediately, it becomes necessary for me to request a warrant, placing at my disposal a part of the above-mentioned sum of $50,000, sufficient, after paying the Committee, to meet the further demands that will be made. The workmen's wages alone amount to about $1000 per week; of the probable expenses for materials I can form no accurate calculation.

I have, &c.,
(Signed) THOS. CADWALADER,
Brig.-Gen. Commanding.
HON. JAMES MONROE,
Secretary of War.

(EXTRACT.)

FOURTH MILITARY DISTRICT.

HEADQUARTERS,
PHILADELPHIA, *January* 1st, 1815.

I request your attendance to my letter of 23d December, respecting funds to carry on the works at the Pea Patch. The workmen's wages for the last week remain unpaid, and there is reason to apprehend a stoppage of their labors, unless a supply of money is speedily furnished. There are, moreover, several bills for lumber unsatisfied.

I have, &c.,
(Signed) THOS. CADWALADER.
HON. JAMES MONROE,
Secretary of War.

PEA PATCH, *January* 5th, 1815.
SIR:
I yesterday received your letter of the 2d instant, by Mr. Skellinger, who, with a shallop load of stone, ar-

rived very opportunely yesterday morning. The wharf is ready to sink. The stone would have been thrown into it last night, but the tide was too low; it will however be done this morning.

I begin to be uneasy about funds. I brought only a thousand dollars with me, out of which I have spent six hundred, paying my people and purchasing contingent articles. It is absolutely necessary that I should be punctual in all my engagements. It will be impossible for me to proceed to Philadelphia. I could on no account be absent a night from this place. I therefore earnestly request some arrangement may be made to send me funds. General Cadwalader was the person in whose hands funds to a small amount were deposited when I left Philadelphia. He has been very punctual and prompt in meeting all demands while this sum held out. I now scarcely know in whose hands moneys for this place are left. I would thank you to make mention of the above circumstances to the gentlemen who may be empowered to obviate the pecuniary difficulties I am likely to encounter. But for God's sake let me have some money by the ensuing week; if it be only a thousand dollars, it will keep the credit of the place good until better arrangements can be made. Mr. Senton, who proceeds to town. would be a proper person to take charge of money for me. The wharf is sunk, and perfectly secure; we now need fear no weather. Mr. Teal's shallop load of stone was thrown into the wharf, as was also that Mr. Skellinger brought with him.

Inclosed is a receipt for the sloop Adventure; the other receipts were forwarded to you a few days ago.

I am, &c.,

(Signed) THOS. CLARK,
Captain Commanding Engineers.

CAPTAIN JOSIAH.

Thereupon, upon motion of General Cadwalader,

Resolved, That whereas, it being stated to the Committee that the commanding officer at this port has no funds in his hands for payment of the expenses of fortifying the Pea Patch, and it being uncertain when warrants may be received from the War Department, placing at the disposal of the commanding officer such moneys as may be necessary to carry on the work, to prevent an interruption of the work, therefore be it

Resolved, That the Chairman be directed to give his warrant on the Treasurer for five thousand dollars, in favor of Colonel Irvine, the officer at present commanding at this port, to be applied specially to that work, Colonel Irvine engaging to repay the amount out of the fifty thousand dollars lodged in bank to meet the expenses of that work, as soon as those funds, or a sufficient part thereof, shall be at his disposal.

Resolved, That an order be drawn in favor of the Chairman of the Sub-Committee of Defence for two hundred dollars.

The Committee of Accounts report that they have

examined the accounts, with the vouchers, handed to them by the Committee of Supplies, for expenditures made by them; the following is the result, viz.:

For account of United States, making cartridges, &c., per order General Bloomfield	$1693 70
For account of United States, for repairs to gun-carriages, blocks, for casting ball, port-fires, &c.	1052 88
	$2746 58
Captain Samuel Swift, advanced to make uniform for his company, to be deducted out of their pay	250 00
Captain G. W. Westfall, advanced to make uniform for his company, to be deducted out of their pay	750 75
Expense account and for general purposes	760 72½
Donation account, for making blankets, coats, purchase of shoes, &c., for men in service	458 33
General account of purchases, cooperage of bread barrels	25 49
	$4991 87½

Resolved, That the above sum of four thousand nine hundred and ninety-one dollars and eighty-seven cents be placed to the credit of the Committee of Supplies on the books of the General Committee, and the vouchers thereof be placed in charge of the Secretary to the General Committee.

The Committee for the Defence of the Delaware, to whom was referred the bill of Mr. Joseph Grice, for services at Fort Mifflin and in Philadelphia, taking all the circumstances into consideration, are of opinion that Mr. Grice has no claim on the General Committee whatever.

(Signed) JAMES JOSIAH,
HENRY HAWKINS,
WM. McFADEN,
PETER MIERCKEN,
JNO. NAGLEE.

January 4*th*, 1815.

Resolved, That the Committee of Supplies be instructed to dispose of the provisions belonging to the Committee to Colonel Irvine, taking such securities of the United States as to them may appear best.

A communication was received from a committee of the City Councils, relative to the expenditures of the Committee. Referred to the committee appointed to confer on a former application from the Corporation, dated 10th November last.

The committee to whom was referred the letter of Mr. Fulton, of the 1st inst., proposing a mode of annoying the enemy, by a newly invented torpedo-boat, report:

That it being unwise to go to a great expense before a satisfactory experiment be made, the committee recommend that one boat be first constructed, and that the power of movement with a submarine wheel be fully ascertained before any further expense be incurred. That in case the plan be adopted, the committee think it would be expedient to send a carpenter to New York to be instructed in such manner as to make the experiment in the most perfect way.

That Mr. Fulton's proposition of having one-quarter of the bounty allowed by the Government of the United States, for the destruction of ships of war belonging to the enemy secured to him is reasonable; but the committee cannot recommend any contract in the nature of a privateer, as suggested by Mr. Fulton. If a company of citizens were formed for this purpose, the committee think they ought to be encouraged as far as is consistent with propriety.

The committee is of opinion, that if the experiment should succeed to satisfaction, and this mode of defence be adopted, no time ought to be lost to carry it into effect, so that the torpedo-boat may be ready to attack the first ship of the enemy that may appear in the spring.

Resolved, That the Committee of Correspondence be instructed to write to the Secretary of the Navy, and to know of him whether Mr. Fulton's torpedo-boats have been approved by him, and whether they will be accepted as a temporary substitute for the steam-frigate proposed to be built, and which cannot be prepared in time to meet the enemy, and if the plan of the torpedo-boat be accepted, whether a loan for the purpose of constructing them will be accepted in part of the loan for the steam-frigate.

COMMITTEE OF DEFENCE. 343

SIXTY-SEVENTH MEETING.

PHILADELPHIA, *January* 13*th*, 1815,
3 o'clock P.M.

The Committee met.

Present:—Messrs. Goodman, Latimer, Leib, Williams, Reed, Ferguson, Whitehead, Leiper, Connelly, Ronaldson, Miercken, Josiah, Eyre, Hawkins, Ross, Biddle.

Mr. Goodman was called to the Chair in absence of Mr. Biddle on a jury.

The minutes of the last meeting were read.

The Committee of Correspondence reported the following letter:

PHILADELPHIA, *January* 7*th*, 1815.
SIR:

The inclosed resolution of the Committee of Defence of this city will sufficiently explain their views on the subject of it. We are instructed to inquire whether Mr. Fulton's late invention of torpedo-boats, with the means of submarine attack, has received the approbation of the Navy Department, and whether it is the intention of the Government to make an experiment of their efficacy. From the representations which have been made by Mr. Fulton to the Committee, they are disposed to think favorably of the plan, and, under the sanction of the Navy Department, would be willing to make the necessary advances to construct one or more for the defence of the Delaware, it being understood that the Government will accept a loan for that purpose on the terms proposed by the late Secretary of the Navy for the construction of the steam-frigate, for which these boats, in the opinion of Mr. Fulton, would be an efficient substitute. Your early answer to these inquiries will confer a favor on the Committee, and enable them to proceed immediately with the building of the boats, to be in readiness for the opening of the campaign in the spring.

NAVY DEPARTMENT, *January* 10*th*, 1815.
GENTLEMEN:

I have the honor to acknowledge the receipt of your letter of the 7th instant, covering the copy of a resolution of the Committee of Correspondence.

Mr. Fulton has lately been at this place, and obtained the sanction of the President of the United States to a new contrivance called a "bullet-proof boat;" but as Mr. Fulton did not condescend to make application to this department, nor to exhibit either a model, plan, or estimate, I am under the unpleasant necessity of informing the committee that the Navy Department has no knowledge or information upon the subject whereon to found its sanction or opinion.

In the temporary exercise of the duties devolving upon me, it is my highest ambition to discharge them promptly and faithfully. I therefore have the more to

regret the course pursued by Mr. Fulton, which puts it out of my power to comply fully with your request.
I have the honor to be,
With great consideration,
Most respectfully,
Your obedient servant,
(Signed)   BENJAMIN HOMANS,
Acting Secretary of the Navy.

GEO. LATIMER, JOSEPH REED, ESQUIRES,
Committee of Correspondence, Philadelphia.

WASHINGTON, *January 9th*, 1815.
GENTLEMEN:

We have the honor to acknowledge the receipt of your letter of the 4th inst., the contents of which we made known this morning to the Secretaries of War and the Treasury; the former of whom will immediately give the necessary orders for placing the fund in question under the direction of General Scott, for its application to the purposes to which it is appropriated.

We remain, your most obedient, &c.,
(Signed)   ADAM SEYBERT,
W. ANDERSON,
C. J. INGERSOLL.

GEO. LATIMER, JOHN SERGEANT, JOS. REED, ESQS.

PHILADELPHIA, *January 13th*, 1815.
GENTLEMEN:

The fund placed in my hands by your body, on the credit of the United States, to be appropriated in erecting fortifications on the Pea Patch, is nearly expended; the payment of the workmen for the present week will exhaust it entirely. I am therefore compelled to solicit from you the appropriation or loan of three or four thousand dollars, to meet the necessary expenses of the ensuing week.

Very respectfully, I am,

Gentlemen, your most obedient servant,

(Signed) W. N. IRVINE,

Colonel 42d M. f. y.

THE COMMITTEE OF DEFENCE.

Resolved, That the Chairman of this Committee be directed to give his warrant on the Treasurer, for four thousand dollars, in favor of Colonel Irvine, the officer at present commanding at this post, to be applied especially to the defence of the Pea Patch, Colonel Irvine engaging to repay the amount out of the fifty thousand dollars lodged in the bank to meet the expenses of that work, as soon as those funds, or a sufficient part thereof, shall be at his disposal.

The committee appointed on the 6th instant to confer with a committee from the Councils of this city, on the subject of the expenditures of money by the Committee of Defence, report:

That they inclosed in a letter to the committee from the Councils a statement of account, of which a copy is annexed, and which they conceive contains all the information required in their communication of the 3d instant.

COMMITTEE OF DEFENCE.

The City Councils appropriated $300,000, of which
the Committee received $175,000
The Corporation of Northern Liberties, $41,000,
of which the Committee received.................. 10,000
The Corporation of Southwark, $20,000, of which
the Committee received............................ 10,000

$195,000

An account of expenditures by the Committee,
and cash in the Treasury, viz.:

For fortifications near Schuylkill......	$3,886	46
For provisions	21,700	00
For general purposes of defence.......	2,973	11
For hulks.................................	21,651	99
For Fort Mifflin, Fort Gaines, and gun-boats...............................	33,532	69
For making cartridges, casting balls, repairs to gun-carriages, &c..........	3,397	50
To General Cadwalader, to enable him to pay the militia under General Spering, whose necessities required it to prosecute their march to their homes, on condition that the same be deducted from their pay, and returned to the Committee by the paymaster...............................	4,000	00
To advance to Captain Swift, in aid of procuring uniform for his company of militia, to be deducted out of their pay, and returned to the Committee by the paymaster.........	250	00
To advance to Captain Westfall, in aid of procuring uniform for his company of militia, to be deducted out of their pay, and returned to the Committee by the paymaster........	750	00
To advance to Captain Sparks, in aid of procuring uniform for his company of militia, to be deducted out of their pay, and returned to the Committee by the paymaster........	360	00

To advance to Captain Fesmeyer, in aid of procuring uniform for his company of militia, to be deducted out of their pay, and returned to the Committee by the paymaster....	$94 50	
To advance to General Gaines, to be repaid out of the loan from the Committee for the purpose of fortifying the Pea Patch..........................	10,602 50	
To advance to Colonel Irvine, to be repaid out of the loan from the Committee for the purpose of fortifying the Pea Patch...........................	5,000 00	
To cash loaned to United States, in part of $100,000, for the purpose of fortifying the Pea Patch, and for which sum the Committee have received 6 per cent. stock...............	50,000 00	
To cash in treasury......................	36,801 25	
		$195,000

For these expenditures the Committee have property and claims, as follows, viz.:

Provisons on hand (to be sold)...	$11,700 00	
Hulks, valued at.....................	21,651 99	
United States, for repairs to Fort Mifflin, Fort Gaines, gun-boats, making cartridges, repairs to gun-carriages, by order of General Bloomfield....................	36,930 19	
		$70,282 18
Loan to United States, for which the Committee have received 6 per cent. stock.....................	50,000 00	
General Cadwalader, advanced for the troops of General Spering's brigade, to be repaid by the paymaster.....................	4,000 00	
Captain Swift's company, to be repaid by the paymaster.........	250 00	
Captain Westfall's company, to be repaid by the paymaster	750 00	

COMMITTEE OF DEFENCE. 349

Captain Sparks' company, to be repaid by the paymaster	$360 00	
Captain Fesmeyer's company, to be repaid by the paymaster	94 50	
General Gaines, to be repaid out of the money appropriated to fortifying Pea Patch	10,602 50	
Colonel Irvine, to be repaid out of the money appropriated to fortifying Pea Patch	5,000 00	
Intrenching tools, &c., valued	1,000 00	
Cash in treasury	36,801 25	
		$179,140 43
Balance, which has been appropriated for general purposes of defence, and for which the Committee do not expect to be reimbursed	$15,859 57	

The following letter was read, and, by special order, directed to be placed on the minutes:

PHILADELPHIA, *December* 19*th*, 1814.

THE COMMITTEE OF DEFENCE FOR THE CITY AND COUNTY OF PHILADELPHIA.

GENTLEMEN:

I am induced to make application to the gentlemen composing the Committee of Defence, in behalf of the troops under my command, in consequence of their present destitute situation, believing it to be the wish of the Committee to give them such relief as may be requisite and in their power to afford.

The men belonging to the brigade left their homes from motives which require no comment, and have submitted to difficulties and privations without a murmur.

They appeared at their post in the hour of danger, and were welcomed as a part of the band destined to insure safety to the City of Philadelphia. The object has been obtained. The soldiers, now that their services are no longer necessary, are desirous of returning to their homes. They were the last in the field. They have been detained until the inclement season has not only commenced, but until they have suffered from its effects; and they were the only troops in the service that had a a long journey to perform before they could reach their homes.

Most of the men marched clothed in summer dress, calculating that they would be discharged before the commencement of winter. Many, who at home, were comfortable, many wealthy, have, from assisting their fellow-soldiers, expended all they brought with them, to which, as additional cause of want, may be stated frequent disappointment in receiving rations, when they were compelled to supply themselves in a poor and uninhabited neighborhood, where little was to be had, and that little at extravagant prices.

From what is already stated, the present wants of the brigade require little further exposition. Many are destitute of shoes and stockings—all without money— some have to cross the Blue and the Broad Mountains, a dreary tract of considerable extent, and at this season generally covered with snow. A proportion will have to march from 120 to 160 miles; without shoes, without stockings, without money, this march cannot be performed. Therefore, as there is no provision made by the Government of the United States, nor by the State of Pennsylvania, to my knowledge, for the payment of the troops, nor for their subsistence on their journey, the Committee of Defence of the City and County of Philadelphia are requested to advance such a proportion of the pay to the men (say five dollars each) as will enable them to return to their homes, to be repaid when funds are received by the regimental paymasters, Doctor John Erb for Lieutenant-Colonel Hutter's regiment, and Lieutenant Scott of Colonel Wirick's, for whose faithful performance of any contract entered into by them with the Committee of Defence, or with any gentlemen on the part of the Committee of Defence of the City and County of Philadelphia, I hold myself responsible.

The number of men at present belonging to the brigade, present, amounts to from ten to twelve hundred.

(Signed) W. SPERING,
Brig.-Gen. of the Militia of Lehigh, Pike, Northumberland, Union, and Columbia Counties.

Resolved, That Messrs. Leib, Goodman, and Connelly be a committee to prepare and report a circular addressed to both Houses of the Legislature of this State, relating to auctions in the city, and bounds prescribed by law. And stating reasons why the citizens of this part of the State may in justice calculate on an appropriation of the duties arising from the sales at auction for their defence.

The Committee of Accounts reported, that they have examined the accounts of the following committees, for disbursements made by them since the last report, for sundry purposes, and the following is the result, viz.:

By Committee for Defence of Delaware:
For Fort Mifflin, repairs, &c.........	$1576 62½	
For Fort Gaines, "	1769 83	
For gun-boats, "	8 96	
For hulks.................................	181 35	
For general purposes of defence....	4 00	
	———	$3540 76½

By the Committee of Supplies:
For United States, hauling cannon to Fort Hamilton, &c..............	$94 50	
For general purposes of defence....	36 10	
For Captain John Fesmeyer, advance for rifle-frocks, &c., for his men, to be deducted out of their pay...................................	90 00	
	———	220 60

By the Sub-Committee of Defence:
Fortification account, for sundries..	$379 50	
Expense account, for doorkeeper to the Committee....................	44 99	
General Jon'n Williams, on account of contract with Mr. Lukens, for making a carriage-rifle.............	500 00	
	———	924 49

Resolved, That the following sums be credited to the accounts of the several committees on the books of the General Committee, viz.:

To the Committee for Defence of the Delaware..	$3540 76½
To the Committee of Supplies......................	220 60
To the Sub-Committee of Defence................	924 49

On motion of Mr. Reed,

Resolved, That the accounts of Captain Ross' corps of vidcttes be referred to a committee, consisting of the Committee of Accounts and the committee appointed on the 4th November last, to confer on a letter from Mr. Bryant, of that date, in behalf of Captain Ross.

Resolved, That the Chairman be instructed to forward, with all convenient expedition, the memorials relative to the appropriation of the auction duties to the defence of this city, as they are signed, and separately received by him, to our representatives in the State Legislature, in order that they may present them to the Senate and Assembly, and to inform them that more will be forwarded as they are received.

SIXTY-EIGHTH MEETING.

PHILADELPHIA, *January* 20*th*, 1815,
3½ o'clock P.M.

The Committee met.

Present:—Messrs. Biddle, Goodman, Latimer, Whitehead, Ross, Huff, Leib, McFaden, Leiper, Groves, Ronaldson, Hawkins, Williams, Josiah, Miercken, Sergeant, Reed, Connelly, McMullin, Ferguson, Peltz.

The minutes of the last meeting were read.

A letter from Joseph Grice, requesting to be heard before this Committee, relative to a claim which he makes against them, was read.

A motion was made by Mr. Leib to grant his (Mr. Grice's) request, which was negatived. Whereupon

Resolved, That the Secretary of the Committee be instructed to inform Mr. Grice that the Committee of Defence will receive any written communication from him on the subject.

The following letter was read:

SPRING GARDEN, *January 9th*, 1815.

SIR:

I am directed by the Board of Commissioners of the District of Spring Garden, to inform you that they have examined the state of the funds of the Corporation, and that they are of the opinion that it will be impolitic in them at this time to grant any money for the use of the Committee of Defence.

I am, Sir,
Your most obedient servant,
JACOB FRICK,
Clerk.

CHAIRMAN OF COMMITTEE OF DEFENCE.

The following letter was read:

TO THE HONORABLE COMMITTEE OF DEFENCE, PHILADELPHIA.

GENTLEMEN:

By an Act of the Legislature of this State the Governor is authorized to contract for a quantity of repeating-arms, &c. at a specified price. And to draw his warrant for payment upon the Treasurer, "When the said arms are completed and delivered, or when sufficient security shall be given for the due performance of such contracts, &c." The amount is about seven thousand dollars. And it has been suggested, as an eligible mode of carrying the business into effect, that the honorable Committee of Defence shall, in public or individual capacity, furnish the requisite surety to sustain the said contract. The manner in which the arms are furnished to the General Government is to pay the workmen down, as fast as the several portions of the arms are completed and delivered. And this may be most conveniently done in the present case. I therefore propose that, for carrying into effect such contracts, one-tenth part of the sum shall be taken for the necessary preliminary expense of furnishing barrels, tubes, &c. And the remainder deposited with the gentlemen sureties, as a fund for the successive payments, as fast as the arms shall be completed and delivered in.

If unable to apprise the Governor of such proposition, we can have to forward duplicate contracts, with all necessary orders, for the immediate progress of the business, which is important to the object of the occasion, &c.

All of which is respectfully submitted, by,
Gentlemen,
Your most obedient humble servant,
(Signed) JOSEPH G. CHAMBERS.
January 20*th*, 1815.

Resolved, That Messrs. Reed, Hawkins, and Miercken be a committee to confer with Mr. Chambers on the subject of the above letter.

The committee appointed to confer with Joseph G. Chambers on the subject of his letter, this day received, reported:

That to enable him to make his contract with the Commonwealth, the interference of this Committee is requested to procure the necessary security. Considering the importance of the object, we recommend that such surety be authorized, and that a committee be appointed for that purpose. They offer the following resolution:

Resolved, That a committee be appointed to give such surety, on behalf of this Committee, to the Governor of the Commonwealth, for the performance of Mr. Chambers' contract, on condition that the money to be received from the State be paid into the hands of said committee, who are authorized to advance the same to Mr. Chambers as the arms are delivered into the State Arsenal, or in such sums as they may think proper, to accomplish the objects of the contract as speedily as possible.

Adopted.

Resolved, That Messrs. Reed, Whitehead, and Miercken be a committee to confer with Colonel Irvine, upon a plan for the subsistence of the men employed in the works at the Pea Patch, and to report what they may deem requisite to be done for that purpose.

Resolved, That the said committee be also requested to confer with the commander of the district on the state and progress of the work, and to offer him their services in the execution of it.

The committee appointed by a resolution of 13th inst., to confer on the accounts of Captain Ross, of the videttes, reported:

That on the 27th of August last, when considerable alarm prevailed in the city, and it was considered of great importance to obtain early and authentic information of the movements of the enemy, the Sub-Committee of Defence, in a conference with the then commanding general, requested him to order out a portion of the cavalry to aid as videttes. The general, as your Committee are informed, suggested a difficulty arising from a want of funds, he having no public moneys under his directions, upon which the Committee assured him, that if he would order out the men, the funds should not be wanting; upon which he agreed to comply with their request. The result of this conference was reported to the General Committee the same day, viz.:

"At the request of your Committee, the general has ordered on duty thirty men of the First Troop of Cavalry, under Captain Ross, who is to march to-morrow, to form a chain of videttes from this city to Port Penn, on the Delaware, and the mouth of the Elk River, in order that intelligence may be rapidly conveyed of the enemy's movements."

Which report was accepted by the Committee, and the next morning the following general order was issued, viz.:

"GENERAL ORDERS.

"Captain Ross, with thirty men of his troop of cavalry, are called into service, to act as videttes between this city, the Delaware, and the Chesapeake, &c."

And Captain Ross marched the next morning, and established the line, the Committee placing funds, to the amount of five hundred dollars, in the Bank of Wilmington, to his credit to meet the expenses.

The first establishment was between Port Penn and the city, and between the city and Turkey Point; the latter portion being considered a dangerous one, and the men liable to be cut off by the enemy, an application was made to the Committee and General Bloomfield, requesting a detachment of infantry to protect them, to which the following answer was returned by the Committee and by the general:

PHILADELPHIA, *September 4th*, 1814.

SIR:

The Committee of Defence have received your dispatch, dated Outpost Videttes, September 3d, 1814, 10 A M., and have instructed us to suggest to you in answer, that there is a corps of volunteer infantry, from the State of Delaware, now stationed at or near Elkton, who would, no doubt, upon the application of your commanding officer, Captain Ross, furnish such an outpost of infantry as may be necessary.

You will therefore be pleased, immediately, to communicate to Captain Ross the contents of your dispatch of the 3d instant, and of this answer, requesting him to make the answer suggested to the commanding officer of the Delaware volunteers, and in the name of the Committee of Defence, to ask their co-operation in this branch of the service, *to the extent that may be thought necessary by Captain Ross.*

We are, respectfully,
Your most obedient,
GEORGE LATIMER,
JOHN SERGEANT,
JOS. REED,
Committee of Correspondence.

Mr. John R. C. Smith,
Commandant, &c.

FOURTH MILITARY DISTRICT.

PHILADELPHIA, *September 5th*, 1814.

CAPTAIN ROSS:

SIR,—Mr. Smith, in his communication of 3d inst., intimates the advantage of infantry in front of the outposts of the videttes, but being without my district of command, a picket cannot be sent from Turkey Point. It may, however, probably be arranged by you with some of the militia of Maryland or Delaware.

(Signed) JOS. S. BLOOMFIELD,
Brig.-General Commanding.

By which it appears that so far from there being an objection to the increase of the force, the Committee were anxious to have infantry in addition for its protection.

On the 14th September, when the public anxiety as to the state of Baltimore was at its height, the following letter was addressed to Captain Ross by the Chairman of the Committee:

PHILADELPHIA, *September* 14*th*, 1814.

SIR:

We had no stage last night, and no mail to-day from Baltimore.

You will please therefore, immediately upon receipt of this, *to establish a line of videttes*, from the nearest point *on the present line* to some point as near as practicable to Baltimore, and send us intelligence, as speedily as possible, of whatever may occur.

If at the extremity of the line, or indeed at any part of it, you should think it best to employ persons not of the cavalry, or without uniform, you are authorized to do so, and the Committee will pay the expense.

Your most obedient servant,

(Signed) CHARLES BIDDLE.

CAPTAIN ROSS.

Employ any number of expresses you may think necessary.

In consequence of this letter a double line of videttes was established, the last extending to Baltimore.

Very soon after the arrival of General Gaines, conferences on the subject of the videttes were had with him, in consequence of applications by Captain Ross to the Committee for advances of money, and the Committee resolved that Captain Ross should be requested to consider himself under the orders of the commanding general.

On the 6th of October a committee was appointed to call on the commanding general, to confer on the subject of the videttes, and ascertain at whose expense this troop has been and is to be kept in service; and on the 10th the following report of the Committee was received, which relieves the Committee from any danger of continual loss. As the troops were ordered out at the request of the Committee of Defence, under an engagement to defray their expenses, your Committee are of opinion that it would be proper to make a further advance of money to Captain Ross, to enable him to discharge such engagements for the troops as the United States may eventually be responsible for, under an engagement from him to furnish the necessary vouchers to charge the United States, not only with the advance which shall be now made, but which has been already paid, which without such vouchers cannot be expected. They therefore offer the following resolution:

Resolved, That the sum of three thousand two hundred dollars be advanced to Captain Ross, on his engagement to the Treasurer to furnish the necessary documents to enable this Committee to demand repayment of all their advances on account of the United States, he being responsible for all sums beyond the same.

Resolved, That an order be drawn on the Treasurer, in favor of the Chairman of the Committee of the Delaware, for one hundred dollars.

Resolved, That an order be drawn in favor of the Assistant Secretary for one month's salary, forty dollars.

The Committee of Correspondence reported the following letters:

WILMINGTON, *January* 12*th*, 1815.

GENTLEMEN:

I am desired by the Borough Council to inform you that the sum of $5000, being part of the fifteen thousand dollars appropriated as a loan to the General Government, is now ready to be deposited to the credit of the Committee of Philadelphia; you will therefore be pleased to inform me in what manner and in whose name the deposit shall be made.

Upon the point of interest, I presume it is understood that the interest runs, upon each deposit, from the time it is made, that is, from the date of the receipt given by the cashier of the bank in which the money is placed.

I am, gentlemen,
Your obedient servant,
JAS. BROBSON,
First Burgess.

THE COMMITTEE OF SAFETY, PHILADELPHIA.

PHILADELPHIA, *January* 16*th*, 1815.

SIR:

We have the pleasure of acknowledging the receipt of your letter of the 12th inst., informing us "that the sum of five thousand dollars, being a part of the fifteen thousand dollars appropriated as a loan to the General Government, is now ready to be deposited to the credit of the Committee of Philadelphia," and requesting us to inform you in whose name the deposit shall be made.

You will please to place it in any of the banks at Wilmington, to the credit of George Latimer, Esquire, Treasurer of the Committee of Defence of Philadelphia, advising us of the same, and inclosing the cashier's receipt. The amount will have interest from the date of the cashier's receipt.

We are, Sir,
Your obedient servants,
(Signed)   GEO. LATIMER,
JOHN SERGEANT,
JOS. REED.

JAS. BROBSON, ESQ., *Wilmington, Delaware.*

SIXTY-NINTH MEETING.

PHILADELPHIA, *January* 24*th*, 1815,
3 o'clock P.M.

The Committee met.

Present:—Messrs. Biddle, Latimer, Whitehead, Leiper, McMullin, Huff, McFaden, Peltz, Ronaldson, Miercken, Connelly, Reed.

The minutes of the last meeting were read.

The Committee of Correspondence reported the following letter:

WILMINGTON, *January* 21st, 1815.
GENTLEMEN:

Inclosed you will find the cashier's receipt for five thousand dollars, deposited by the borough treasurer, to the credit of George Latimer, Esquire, Treasurer of the Committee of Defence of Philadelphia, being a part of the fifteen thousand dollars appropriated as a loan to the General Government. You will be pleased to acknowledge the receipt.

I am, gentlemen,
Your obedient servant,
JAS. BROBSON,
First Burgess.

P. S.—You will please to forward the certificate of stock as soon as convenient.

COMMITTEE OF CORRESPONDENCE.

Resolved, That the Committee of Correspondence be instructed to acknowledge the receipt of the sum of five thousand dollars, paid on the 21st inst. by the Corporation of Wilmington, to the credit of the Treasurer, at the Bank of Wilmington and Brandywine, and that they be desired to request that the balance of the sum appropriated by the Borough of Wilmington be paid as speedily as possible. And that the same committee be also instructed to request the Town of New Castle to make payment of the sum which is intended to be appropriated by the inhabitants of that town for the fortifications at the Pea Patch.

Resolved, That the sum of twenty-five thousand dollars be paid to the credit of the Treasurer of the United States, on account of the appropriation for the erection of the fortifications at the Pea Patch, and that the Committee of Correspondence be instructed to inform the Secretary of the Treasury of such payment, and request a certificate of stock for the same, according to the terms of the loan.

The Committee of Accounts report that they have examined the accounts of the Committee of Relief, and the Committee of Supplies, and the following is the result:

The Committee of Relief have for the relief of absent soldiers' families:
23d November, cash $903 00
30th November, cash........................ 719 00
7th December, cash........... .... 519 75
——— $2141 75
The Committee of Supplies:
Paid for casting ball to Thomas Sparks
on account of United States........... $88 96
Expense account, paid Jas. McGlathery
for wages, and one month due 14th
inst....................................... 40 00
——— $128 96

Resolved, That the above sum of $2141.75 be placed to the credit of the Committee of Relief, which balances their account with the Board. And that the sum of $128.96 be placed to the credit of the Committee of Supplies.

The Treasurer (Mr. Latimer) reported that he had

received from Mr. Reed, Treasurer of the Committee of Supplies, the sum of $532.94, which balances their account with the General Committee.

SEVENTIETH MEETING.

PHILADELPHIA, *January 27th*, 1815.

The Committee met.

Present:—Messrs. Biddle, Goodman, Whitehead, Huff, McMullin, Leib, McFaden, Leiper, Williams, Peltz, Eyre. Reed, Ross, Ferguson, Josiah, Connelly, Sergeant.

The minutes of the last meeting were read.

A letter from John Towers, expressing his objections to the fortifications on the Pea Patch, was read, and referred to the committee appointed to confer with the commanding general on the subject of the Pea Patch.

The following letter from Joseph Grice was read:

PHILADELPHIA, *January 27th*, 1815.

COMMITTEE OF DEFENCE, &C.

GENTLEMEN: Having only this minute been officially informed from you, that the Committee are ready to receive any written communication from me, I again take the liberty to ask for the payment of one hundred and thirty-five dollars, as stated in my former application to you, for my services, &c., rendered for assisting to superintending of the works for repairing Fort Mifflin, which I feel myself entitled to have. If the Committee are yet of the opinion I am not deserving any pay, I shall make request of them to refer the same to men where I shall have an opportunity of stating the demand of your fellow-citizen,

(Signed) JOSEPH GRICE.

Resolved, That the Secretary be instructed to inform Mr. Grice, that before they submit his account to arbitration, they must receive from Mr. Grice a written communication upon what ground his claim is founded, and the manner in which his services have been performed.

Resolved, That the future meetings of this Committee be held on Fridays, weekly.

SEVENTY-FIRST MEETING.

PHILADELPHIA, *February 3d*, 1815.

The Committee met.

Present:—Messrs. Biddle, Goodman, Latimer, Reed, Whitehead, Groves, Connelly, Eyre, Josiah, Williams, McMullin, Ferguson, Ronaldson, Leib, McFaden, Hawkins.

The minutes of the last meeting were read.

A letter from Joseph Grice, dated this day, stating his grounds for his claim on the Committee.

Resolved, That Mr. Grice's claim be referred to arbitration, and the Committee appoint Captain McAllister as an arbitrator on their part.

A letter from T. Clark, of the engineers, now employed in superintending fortifications at the Pea Patch, was read.

Resolved, That the Chairman of this Committee be instructed to write to the Secretary ——— in behalf of Mr. Clark.

The Committee of Correspondence reported the following letters:

WILMINGTON, *January* 30*th*, 1815.
GENTLEMEN:

I have received your letter of the 21st instant, and now inform you to have the certificate of stock issued in the name of Allen Thomson, Treasurer of the Borough of Wilmington. Your request that payment of the balance of the fifteen thousand dollars, appropriated by the Borough of Wilmington for the fortifications at the Pea Patch, be made as speedily as possible, shall be duly attended to.

  I am, gentlemen,
   Your obedient servant,
    (Signed) JAMES BROBSON,
            First Burgess.

To GEORGE LATIMER, JOHN SERGEANT, AND
  JOSEPH REED, ESQUIRES.

PHILADELPHIA, *January 25th*, 1815.
GENTLEMEN:

The committee of this city and its vicinities have instructed us to address you as a committee of the inhabitants of New Castle, on the subject of a loan to the United States for the special purpose of making defences on the Delaware at and near the Pea Patch.

In confidence that money competent to the object would be provided by loans, the Government have given directions to their officers to proceed with as much expedition as possible to erect the necessary defences at that important situation. General Gaines, while in command, zealously commenced the works, and Colonel Irvine, who succeeds him, is no less earnestly engaged to have them completed. Part of the works are going on here to begin the fortifications, contracts have been made in New Jersey for large quantities of timber for chevaux-de-frise, &c., and you no doubt know that Captain Clark, an officer of the corps of engineers, has a considerable number of men employed under his immediate directions at the Pea Patch. Everything is in a state of forwardness, and arrangements are making to engage the necessary workmen that the chevaux-de-frise and wharves may be sunk. The General Government has no money at command, but have given assurance to apply solely to the purpose intended whatever sums may be loaned for these defences, and there can be no doubt but the same will be so applied.

For the amount loaned certificates of funded debt, on

the terms of the loan of 1812, will be issued, bearing equal date with the deposit in bank.

In this way we have already received certificates for $50,000, deposited in November, and will no doubt receive the same evidence of debt for our subsequent advances.

The Borough of Wilmington have agreed to loan fifteen thousand dollars, of which $5000 has been deposited in the Bank of Wilmington and Brandywine to the credit of our Treasurer. This sum will be expended by or under the direction of the engineer to whom the Government have intrusted the superintendence of the works, and expended as far as practicable in the vicinity of that place; in like manner, whatever sums you may lend, will be deposited in your bank, drawn from thence and used in like manner. Our Committee will charge itself with procuring for you the certificates of stock, you advising us in whose name or names you wish them to be issued.

While the labors and expenditures of the Committee were confined to our own immediate vicinity it was not intended to call on you to aid us with money, but as the contemplated defences on the Delaware are as important and perhaps more so to the citizens of New Castle than to us, we now solicit your aid. As you will receive certificates of funded debt, with interest, payable quarterly, you only interpose your credit, even if you borrow of the bank, between the Government of the United States and bank.

Whatever sum you may loan you will be pleased to deposit in your bank to the credit of George Latimer, Esquire, Treasurer of the Committee of Defence of this city, and send us the receipt of the cashier. For the sum so deposited we will procure you a certificate or certificates of six per cent. stock in the names of such persons as you shall appoint.

  We are, gentlemen,
    Your obedient humble servants,
    (Signed) GEO. LATIMER,
          JNO. SERGEANT,
          JOS. REED,
      Committee of Correspondence.

N. B.—We have this day placed to the credit of the Treasurer of the United States twenty-five thousand dollars, in addition to the fifty thousand dollars paid in November last, in part of $100,000 agreed to be loaned by the city, &c.

JAMES RIDDLE, GEORGE REED, NICHOLAS VAN DYKE, ESQUIRES, *New Castle.*

    TREASURY DEPARTMENT, *January 30th*, 1815.
GENTLEMEN:

I have received your letter of the 26th instant, inclosing a bank receipt for twenty-five thousand dollars, paid on the 25th inst., on account of the fortifications of the Pea Patch. The Comptroller has been requested to give the necessary instructions to the Commissioner of

Loans for Pennsylvania to issue the stock in the manner you desire.

I am, very respectfully,

Gentlemen, your obedient servant,

(Signed)   A. J. DALLAS.

MESSRS. LATIMER, SERGEANT, AND REED,
Committee, &c., Philadelphia.

The Committee of Accounts reported as follows:

The Committee of Accounts report, that they have examined the accounts of the Committee for the Defence of the Delaware, and find they have expended on account of United States:

```
For repairs to Fort Mifflin.......................... $101 25
For hulks............................................    7 37
                                                     --------
                                                     $108 62
```

Resolved, That the above sum of $108.62 be placed to the credit of the Committee of the Delaware, and that the vouchers thereof be put in charge of the Secretary to the General Committee.

Resolved, That an order be drawn in favor of the Chairman of the Committee for the Delaware for one hundred and thirty dollars.

Resolved, That a warrant for forty dollars be drawn in favor of Samuel Field for one month's salary, due 23d of the present month.

COMMITTEE OF DEFENCE.   373

PHILADELPHIA, *February* 3d, 1815.

The committee to whom was referred a letter, dated January 10th, and signed John Towers, offer the following report:

Mr. Towers introduces his subject in these words: "I am informed you are about building fortifications on the Pea Patch. I, being a native of this city, and has its interest at heart, feel it my duty to give you my opinion, and to point out the inconveniences that will attend the fortifying there, and should you persist in it, probably you may see your error when too late, if the enemy should take advantage of it, therefore I will make a few observations for your consideration."

Your Committee will not suppose that Mr. Towers meant the apparent, and not very decorous insinuation, that he enjoys a pre-eminence over the members of the General Committee, by qualities which they do not possess, as if none of them were *natives*, nor had the *interest of the city at heart;* but it is evident that his self-complacency has induced him to assume the office of censor, and after giving an authoritative admonition, he becomes an instructor.

To show the importance and urgent necessity of his instructions, he takes it for granted that the Committee are about to build on the island called the Pea Patch, an open and extensive work, which would require "at least two thousand men to defend it in case of an attack;" so devoid of power as to suffer "ships to lay at anchor within musket-shot," so completely uncovered as to enable the enemy to pick off the men at their guns "by rifles from his tops," and, finally, so deficient in every means of resistance, or self-protection, as to expose the whole garrison to certain death or imprisonment. He also takes it for granted that the Committee have not "studied the public utility of fortifying at this place previously to undertaking the works, and (by implication at least) that they are unacquainted with its situation or soundings."

What opinion Mr. Towers has formed of the judgment or talents of the General Committee of Defence may be inferred from the language he has adopted, and your Committee will not deny, that if they had done what he appears to suppose they have done, they would have deserved the reprehension Mr. Towers has indirectly bestowed upon them, but the General Committee can never be justly blamed for what is out of their control, both as it respects advice or directions.

To pursue this monitory letter through all its parts would have the appearance of engaging in a controversy, which for many reasons would be improper, especially as your Committee are willing to admit that Mr. Towers has been influenced by zeal for the public welfare unrestrained by ordinary bounds, and that this excess of zeal has dictated expressions which, strictly considered, would appear indecorous in an address to this General Committee.

But since it is evident, from this letter, that erroneous impressions are abroad, respecting their past conduct and future intention on the subject of defence at and near the Pea Patch, the Committee have requested one of its members to furnish the plan which was some time since made by him, at the request of General Gaines, with such explanations and observations connected therewith as might be requisite. The report of their member is hereto annexed, and submitted as part thereof.

Respecting the letter from Mr. Towers, the Committee propose that it be disposed of in the same manner as other letters from respectable citizens, and that it lie on the table.

(Signed)   JAMES JOSIAH,
Chairman.

PHILADELPHIA, *February 2d*, 1815.

In compliance with the request of the Committee of Defence of the River Delaware, the subscriber herewith communicates a plan for fortifying the island called the Pea Patch, a few miles below New Castle, which was made at the request of, and communicated to General Gaines, when he commanded in this district; but as this work is not to be understood alone sufficient, being necessarily connected with others to be erected on the shores of the Delaware and Jersey, and all combined with obstructions to be sunk in the channel in advance of them, it is necessary to take a view of the subject with respect to locality, and a combined system of defence.

From the analogies of natural history respecting rivers, it may be concluded that this island has been formed by accumulations of alluvium from time to time, and, consequently, that it has not a solid bed of rock for its foundation; whence the conclusion is obvious, that whatever work of defence be constructed here, the mode of making the foundation should be first well considered. It is in this place proper to remark, that a foundation by piles and gratings, which would be necessary for even an ordinary work, might, without any great additional expense, be made ample for one of the most solid and formidable kind; the western piers of the permanent bridges over the River Schuylkill fully exemplifying this assertion, the bottom there being as soft as that of the Pea Patch.

On each side of this island is a channel sufficiently deep for a ship of any size, the whole way up to New Castle; it would of course be a very absurd undertaking to fortify the front of this position without also fortifying its opposite shores, and sinking obstructions in both channels, within the distance of cannon-shot.

Beginning at the entrance point, in advance, it is self-evident that the chevaux-de-frise proposed to be sunk in both channels, the piers between which our own vessels are to pass and repass, and the mode of obstructing the passage between these piers, at a very short warning, should all be carried into full effect before any fortifications are so far advanced as to invite an enemy to attack them. But this once done, and a few guns being mounted on temporary works, to prevent the enemy from removing any part of the obstructions by craft, so as to obtain a passage for his ships of war between them, we may proceed with our permanent works in such a manner as to render the River Delaware safe against the approach of an enemy however numerous or formidable. On the Delaware and Jersey shores positions may be chosen for batteries of earth, presenting, by their thickness, an impenetrable front, with wet ditches, and an inclosure in their rear. These batteries need not be bomb-proof, because the fire of the Pea Patch would effectually prevent their being annoyed in that way; nor need they be extensive, the object in placing them in these shores being solely to force any ship that might pass the obstructions to keep in mid channel, as the farthest distance from either fort; for, were there no forts here, a ship might keep itself close to the farther edge of the channel, at too great a distance for destructive fire from the Pea Patch, though they would certainly be annoyed even there.

Although these works be open, there can be no danger from the enemy's tops, for with such a fort on the Pea Patch, as will hereafter be described, no ship in the world would come to an anchor within range of its heated shot.

It is also unnecessary to delineate the forms or modes of constructing these forts, for the ordinary principles of fortification, generally understood, will be sufficient to indicate all that is requisite on this head.

The position of the work on the Pea Patch (the central points and the keystone of the system) is now to be described, and deserves particular consideration. A line drawn through the centre of the island, as nearly as possible in continuation of that formed by the course of the channel below it, should be taken as one that would divide the proposed fort into equal halves; taking the form of a pentagon, as most advantageous for the best distribution of the fire of the fort, this line would equally divide the courtine in front and the bastion in the rear. This position gives the whole fire of one front and half the fire of two bastions, on the right and left, against a ship entering either channel as soon it appears to be within cannon-shot; and this raking fire, of about twenty guns of the heaviest caliber, would be incessant as the ship advanced, till she comes on either side, when the guns of another front come into play, and bear upon her along the waist, from the bow to the quarter; passing this fire, the fourth or fifth front (according as the ship may be in the eastern or western channel) attacks her on the quarter, and the fire continues more and more raking until the ship has passed out of the reach of the shot up the river. At the most moderate calculation, a ship so passing would be exposed to the effect of an hundred shot, some of them at red heat, without being able to make any impression on the fort in return. Should another ship come on in succession the same attack would be repeated, and they would both have to expect the same salutation on their retreat.

It is now necessary to show that the enemy could not silence the fort by the fire from ships of the line, by shells from bomb-ketches at anchor, by escalade, with troops to be landed from their barges, nor injure it materially by their rockets, or any other missile incendiary. To do this with perspicuity it is necessary to describe the whole work from its foundation to its completion.

There are several ways of procuring a foundation on soft ground, but that by piles is uniformly used as the best, where the expense, or other circumstances relative to the procuring or driving them, do not prevent it. Open gratings, and even a floor of plank, is found to be sufficient where the superstructure is not too ponderous, nor the bottom too yielding. The matter of the Pea Patch being less yielding than mere mud in a semi-fluid state, and less resisting than compact earth, it is presumed that a combination might be made which would diminish the requisite number of piles to about a ninth part of the surface, and be sufficiently resisting to the pressure. Suppose that in a surface of nine square feet we were to drive piles of a foot in diameter and twenty or thirty feet long, in three rows, each row three feet distant from the other, and each pile three feet apart, filling the spaces with logs in a horizontal position; on these piles, stone, at least four feet long, should be laid athwart, in opposite directions, connecting the outside row of piles on each side with the centre row; cross stones being again placed on those, and all the interstices being accurately filled, it will be evident that the superstructure would bear principally on the piles, and but partially on the logs between, forming a sort of arched-work, which it is presumed would afford an ample resistance; but as the matter of the Pea Patch is nearly homogeneous, and of course would yield uniformly under a uniform pressure, it would be proper to complete the whole foundation in the first instance, and raise the superstructure gradually, in every part alike, till it came to the spring of the arches, by which time, it is presumed, the weight would have obtained its utmost point bearing, and the foundation become immovable.

In the foundation part of the plan hereto annexed it will appear that each courtine is a casemate of twenty feet wide, eight feet long, and of sufficient height to admit of two tiers of bunks. (The word casemate is a compound of two Italian words, casa-armata, and literally signifies an armed house; as the word will frequently occur, this explanation may not be improper.) The light and air are admitted through large doors, opening within, and loop-holes, which also serve for defence; in each tower bastion are six casemates; that one which contains the magazine, being necessarily larger, may contain more. All these casemates are under the parapets, covered with bomb-proof arches, and would afford protection, in case of a bombardment, for more men than the fort would require, beside furnishing ample room for provisions and munitions of war sufficient for a long siege. But it is not designed to keep men in bomb-proofs when wanted for action; in case of an attack by ships of war they will be found on the ramparts, and here they will fight with nothing exposed below the muzzle of the gun, behind impenetrable walls, while the men in the ships are everywhere vulnerable.

In one case the fire is from a point at rest, in the other from an unsteady and moving surface; in one case the enemy's shot, either below or above the diameter of the gun, are harmless, being stopped in the first instance, and spent in open air in the second; in the other case every shot tends to disable a ship somewhere; and one red-hot shot, well embedded in her hull, would be fatal. It has been by some naval character reduced to almost an axiom, that four guns from such a fort is a full balance from the fire of a whole broadside, and it is consequently settled that no prudent commander would ever drop his anchor within such a range. It will be remarked that the bastions are round, and not, according to a long-received system, angular; this at first sight appears an error, because it is a fundamental maxim in fortification that every point without must be defended from some point within, otherwise there would be points exposed to an escalade with impunity. This maxim, however, presupposes that the work is not casemated, and in such a case it would be an indispensable condition, but the fire from the casemates below render that part of the curve which takes place of the flanked angle of the bastion better defended, inasmuch as small arms at a few feet distance are more effective than at the distance of several hundred feet; an inspection of the plan will be sufficient to establish this fact.

Each tower has, beside this advantage, all the power from its platform that a bastion can have, and as a circle is that figure which inscribes the greatest area with the least extent of wall; so in this instance it must be cheaper. A circular wall is more difficult to batter than an angular one, because a shot cannot strike perpendicularly to its surface, unless it strikes in the line of its diameter, every direction from this line makes the blow more or less oblique, and causes it to fly off in the same angle at which it strikes.

While speaking of battering a fort, it is proper to correct a very common error. We read of sieges and of battering breaches in walls of fortifications, and are apt to apply this effect to an attack from a ship, without considering the circumstances of the two cases. In sieges, before the enemy thinks of making a breach by battering, he makes regular approaches, and finally establishes himself on the corner of the glacis, distant from the works only the width of the ditch and covered way, some thirty or forty yards. Here, by having two batteries attacking the salient angle of a bastion forming a sharp edge by cross-fires, steadily striking at or near the same point at every fire, he at length succeeds in making an excavation below. The wall from above crumbles into the cavity, and the whole becomes a heap of stones, over which he marches into the breach. A ship, on the contrary, cannot attack within as many hundred yards, its fire is uncertain, and can only be high because the glacis covers the lower wall; it attacks from but one point at the same time, for it has only the river to act in, and the fort presents a round wall against which he may spend his whole force without doing any injury to the work or those within it. There is not an angle or edge to be seen. The tower bastions should be carried up six feet higher than the other parts of the work, thereby protecting the guns on all the other platforms from being enfiladed, so that the enemy could do no injury by their shot, unless directly opposite, and that, as before observed, would be comparatively small. These towers might be made bomb-proof over the guns with very little additional expense. The bastion which contains the magazine is directly in the rear, and could not be even visible to the enemy unless he had passed the others; it is presumed that nothing can be imagined more safe from the power of an enemy than the magazine, which is not only bomb-proof, but placed in the rear, at the greatest possible distance from either side, and wholly out of sight of an enemy in front. The gateway is covered by a traverse in a circular form, and a covered way is made along that courtine with a place d'armes in front. If the fuel of the garrison should be wood, here is ample room for the deposit of a large supply; if of coal, there would be sufficient space in the smaller casemates.

Although it is stated that the whole garrison might be kept under bomb-proofs in case of distant bombardment from boom-ketches, yet there will be ample room for comfortable barracks on each side of the parade, and there can be no difficulty of having a plentiful supply of water within the inclosure. The barracks are the only parts vulnerable to rockets, shells, or carcases, but although they might be destroyed, the defensive power of the fort would remain the same. It is presumed, however, that by the attention of a few men, with a supply of water appropriately placed, the fire might always be extinguished as soon as it caught.

In a work of this kind, when the appearance of an enemy, with a numerous and powerful fleet, may be sudden, there should not be kept one invalid, and of effective men five hundred would be a sufficient garrison for an attack by as many thousand. There are three modes of attack—bombardment, battery by ships of war, and escalade. The two former have been shown to be ineffectual against a work of this kind; respecting the latter, it is proposed to take a view of the ground. A landing on this island is so difficult that it has been necessary to make an artificial one for the purpose of erecting the work. Boats designed to land troops therefore must pass through the whole fire of the fort before they can put a foot on shore, and here, as everywhere else, in all directions, they are liable to the musketry of the whole garrison at the moment of landing. To fix their scaling-ladders they must go into a wet ditch, always exposed to an incessant fire, and their ladders would be knocked away as fast as they were fixed, if they could place them against the walls; but the besiegers would be up to the arm-pits in water and mud. Under all these circumstances, what men, however great their numbers, would attempt such an assault?

The conclusion then is, that such a work would be invulnerable by bombardment, impregnable by battery, and unassailable by escalade. Nothing could then remain but to starve the garrison into a surrender; but this is impossible, by its having an inexhaustible source of water within its inclosure, and a supply of provision for the whole season that ships could remain in its vicinity; it would be like a very large ship provided for an East India voyage—to this add the obstructions, and we might rest satisfied that the Delaware would never be attempted.

In our country (where the Genius of Peace has presided ever since it became an independent one) war was never thought of until we were roused out of our lethargy by the declaration of it; no defence of the Delaware has ever been contemplated, and even after we knew, and daily observed, that our river was not invulnerable to a very small force, and that an enterprising enemy might lay the city under contribution, we never attempted any work of defence, or threw any obtruction in his way, till after the capital of the Union was destroyed, and the City of Baltimore besieged, and even in the third year of the war we are but beginning what ought to have been completed before it was declared. "In peace prepare for war," is an old adage, universally admitted to be a wise one; wise sayings are generally considered too trite to deserve notice.

These observations inevitably force themselves upon the subscriber, because he has generally observed that whenever works of defence are spoken of, the time that is requisite to complete them, and the sums of money they will cost, are two first considerations; and whatever is not capable of sudden preparation, or that would require considerable expenditure, is thrown aside, and any scheme that presents itself in the moment of alarm is adopted with alacrity, although the slightest inspection by professional men would pronounce it to be defenceless.

If five months ago we had been in a hurry about the Pea Patch, and had begun by sinking the obstructions which common sense alone indicated, we might at this moment have had the foundations laid for a work on the plan hereto annexed, and by amassing materials during the winter, have had it completed in the course of the ensuing season, so as to form a perfect defence at the beginning of the year 1816. But, then, it may be said, we shall be in peace! To this delusion there is but one reply, unless we place our harbors and rivers in a state of security, *at all events* (actual or expected peace notwithstanding), our country will remain assailable, and invite rather than deter hostile powers from attacking or injuring us; thus by being subject to repeated alarms, and always relying on temporary means, we waste that money which would be sufficient for permanent defence, and leave the country as much unprotected as if nothing had been done. This might be illustrated by many examples; but lest the subscriber should appear invidious, he will drop the subject.

Nothing is further from the intention of the subscriber than to convey a sentiment of reproach to any men or class of men; he believes that a want of precaution, generally speaking, is a defect belonging to human nature, and in republican governments, where the general opinion is the criterion by which the prosperity of public measures are decided, such opinions must partake of the qualities inherent in society at large. A community rolling on in the paths of prosperity, dreaming about perpetual peace, because it feels itself indisposed to give a just cause of war, may be brought to listen to an expectation that the millennium is about to arrive; but the very names of war, and its attendants, fortifications, armies, and navies, are considered like a repetition of ancient fables, made to amuse or frighten, without possessing any reasonable claim to their belief.

The attention of the community, however, has lately been excited by events that will not be deemed fabulous. It may therefore be proper for the General Committee to recommend a permanent system of defence to the constitutional authorities of the State, or at least to take some measures to show to their constituents that, although they have been obliged to submit to circumstances in their nature imperious, because pressing under the apprehension of danger, they are nevertheless persuaded that a permanent defence of the River Delaware ought to be determined on, whatever may be the expense, and pursued with vigor until completed, whether the war should continue or not.

Respecting the expense of such a work, it is not believed that it would exceed one hundred and fifty thousand dollars. A similar work is now erecting on Staten Island, in New York, under the subscriber's direction, according to his plan; two of its sides are completed as far as the rampart, and a great mass of materials are collected, yet not one-third of this sum was expended when the subscriber last saw it; and the calculation made does not much exceed one hundred thousand dollars. A considerable allowance may be made on account of a foundation, which is all the preference the site on Staten Island has respecting expense over the Pea Patch.

SEVENTY-SECOND MEETING.

PHILADELPHIA, *February* 10*th*, 1815, 4 o'clock P.M.

The Committee met.

Present:—Messrs. Biddle, Goodman, Latimer, Leib, McFaden, Williams, Leiper, Cadwalader, Whitehead, Hawkins, Josiah, Miercken, Ronaldson, Steel, Groves, McMullin, Reed, Naglee.

The minutes of the last meeting were read.

A communication from Messrs. Smith and Wallace, requesting a committee to be appointed by the Committee of Defence to meet a committee from the Select and Common Councils.

Referred to the former committee.

Resolved, That the Committee of Correspondence be instructed to write immediately to the members in Congress representing this district, requesting the immediate presentation to Congress of the memorial of the Committee of Defence, soliciting a local force to be authorized for the defence of this district.

Resolved, That Messrs. Leiper, McMullin, and Whitehead be authorized and requested to transfer the sum of five thousand dollars in the six per cent. stock of the United States, held by them in trust for this Committee, to Allen Thompson, Treasurer of the Borough of Wilmington, the same being the amount loaned to the United States by the Corporation of Wilmington for the erection of fortifications on the River Delaware at and near the Pea Patch.

The committee to whom was referred the claim of Joseph Grice, with instructions to agree to an arbitration, reported that an arbitration had taken place, and an award given in favor of Mr. Grice for fifty dollars. Whereupon

Resolved, That a warrant be drawn in favor of Mr. Grice for fifty dollars.

Resolved, That the thanks of the Committee be presented to Messrs. Anthony Cuthbert, Samuel Humphreys, Charles Penrose, and Captain Bankson Taylor, for their patriotic services in aid of the Committee appointed on the Defence of the River Delaware, and that the Chairman be requested to communicate the resolution to the above-named gentlemen.

The committee appointed to prepare a digest of the whole proceedings of the General Committee of Defence. up to the 31st of January last, report:

That they have arranged the said proceedings in as concise a form as appears to them consistent with perspicuity, and have separately arranged the documents in an appendix, with reference to each in the main report, under the proper head. That this form is susceptible of continuation up to the time when it shall be deemed proper to conclude the digest, and that the Committee mean to continue it accordingly.

As the manner of disposing of this digest is, in the opinion of the Committee, of much importance, in which every member of the Committee must consider himself more or less concerned, your Committee beg leave to submit the following resolution:

Resolved, That individual notices be issued, and left at the place of abode of every member of the General Committee of Defence, informing him that on Friday, 17th instant, a digest of all the proceedings of this Committee will be taken into consideration, and that he be requested to attend punctually at 4 P.M.

Resolved, That General Cadwalader be added to the committee on the above digest.

The Treasurer reported, that pursuant to a resolution of this Committee, of the 26th November last, he called upon the Mayor of this city for a warrant for one hundred thousand dollars, to place in the treasury of this Committee, being part of a loan appropriated by the City Councils for defence of the city and districts adjoining, and obtained from him a warrant on the City

Treasurer for the same. That the Treasurer of the City issued a check on the Bank of Pennsylvania for the same, which the bank refused to pay, declining to make any further loans on that account. The object therefore of that resolution could not be executed, and the warrant and check were returned and cancelled.

An account was exhibited from D. Brown. Whereupon

Resolved, That as the Committee of Defence did not authorize the expenditure, they deem it inexpedient to pay the account.

SEVENTY-THIRD MEETING.

PHILADELPHIA, *February* 17*th*, 1815,
4 o'clock P.M.

The Committee met.

Present:—Messrs. Goodman, Latimer, McMullin, Eyre, Whitehead, Ronaldson, Thompson, McFaden, Brown, Reed, Miercken, Hawkins, Leiper, Josiah, Huff, Naglee, Peltz, Williams, Ross, Sergeant.

Mr. Biddle being absent, Mr. Goodman was called to the Chair.

The minutes of the last meeting were read.

The Committee of Correspondence reported the following letter:

WASHINGTON, *February* 15*th*, 1815.

GENTLEMEN:

Not having received instructions from you to present the Philadelphia memorial to Congress, after we did ourselves the honor to answer your first letters on this subject, we took it for granted that you acquiesced in the opinions we then entertained, that it would be better to endeavor to accomplish the object in view without making it a matter of notoriety. A peace having now taken place, we presume that you will not consider it necessary to press the matter further at this moment.

We remain,

Your most obedient and humble servants,

(Signed) C. J. INGERSOLL.

GEO. LATIMER, JOHN SERGEANT, JOS. REED, ESQS.

An account from William Powell, for three dollars and twenty-five cents, was presented.

Ordered, That Mr. Whitehead be requested to pay the same.

An account from William McGlathery, for services, amount twenty dollars, was presented, and referred to the Committee of Supplies.

Ordered, That the expense of sending the plough ——— be sent home to the Commissioners of Southwark, and the expense be paid by Mr. Whitehead.

The committee appointed to confer with a committee from the Councils of the City, relative to the money

COMMITTEE OF DEFENCE. 393

appropriated for the purpose of the defence of the City of Philadelphia, and paid to the Treasurer of the Board, reported:

That they had a conference with the said committee on the 13th instant, and exhibited to them the two annexed accounts, marked A and B. The one marked A being an account current with the Board and the Treasurer. That marked B shows the object of each expenditure, as well as the means which the Committee possess to reimburse the Councils for the money placed at their disposal, and with which they were perfectly satisfied, as containing all the information they required:

DR. *The Treasurer in account current with the Committee of Defence.*

1814.
Sept. 1. To cash received from City Councils.... $100,000
" 19. " Commissioners of District of Southwark...................... 7,000
Oct. 4. " Commissioners of N. Liberties.. 10,000
" 4. " City Councils...................... 25,000
" 17. " " " 25,000
" 20. " " " 25,000
Nov. 18. " Commissioners of District of Southwark...................... 3,000
1815.
Jan. 24. " Borough of Wilmington......... 5,000

$200,000

By cash paid for purchase of hulks............ 21,659 36
" " loan to fortify Pea Patch........ 75,000 00
" " United States for repairs to Fort Mifflin, Fort Hamilton, &c........................ 37,190 49½

By cash paid for expense account for general
   purposes of defence........... $10,595 75½
" " general account of purchases for
   provisions....................... 9,645 00½
" " fortifications near Schuylkill ... 3,669 86
By cash advanced General Cad-
walader.............................. $4,000 00
By cash advanced Captain John
Fesmeyer........................... 90 00
By cash advanced Captain Charles
Ross................................. 5,500 00
By cash advanced Captain Jacob
Sparks.............................. 360 00
By cash advanced Captain Charles
Swift................................ 250 00
By cash advanced Captain Charles
Westphall.......................... 750 75
            10,950 75
By cash paid Jonathan Williams, carriage rifle 500 00
" " N. Dilhorn 408 27
" " Robt. McKoy..................... 426 63
" " Sub-Committee of Defence....... 144 11
" " Committee for Defence of Dela-
   ware 169 32½
By cash in Treasury........................... 29,640 44

            $200,000 00

Amount of expenditures by the Committee... $170,359 56
On account of the above ex-
penditures, the Committee
have received in six per
cent. stock, for the amount
loaned to the United States
for the purpose of fortifying
the Pea Patch, in which is
included the $5000 re-
ceived from the Borough
of Wilmington for that
object...................... $75,000 00
They claim from the United

COMMITTEE OF DEFENCE.

States, the expenditures made in repairs to Fort Mifflin, &c. $37,190 49½
The hulks they value at cost, &c. 21,659 36
The provisions on hand valued at..................... 9,645 00½
           ——————— 143,494 86

The sum advanced General Cadwalader, to pay the troops of General Spering's brigade of militia, was on condition that it should be reimbursed the Committee out of the pay of the troops................ 4,000 00
The sums advanced to the following officers, for the purpose of clothing their men for services in the field, was on the same condition as above:
 Capt. John Fesmeyer... 90 00
  " Jacob Sparks..... 360 00
  " Chas. Swift....... 250 00
  " Chas. Westphall.. 750 75
        ——— 1,450 75

The sum advanced to Capt. Ross, on account services of videttes, is to be repaid so soon as the accounts shall be settled with the United States............... 5,500 00
        ——— 10,950 75

Balance due from N. Dilborn........................ 408 27
Balance due from R. McKoy........ .... 426 63
        ——— 834 90
          ——————— 155,280 51

            $15,079 05

The deficiency being expended for general purposes of defence, and for which the Committee do not expect to be reimbursed, though they intend to claim it from the United States.

SEVENTY-FOURTH MEETING.

PHILADELPHIA, *February* 20*th*, 1815,
4 o'clock P.M.

The Committee met.

Present:—Messrs. Biddle, Goodman, Latimer, Williams, Cadwalader, Leib, Reed, Josiah. Hawkins, McMullin, Huff, Leiper, Ross, Thompson, Whitehead, Eyre, Ferguson, Barker, Groves, Sergeant, Miercken, Peltz, McFaden.

The minutes of the last meeting were read.

Resolved, That the Committee for the Defence of the River Delaware be authorized and requested, as soon as they shall deem it expedient, to sell the vessels that were purchased for sinking in the channel near Fort Mifflin, in such manner as they shall think fit, and for that purpose to employ such person or persons, and allow such compensation as they may think fit.

Resolved, That the Committee of Supplies be authorized and requested to sell, as soon and in such manner as they may deem expedient, whatever property they have under their care belonging to the Committee, excepting the blankets received as donations, and for that purpose to employ such person or persons as they may think proper.

Resolved, That the Committee of Accounts be requested, as soon as they can make it convenient, to proceed to Washington, and there have all the accounts of this Committee against the Government of the United State liquidated, adjusted, and settled by the proper department, and obtain for the amount that shall be found due, such security or evidence of debt as to them shall seem most for the advantage of our constituents.

Resolved, That the Committee of Supplies be authorized to present the blankets remaining on hand to the American Patriotic Fund Society, to be by them distributed to the wives and children of the soldiers and sailors whose husbands and fathers have been in the service of the United States, and that a barrel of beef, and such articles of clothing as may be in the possession of the Committee, be given to the said Society for the aforesaid purpose.

SEVENTY-FIFTH MEETING.

PHILADELPHIA, *March 3d*, 1815,
4 o'clock P.M.

The Committee met.

Present:—Messrs. Biddle, Miercken, Hawkins, Leib, McFaden, Thompson, Eyre, Josiah, Reed, McMullin, Leiper, Naglee, Ronaldson, Williams.

The minutes of the last meeting were read.
The following letter was read:

PHILADELPHIA, *March* 1*st*, 1815.

To the Committee of Defence.

Gentlemen:—Presuming the happy change that has taken place in our foreign relations will render it unnecessary to hold Fort Hamilton longer in your possession, and although I sustain considerable injury, yet as the three works thrown up on my estate were for the safety of the city, it is not my desire to make a claim for damages, yet hope, as some little indemnity, I may with propriety ask you for all the lumber, materials. pump, &c., now in Fort Hamilton (guns and munitions of war excepted).

I am, very respectfully,
Gentlemen, your most obedient,
(Signed) JAMES HAMILTON.

N. B.—I wish it to be understood that if the above request is granted it is to extinguish Mr. Tomlinson's claim on the Committee.

Resolved, That an order be drawn in favor of the Chairman of the Committee of the Delaware for three hundred dollars, for rigging and fitting the hulks for sale.

The Committee of Accounts report, that they have examined the vouchers for expenditure of money by the

COMMITTEE OF DEFENCE. 399

Committee for the Defence of the Delaware, and it appears that they have disbursed:

For repairs to Fort Mifflin............................ $53 48
On account of hulks..................................... 58 50
                                                       ———
                                                       $111 98

Resolved, That the above amount of one hundred and eleven dollars and ninety-eight cents be placed to the credit of James Josiah, Chairman of the Committee for the Defence of the Delaware.

Resolved, That the Secretary be requested to call upon the officers to whom arms have been delivered under the authority of this Committee to return them to the store-house of the Committee.

Resolved, That the Committee of Correspondence be instructed to write to the Secretary of War, and to suggest to him the propriety of employing the moneys appropriated for erecting fortifications at and near the Pea Patch on permanent works for the defence of the River Delaware, and that the materials purchased for the fortifications be employed in the commencement of a permanent defence instead of a temporary one; and that the committee inform the Secretary of War that the balance (twenty-five thousand dollars) of the appropriation is ready to be placed at the disposal of the War Department to accomplish the object.

SEVENTY-SIXTH MEETING.

PHILADELPHIA, *March* 17*th*, 1815.
4 o'clock P.M.

The Committee met.

Present:—Messrs. Biddle, Goodman, Ronaldson, Eyre, Connelly, Hawkins, Whitehead, Raguet, Leib, Ferguson, McFaden, Leiper.

The minutes of the last meeting were read.

The Committee of Accounts reported, that they have examined the accounts of the Sub-Committee of Defence, and find that they have disbursed for the following purposes, viz.:

For fortifications west of the Schuylkill.............	$29 94
For expense account.................................	86 16
For United States...................................	66 70
	$182 80

Resolved, That the above sum of one hundred and eighty-two dollars and eighty cents be placed to the credit of the Sub-Committee of Defence.

The committee appointed to have the hulks fitted for sale, report:

That they have got up to the city nine of the hulks. The six remaining are at Fort Mifflin and the Pea Patch. Those at Fort Mifflin, in charge of Major Beal, for the accommodation of some of the garrison, are thrown up on the bank by the ice and tide, that it will take some time and expense in getting them off. Those in charge of Captain Clark, at the Pea Patch, are not returned, for want of accommodation on the island for the men employed. Captain Clark writes that he will send them up the next week.

The Committee has not been able to accomplish the fitting the hulks as soon as they contemplated, owing to the great demand for sailors and riggers to fit the vessels in port for sea.

Five of the hulks will be sold the next week at auction.

JAMES JOSIAH,
Chairman.

Resolved, That Messrs. Williams, Josiah, Eyre, McFaden, and Leiper be a committee to wait upon Mr. Dallas and General Scott, to consult with them about the fortification on the Pea Patch, and also to confer with General Scott respecting field-pieces at Fort Hamilton.

Resolved, That Messrs. Eyre, Goodman, and Whitehead be a committee to inquire what damages have been sustained by Mr. Raguet and others by the erection of fortifications on their land.

SEVENTY-SEVENTH MEETING.

PHILADELPHIA, *March* 31*st*, 1815,
4 o'clock P.M.

The Committee met.

Present:—Messrs. Biddle, Goodman, Latimer, Williams, Hawkins, Leib, Whitehead, Connelly, Leiper, Ronaldson, Josiah.

The minutes of the last meeting were read.

On motion,

Resolved, That the Treasurer of this Committee be instructed to place in the Bank of Pennsylvania, to the credit of the Treasurer of the United States, the sum of twenty-five thousand dollars, being the balance of the one hundred thousand dollars agreed to be advanced the Government by this Committee for the purpose of erecting fortifications at and near the Pea Patch.

Resolved, That Messrs. Whitehead and Latimer be a committee to make an apportionment of the funds of this Committee, preparatory to a division thereof among the corporations of this city.

Resolved, That a warrant be drawn in favor of the Assistant Secretary for forty dollars, being the amount of salary due him on the 23d inst.

Ordered, At the request of General Williams, that his name be withdrawn from the committee appointed by a resolution of 17th ultimo to wait on Mr. Dallas.

Resolved, That Messrs. Goodman and Ronaldson be a committee to settle the books at the Arsenal.

The committee appointed to wait on Mr. Dallas, by a resolution of the 17th ultimo, reported verbally:

That they had called on Mr. Dallas, agreeably to the resolution, and that he had told them that the money appropriated by the Committee for the defence of the Pea Patch would be applied to that purpose.

SEVENTY-EIGHTH MEETING.

PHILADELPHIA, *April* 14*th*, 1815,
4 o'clock P.M.

The Committee met.

Present:—Messrs. Biddle, Hawkins, Miercken, McFaden, Connelly, Whitehead, Reed, Josiah.

The minutes of the last meeting were read.

The following report from General Williams was read:

The subscriber, to whom was referred the proposition of Mr. Lukens for making a carriage-rifle, begs leave to report that, in conformity to the orders of the General Committee of Defence, he directed the work to be commenced, and in due time the cannon was forged and turned ready for boring. That it was afterward carried to the Water-works, near the River Schuylkill, in Market Street, and fixed on a lathe for the purpose of being bored by the power of that engine. That it was found, in attempting this operation, that the lathe was inadequate to the object, and it became necessary to use other machinery.

That besides the delay incident to this circumstance, the artist employed for this purpose, having met with some family afflictions, has been unable to attend to the business for a considerable length of time, and it has not been in the power of Mr. Lukens to find another artist to perform a work of so much delicacy (which requires perfect accuracy) and in whom he has so great a degree of confidence as he has in the one first engaged.

That this dependence on a single individual not only has occasioned a submission to delays, arising from the causes above mentioned, but has hitherto forced a submission to unreasonable neglect.

That in order to put an end to this uncertainty, the subscriber has declared that, if the cannon be not ready for proving on or before the 20th instant, he will abandon the object. As the time allowed is ample for the purpose, he is in hopes to make a more satisfactory report at the first meeting of the Committee after the 20th instant.

He has been induced to make present imperfect report, that the Committee may know the causes of a delay, which has certainly been unreasonable, but which it has not been in the power of Mr. Lukens or himself either to foresee or prevent.

He would have abandoned the object immediately after the peace, had it not been for the considerations that the unbored cannon is only worth its weight as old iron, and that if completed it may prove an important addition to the ordnance of the United States, and of course worth all its cost.

(Signed)   JONA. WILLIAMS,
Chairman Sub-Committee of Defence.

Philadelphia, April 10th, 1815.

Ordered, That the above report be entered on the minutes of this Committee.

The following letter was read:

TREASURY DEPARTMENT, *April* 11*th*, 1815.

SIR:

Your letter of the 4th instant, inclosing a bank receipt for twenty-five thousand dollars, paid on the 1st instant, to complete the loan of 100,000 dollars, made by the Committee of Defence of Philadelphia for the fortifications of the Pea Patch, has been received, and the Comptroller of the Treasury has been requested to instruct the Commissioner of Loans for Pennsylvania to issue the stock as heretofore for the sum thus paid.

I am, very respectfully,
Sir, your obedient servant,
(Signed)   A. J. DALLAS.

JOS. REED, ESQ., Philadelphia.

The committee appointed at the last meeting to make an apportionment of the funds of this Committee, preparatory to a division thereof among the corporations of this city, report that there be paid

To the Corporation of the City of Philadelphia.. $11,666 64
To the Corporation of the Northern Liberties...   666 67
To the Corporation of Southwark.................   666 67
                                                 _____
                                                 $13,000 00
That of the stock, there be transferred
  To the Corporation of the City of
    Philadelphia........................... $85,258
  To the Corporation of the Northern
    Liberties.............................   4,871
  To the Corporation of Southwark....   4,871
                                             _____
                                                     95,000 00
                                                    _____
                                                    $108,000 00

Resolved, That the trustees of the six per cent. stock belonging to this Committee be authorized and requested to transfer the same to the Corporations of the City, Northern Liberties, and Southwark, according to the apportionment this day made by the committee appointed at the last meeting, and that the Treasurer of the Committee be authorized and requested to pay to the said corporations, respectively, in the same proportions, the moneys now remaining in his hands, or which he may hereafter receive.

Resolved, That a warrant be drawn in favor of John Dorsy, for commission on sales of provision at auction, for thirty-five dollars and fifty-one cents.

Resolved, That the Chairman of this Committee be instructed to furnish the members who proceed to Washington to settle the accounts of this Committee with the General Government, with papers signed by him as Chairman of the Committee of Defence, authorizing them to settle and liquidate the accounts.

SEVENTY-NINTH MEETING.

PHILADELPHIA, *April 29th*, 1815,
4 o'clock P.M.

The number of members who attended was insufficient to form a quorum. The Secretary was directed to call a meeting (by notices) for Friday the 7th proximo.

EIGHTIETH MEETING.

PHILADELPHIA, *May 5th*, 1815,
4 o'clock P.M.

The Committee met.

Present:—Messrs. Biddle, Leib, Latimer, McFaden, Hawkins, Josiah, Raguet, Steel, Ferguson, Eyre, Whitehead, Miercken, Thompson, McMullin, Sergeant, Snyder.

The minutes of the last meeting, 14th ultimo, were read.

The committee appointed at the meeting of this Committee on the 31st March last, to make an apportionment of the funds of this Committee, preparatory to a division of them among the corporations of this city, reported that, agreeably to a resolution of the General Committee of the 14th ultimo, they have paid to

(Chk. Penna. Bank............ $6,666 64
" Bank W. & B............ 5,000 00)
The Corporation of the City of Philadelphia... 11,666 64
The Corporation of the Northern Liberties...... 666 64
The Corporation of Southwark.................... 666 64

$13,000 00

The Committee of Accounts reported, they have examined the accounts of the Committee for the Defence of the Delaware, for sales of hulks and expenses attending it, &c., and which they report as follows, viz.:

Amount of sales at auction by John Humes, deducting auction commission, and with which sum they have charged the said Committee............ .... $16,983 33
The Committee have been credited as follows, viz.:
For cash paid Treasurer..................... 8,000 00
For sundry notes received for sales of hulks, and delivered to Treasurer...................... 7,350 70
For expenses paid by them, getting hulks from Fort Mifflin, rigging, &c. 862 02

Expense Account.

For carriage to Fort Mifflin, to obtain certificates from Major Beal, relative to the repairs done by the Committee..................... 2 62
Commission to James Josiah, superintending the getting hulks from Fort Mifflin, rigging them, &c... 512 60

The following letter was read:

QUARTERMASTER-GENERAL'S OFFICE,
PHILADELPHIA, *May 5th*, 1815.

SIR:

I am directed to collect 178 Dutch muskets, delivered to the Committee of Safety last fall. I am told they are in the State-house, but cannot be had without an order from the Committee. As you are Chairman of that Committee, I have taken the liberty to ask the favor of you to give the bearer an order to receive them.

With sentiments, &c.,
(Signed) WM. LINNARD,
Quartermaster-General.
CHARLES BIDDLE, ESQ.,
Chairman Committee of Defence.

A letter from Mr. McKoy, Contractor, claiming compensation for damaged bread, was read, and referred to the Committee of Supplies and Mr. Whitehead.

EIGHTY-FIRST MEETING.

MONDAY, *June* 12*th*, 1815.
The Committee met.
Present:—Messrs. Biddle, Latimer, Ferguson, Eyre, Hawkins, Connelly, Steel, McFaden, Whitehead, McMullin, Cadwalader, Reed, Leiper, Raguet, Sergeant.
The minutes of the last meeting were read.

Resolved, That a warrant be drawn in favor of S. Field for $80, being the amount of salary due him 23d ultimo.

EIGHTY-SECOND MEETING.

PHILADELPHIA, *August* 16*th*, 1815,
4 o'clock P.M.

The Committee met.

Present:—Messrs. Biddle, Goodman, Latimer, Leib, McFaden, Whitehead, Leiper, Brown, Naglee, Ronaldson, Sergeant, Reed.

The following letters were read:

SIR:—If the Committee of Defence approve the inclosed contract with Mr. Clark, relative to the Pea Patch, it will receive the sanction of the War Department. The subject is submitted to them, in order to obtain the benefit of their experience and observation, in ascertaining that the works proposed to be executed by the contract will be efficient for the immediate purpose contemplated, and that the terms are reasonable.

I am, Sir, &c.

(Signed) A. J. DALLAS.

CHARLES BIDDLE, ESQ.

I inclose Major Barker's plan for your perusal.

ARTICLES OF AGREEMENT, made the first day of August, in the year one thousand eight hundred and fifteen, between Alexander J. Dallas, Secretary of War, in behalf of the United States, of the first part, and Thomas Clark, of the City of Philadelphia, late a captain in the Corps of Topographical Engineers, of the second part.

The said Thomas Clark, for the consideration of twenty thousand dollars, to be paid as hereinafter mentioned, doth, for himself and his executors, and administrators, covenant, promise, and agree, to and with the party of the first part, that he, the said Thomas Clark, shall and will, within the space of six months next after the date thereof, in a good and workmanlike manner, well and substantially erect, throw up, and finish, a tide-bank around part of the island in the River Delaware, called the Pea Patch, which, when completed, will inclose between seventy and eighty acres, and forming a circuit from one and a half to two miles; the said bank to be of sufficient breadth and height to prevent any tide or freshet from overflowing the island within its inclosure, and to construct and lay four sluices, with valve-gates for the reception or the discharge of the water, and to dig, or cause to be dug, a number of drain-ditches, sufficient to keep the embanked part of the island perfectly dry; all the girts and breaks to be stopped out by suitable pilings; the lower part of the island to be secured from washing away, by the sinking of hulks or other adequate defences; the tide-bank to be secured against the effect of the tide and sea, by guard-logs properly laid for the purpose. The present wharf to be finished so as to be fit for the landing of all materials for the works, and for the accommodation of the fortress about to be erected on the said island. And the said Thomas Clark doth further covenant, promise, and agree, that he will collect, transport, and put in secure places on the said island, all the timber which has been purchased for the defence of the Delaware, and that pens or yards shall be properly constructed for the reception of the said timber, and to prevent the tide or sea from carrying it away. That the said island shall within the time aforesaid be prepared for the erection of fortifications of any kind; that all rubbish shall be removed, and the ground levelled and dried, and put in a state of preparation for either gardens or meadow. And the party of the first part covenants, promises, and agrees, that the said Thomas Clark shall be allowed to use such materials, and implements, now at the Pea Patch, belonging to the United States, as may be useful and necessary in the construction of the said works; the said implements be returned to an agent of the said United States duly authorized to receive them, after the said work shall be completely finished. And the party of the first part further covenants, promises, and agrees to pay, or cause to be paid, to the said Thomas Clark, five thousand dollars at the execution of this agreement, the further sum of five thousand dollars sixty days thereafter, and the remaining five thousand dollars at the final completion of the work, and after it shall be inspected and approved by persons mutually appointed by the parties. And for the true performance of all and singular the covenants and agreements aforesaid (the party of the first part performing his part of the agreement) the said Thomas Clark bindeth himself, his executors, and administrators, in the penal sum of twenty thousand dollars, firmly by these presents.

In witness whereof, the parties have interchangeably

set their hands and seals, the day and year first above written.

Sealed and delivered in
 presence of

A letter from Mr. Clark, relative to the plan of fortifying the Pea Patch, was read.

Resolved, That in the opinion of this Committee, the proposals of Captain Clark, for an embankment of the Pea Patch, &c., are reasonable, and ought to be accepted.

Resolved, That James Whitehead be authorized to receive from the Bank of Pennsylvania a balance of fifty-nine dollars and fifty-one cents due to the late Jonathan Williams, Chairman of the Sub-Committee of Defence, and to give a full discharge for the same in behalf of this Committee.

A memorial was read from Joseph G. Chambers, relative to his contract with the Commonwealth for furnishing repeating-guns, &c., for the due performance of which the Committee have become his sureties.

It appearing to the Committee that he had not furnished satisfactory evidence of having performed his contract, whereupon, on motion,

Resolved, That the Committee be directed to suspend the payment of the balance of the moneys in their hands to Mr. Chambers, until they should have satisfactory evidence that all the arms have been delivered agreeably to contract.

The committee appointed for the purpose of settling and adjusting the accounts of the Committee of Defence with the Government of the United States, report:

That they proceeded to the City of Washington, and exhibited to the Accountant of the War Department an account, of which a copy is hereto annexed, with the vouchers. showing a balance due to the Committee of $49,913.34.

The account was adjusted, but the following items were rejected, to wit:

Vouchers 114, abstract A deducted, being for carriage hire, inadmissible	$1 25	
Amount overcharged on V, 33, there being no receipt from Louisa O'Neal	66	
Vouchers 17, 24, 29, 52, 54, 59, 62, 64, 66, 67, 72, 75, 83, and 93, deducted from abstract D, being for carriage hire, tavern bills, groceries, which are inadmissible	975 21	
Part of voucher 74, same abstract, for groceries, &c., inadmissible	87 62	
Amount charged for repairs and supplies to gun-boats, abstract E, vouchers withdrawn, not belonging to this department	626 80	
Amount claimed as the balance of interest due on sundry sums of money advanced by them on the requisitions of the commanding generals deducted, the Secretary of War refusing to sanction it	861 08	
		$2,552 62
		$47,360 72

And credit was given to the Committee for a payment made after the account was certified by Major-General Scott, and not included in the account current...... .... $97 50

Making a balance due from the War Department of......... .... $47,458 22

For which the Committee, on the 24th of May, 1815, agreed with the Secretary of the Treasury to receive in payment six per cent. stock at 95.

The item of $626.80 was rejected, as being chargeable to the Navy Department. It has since been paid to George Harrison, Navy Agent.

For the above balance of $47,458.22, the Committee have received six per cent. stock at 95, dated the 10th July, 1815, giving interest from that date, of the final adjustment of the account. Amount, $49,956.

And they have received in cash from the Navy Agent, as above stated, $626.80; to be refunded if the Secretary of the Navy should not allow the payment.

This makes a final settlement of the accounts between the Committee of Defence and the Government, except as to the said sum of $626.80, for which your Committee have given to the Navy Agent an engagement to refund if the same should not be allowed.

Ordered, That the above report be placed on the files of this Committee.

Resolved, That the thanks of this Committee be returned to Messrs. Whitehead and Sergeant, the gentlemen appointed a committee for the settlement of accounts with the Government, for their indefatigable attention to that important business.

[The following order and receipt do not occur in the regular minutes, but are written on one of the fly-leaves of the Minute Book.—COPYIST.]

CAMP MARCUS HOOK, *October* 23d, 1814.

TO THE COMMITTEE OF DEFENCE:

The Committee of Defence is hereby requested to deliver to Samuel Blair two hundred shovels with handles, and one hundred picks with handles, for the use of the camp at Marcus Hook.

ELISHA WILKINSON,
Assistant Quartermaster-General.

Received, October 24th, 1814, from Mr. Jas. Whitehead, Treasurer to the Committee of Defence, two hundred shovels and one hundred pikes, with handles, agreeably to the within order.

SAML. BLAIR, JR.

Resolved, That Messrs. Ronaldson and Reed be a committee to call on Major Sharpe, to endeavor to obtain a settlement of William Shannon's claim on the Commonwealth.

Mr. Whitehead reported that he had received from Captain Charles Ross a warrant on the Treasurer of the United States, at Baltimore, for $3830.81, on account of money advanced him, and that he exchanged the same with Biddle & Wharton for six per cent. stock of the

United States; amount. three thousand eight hundred and thirty dollars and eighty-one cents.

Whereupon

Resolved, That the Committee of Accounts be authorized to transfer the $53,786.83 of six per cent. stock. held in trust for the Committee of Defence, in the following apportionment:

To the Mayor, Aldermen, and Citizens of Philadelphia....................................	$48,270 23
To the Commissioners and Inhabitants of Northern Liberties...............................	2,758 30
To the Commissioners and Inhabitants of Southwark..	2,758 30
	$53,786 83

COPY OF ACCOUNT ANNEXED TO FOREGOING REPORT.

The United States in account with the Committee of Defence of the City of Philadelphia.

DR.				CR.
To am't abstract A, for fortifications, &c.	$22,607 93	1814. Nov. 5.	By sales, sundry intrenching tools, &c., H	$219 38
B, ordnance, &c.	11,927 86	1815.		
C, subsistence for workmen at Fort Mifflin and Fort Gaines	2,046 88	April 17.	By amount nett sales, hulks, ballast, &c., I	16,574 23
D, on account fortifications	5,969 94		Balance due to the Committee	49,913 34
E, repairs and supplies to gun-boats	626 08			
F, purchase of hulks, &c.	22,666 46			
G, balance interest account	861 08			
	66,706 95			$66,706 95
To the above balance	$49,913 34			

[The following is a copy of a letter from N. B. Boileau, Secretary of the Commonwealth, referred to in the minutes of the meeting of the Committee of Defence held September 13th, 1814.—COPYIST.]

PHILADELPHIA, *September* 12*th*, 1814.
SIR:

The Governor concurs as to the propriety and necessity of adopting all the measures suggested in a report of the General Committee of Defence, dated the 8th and presented on the 9th instant by their Chairman, and is willing to adopt any legal or constitutional means in his power to carry those measures into full and complete operation; but he, in common with the Committee, feels not only the responsibility, but the difficulty, if not impracticability of enforcing them, so long as no authority can be "legally exercised to compel their enforcement." He is sensible that, at a crisis like the present, it is expected he will exercise not only all the authority that rightfully appertains to him as the "first civil magistrate" of Pennsylvania, but also that of its military commander-in-chief; nor is he at all desirous to shrink from the performance of any duty, or the exercise of any authority which he can constitutionally exercise in either of those capacities. He has therefore assiduously examined the constitution and laws, and is not aware that it is in his power to compel the people to do the things which the Committee have suggested. Under this view of the subject, he asks permission to observe, that if the General Committee of Defence will prepare for publication a report of the several duties which, under all circumstances, may be imposed upon the citizens as means of impeding, distressing, or any way annoying the enemy, he will cordially and promptly co-operate in recommending their adoption, and in giving them all the effect which can be derived from his official station. He embraces this occasion to state to the Committee, that the removal up the river, as far as the water will admit, of all the ships and craft not contemplated to be employed in the general defence, is a measure imperiously called for. It would now be attended with little comparative expense, and it might hereafter engross funds and men that might be better appropriated.

With high respect and consideration.

Sir, your obedient servant,

N. B. BOILEAU,

Secretary.

CHARLES BIDDLE, ESQ.,
Chairman of the Committee of Defence.

HISTORICAL SOCIETY OF PENNSYLVANIA.

OFFICERS FOR 1867

President.
JOSEPH R. INGERSOLL.

Vice-Presidents.
BENJAMIN H. COATES,
JOHN WILLIAM WALLACE,
JOHN M. READ,
HORATIO GATES JONES.

Treasurer.
CHARLES M. MORRIS.

Recording Secretary.
L. MONTGOMERY BOND.

Corresponding Secretary.
JAMES ROSS SNOWDEN.

Librarian.
RICHARD EDDY.

Library Committee.
RICHARD L. NICHOLSON,
JOHN JORDAN, Jr.,
JOHN A. McALLISTER.

Publication Committee.
FREDERICK D. STONE,
WILLIAM S. PEIRCE,
REV. DANIEL WASHBURN.

Finance Committee.
JOSEPH CARSON,
J. L. FENIMORE,
THOMAS BIDDLE.

Trustees of the Publication Fund.
JOHN JORDAN, Jr.,
AUBREY H. SMITH,
WILLIAM STRONG.

REVISED LIST OF MEMBERS OF THE SOCEITY.

JULY, 1867.

LIFE MEMBERS.

Allen, William H.
Atlee, Washington L.
Agnew, Samuel
Armstrong, Edward
Armstrong, William G.
Ashton, Samuel K.
Ashhurst, William H.
Ashhurst, Lewis
Ashhurst, Lewis R.
Ashhurst, Henry
Ashhurst, Richard
Ashhurst, Richard, jr.
Ashhurst, Richard L.
Ashhurst, John
Ashhurst, John, jr.
Austin, John B.

Balch, Thomas
Bache, T. Hewson
Baird, Matthew
Baker, J. B.
Bell, John T.
Benners, William J.
Bensell, George J.
Bettle, William
Bettle, Samuel
Bettle, Edward, jr.
Betts, Richard K.
Biddle, Alexander
Biddle, George W.
Biddle, Thomas
Biddle, Thomas A.
Brick, Samuel R.
Bowen, Ezra
Bowen, Smith
Bohlen, John
Borie, Adolph E.
Bowers, Edward
Brodhead, L. W.
Brown, J. Johnson
Brown, David Paul
Butler, John M.

Craig, I. Eugene
Carver, Alexander B.
Chambers, William B.
Claghorn, James L.
Chase, Pliny E
Cresson, William P.
Chew, Samuel
Cleveland, Charles D.
Chester, Joseph L.
Childs, Cephas G.
Christian, Samuel J.
Cope, Caleb
Coleman, G. Dawson
Cochran, William G.
Collins, T. K.
Corlies, S. Fisher
Coffin, Arthur G.
Collis, William
Coates, Benjamin H.
Coles, Edward
Conarroe, George W.
Coppee, Henry
Crozer, J. Lewis
Crozer, Samuel A.

Da Costa, John C.
Dallett, Elijah
Day, Alfred
Dreer, F. J.
Drexel, Joseph W.
Dick, Walter B.
Duane, William

Earle, Harrison
Errickson, Michael
Ellis, Charles
Elwyn, A. Langdon
Eddy, Richard

Fahnestock, George W.
Farmer, James S.
Fagan, George R.

Fleming, William W.
Fell, J. Gillingham
Fernon, Thomas S.
Fisher, James C.
Fisher, Joshua F.
Fitler, Edwin H.
Fullerton, Alexander

Gardette, E. B.
Graff, Frederick
Gratz, Simon
Garrett, Philip C.
Grout, Henry T.
Gorton, George W.
Godfrey, Benjamin G.

Harvey, Samuel, jr.
Harvey, Josiah L.
Hart, William H.
Harrison, Joseph
Haseltine, John
Haseltine, Albert C.
Haseltine, Ward B.
Harper, Alexander J.
Hammersley, George
Hazard, Samuel
Helmuth, Henry
Heberton, G. Craig
Hill, Marshall
Houston, William C.
Hutchinson, Charles H.
Hunt, Uriah

Ingersoll, Edward
Ingram, Harlan

James, John O.
Jackman, D. K.
Jordan, John, jr.
Jordan, John W.
Jordan, Francis
Jordan, W. H.
Jones, D. D.
Jones, Andrew M.
Jones, George W.
Judson, William F.

Kane, Thomas L.
Kirkpatrick, Edwin

Lambdin, George C.
Lambdin, James R.
Lambert, John
Lafourcade, Edward
Lee, George F.
Levick, James J.
Lejee, William R.
Lesley, John P.
Livezey, John
Loper, R. F.

Loper, William H.
Logan, J. Dickinson

McAllister, John A.
McArthur, John, jr.
McHenry, George
McIntyre, Archibald
Mann, Rev. W. J.
Martin, Sanderson R.
Matthias, John T.
Man, William
Mason, John
Miles, Thomas J.
Miller, Joseph W.
Miller, John C.
Mitchell, James T.
Middleton, Nathan
Michener, John H.
Morris, Charles M.
Morris, Israel
Morris, Robert
Morris, William J.
Moore, Bloomfield H.
Muirhead, Charles H.
Murphy, Henry F.

Nicholson, Richard L.
Norris, Isaac, jr.
Norris, William F.

Patterson, William C.
Parrish, Dillwyn
Parrish, Samuel
Paxton, Joseph R.
Parry, George R.
Parry, Richard R.
Penington, Edward, jr.
Peirce, William S.
Pepper, George S.
Pepper, Lawrence S.
Peace, Edward
Perkins, Samuel C.
Perot, T. Morris
Price, Eli K.
Plitt, George
Powers, Thomas H.

Reinke, Rev. A. A.
Read, T. Buchanan
Remington, Thomas P
Repplier, John G.
Richards, J. W.
Robins, Edward
Rockey, A. B.
Ruschenberger, W. S. W.

Spackman, Henry S.
Spackman, John B.
Schaffer, Charles
Sparks, Thomas

Sharpless, H. H. G.
Sharpless, Samuel J.
Sargent, Winthrop
Stanton, M. Hall
Smedley, Samuel L.
Stevens, Rev. W. B.
Sergeant, J. Dickinson
Seybert, Henry
Slevin, James
Shipley, Thomas
Smith, Aubrey H.
Smith, Horace W.
Smith, Joseph P.
Smith, Lloyd P.
Smith, Robert
Smith, Thomas
Simons, George W.
Simons, Henry
Sinclair, Thomas
Swift, Joseph
Snowden, James Ross
Sower, Charles G.
Souder, Edmund A.
Sturges, Robert S.
Snyder, W. B.

Traquair, James
Taylor, Stephen
Taylor, Samuel L.
Taylor, William C.
Taws, Lewis
Thomas, William G.
Thompson, Henry C.

Trotter, Joseph H.
Turnpenny, Joseph C.
Tyson, James

Vaux, George
Vaux, William S.

Ward, Townsend
Wagner, Charles M.
Waln, Edward
Waln, S. Morris
Wallace, J. William
Walden, Rev. Treadwell
Wharton, Charles W.
Welsh, John
Welsh, Samuel
Welling, Charles H.
Weber, Paul
Whelen, Edward S.
Williamson, Walter
Winner, William E.
Wilson, Oliver H.
Wilson, William S.
Williams, Henry J.
Wright, James A.
Wright, Richard
Wood, George A.
Wood, Rt. Rev. James F
Woolston, J. W.

Yarnall, Ellis
Yarnall, Francis C.

RESIDENT MEMBERS.

Allen, Prof. George
Ames, Rev. B. O.
Aertson, James M.
Allibone, S. Austin
Africa, J. Simpson
Atkins, Rev. A. B.
Audenreid, Lewis

Barnes, Rev. Albert
Bradford, Charles S.
Bradford, William
Baird, William M.
Bald, J. Dorsey
Bailey, E. Westcott
Blanchard, W. A.
Ball, G. W.
Barton, Isaac
Bailey, M. H.
Bates, Joseph W.
Bray, William K.

Bacon, Alexander
Braidwood, Thomas W.
Beesly, B. W.
Bement, William B.
Benners, Henry B.
Benson, Alexander, jr.
Bottle, Henry
Biddle, Chapman
Biddle, Clement
Biddle, Edward C.
Biddle, William
Briggs, Rev. Lewis L.
Brinton, J. H.
Blight, Atherton
Blight, George
Boker, Charles S.
Boker, George H.
Brock, John P.
Bond, L. Montgomery
Boyd, W. Stokes

Brotherhead, William
Brown, Alexander
Brown, John A.
Browne, John C.
Browne, N. B.
Boardman, Rev. G. D.
Boardman, Rev. H. A.
Bodine, F. L.
Bomberger, Rev. J. H.
Bowen, Franklin H.
Broomall, Lewis R.
Brooks, Rev. Philip
Bullock, Benjamin
Bullock, George
Buckley, Edward S.
Bucknell, William
Budd, John B.
Burgin, George H.
Burt, Nathaniel
Bullitt, John C.
Burroughs, Horatio N.
Busch, Henry E.
Button, Conyers
Bryson, James H.

Cabot, Joseph
Cadwallader, George
Cadwallader, John
Cadwallader, William
Caldcleugh, W. G.
Caldwell, James E.
Callender, Thos. R.
Campbell, St. George T.
Camac, John B.
Cannell, S. Wilmer
Carey, Henry C.
Carpenter, Joseph R.
Carson, Joseph
Case, Robert
Castner, Samuel, jr.
Cassin, John
Cattell, A. G.
Chambers, Herman A.
Chancellor, William
Chandler, Joseph R.
Chapman, Henry
Chauncey, Charles
Clark, Edward L.
Clark, Edward W.
Clark, Rev. W. J.
Clay, H. Gibbs
Craven, Thomas
Cresson, Charles M.
Cresson, John C.
Childs, George W.
Collins, Rev. G.
Collins, Frederick
Colwell, Stephen
Comly, Franklin
Conner, P. S. P.

Cooke, Jay
Cooley, Aaron B.
Cooper, Joseph B.
Cope, Alfred
Cope, Francis R.
Cope, Herman
Cope, John E.
Cope, Thomas P.
Cornelius, John C.
Cornelius, Robert
Corson, Robert R.
Corse, J. M.
Coxe, Brinton
Cross, Michael H.
Crozier, George K.
Crowell, Rev. J. M.
Churchman, C. W.
Cummins, D. B.

Davids, Hugh
Davidson, George
Davis, Lemuel H.
Dawson, Mordecai L.
Derbyshire, A. J.
Drexel, Anthony J.
Drown, William A
Durborrow, Charles B.
Durborrow, Rev. G. A.

Evans, Horace
Engles, Rev. W. M.
Emory, Charles
Elwyn, Rev. Alfred
Edmunds, Henry B.

Fagan, John
Farnum, James A.
Farnum, John
Flanders, Henry
Fraley, Frederick
Frazer, John F.
Felton, S. M.
Fenimore, J. L.
Fitzgerald, Thomas
Findlay, John K.
Foggo, Rev. E. A.
Forney, John W.
Foulke, Francis E.
Fox, Samuel L.

Garrett, Thomas C.
Graeff, Edward C.
Graeff, John E.
Graff, Charles H.
Graff, J.
Glass, A. F.
Gemmill, William D.
Getty, Archibald
Greble, Edwin
Gibbons, Charles

Gilbert, D.
Gilliams, J. Southen
Gilpin, Charles
Gilpin, John F.
Grigg, John W.
Gwinn, John
Gristock, Charles F.
Godon, S. W.
Goodwin, Rev. D. R.
Gordon, N. P.
Gould, John H.
Gulager, William
Gutekunst, F.

Hacker, Morris
Haines, Benjamin H.
Haines, Henry
Hand, James C.
Hand, Thomas C.
Harper, John M.
Hart, Abraham
Hartshorne, Edward
Harmar, Charles
Harding, J. Morris
Heilman, John
Henszey, William C.
Hewson, Addinell
Hickok, Henry C.
Hodge, J. Ledyard
Hodge, Hugh L.
Hofmann, J. William
Hood, Samuel
Hoppinson, Oliver
Howe, Rev. M. A. De Wolfe
Howell, Z. C.
Huddy, Benjamin F.
Hunt, Benjamin P.
Huston, Samuel
Hutter, Rev. E. W.
Hutton, Addison

Ingersoll, Joseph R.

Jacobs, William B.
Jenks, John S.
Jenks, William P.
Jones, Charles Henry
Jones, Horatio Gates
Jones, Jacob P.
Johnstone, Rev. W. O.

Kane, Robert P.
Krauth, Rev. C. P.
Keichline, William H.
Kelley, William D.
Kendall, E. Otis
Kennedy, Alfred L.
Knecht, Charles
Keyser, Peter Dirck
Kimber, Thomas

King, Robert P.
Kinsey, William
Knight, Edward C.
Kline, J. W.
Konnigmacher, A. A.
Kumer, Rev. J. S.

Lardner, James L.
Lardner, Richard P.
Laroche, C. Percy
Lea, Isaac
Lee, Julius
Leedom, B. J.
Leeds, Rev. George
Leeser, Rev Isaac
Letchworth, A. S.
Lewis, Abraham J.
Lewis, Ellis
Lewis, Edwin M.
Lewis, John T.
Lincoln, Ezekiel
Lippincott, Joshua B.
Lockwood, Benoni
Long, William W.
Longacre, James B.
Lovering, Joseph S.
Ludlow, Richard
Lynd, James

McAllister, John, jr.
McAllister, W. Y.
McCall, Peter
McCammon, D. C.
McClellan, J. H. B.
McElroy, Archibald
McElroy, Thomas E.
McElroy, W. J.
McKean, Wm. V.
McKean, Henry P.
McMichael, Morton
McMurtrie, R. C.
MacKellar, Thomas
Mann, William B.
Maris, Matthias
Malcom, Rev. H.
Mayburry, William
Martinez, S. A.
Magarge, Charles
Marsh, Benjamin V.
Mackenzie, R. Shelton
Markle, La Fayette
Markley, Edward C.
Malin, William G.
Meade, George G.
Meredith, William M.
Meredith, William
Mercer, Singleton J.
Merrick, Samuel V.
Messchert, M. H., jr.
Mickley, Joseph J.

Middleton, E. P.
Milliken, James
Mitcheson, McGregor J.
Miskey, William F.
Miller, E. Spencer
Milne, Francis P.
Montgomery, Richard R.
Montgomery, Thomas H.
Morris, Rev. B. Wistar
Morris, Isaac P.
Morton, Henry J.
Morton, Thomas G.
Moran, John
Moses, Horace
Moore, Joseph
Muckle, Mark R.
Muirhead, Henry P.
Myers, Joseph B.

Neal, Daniel
Neill, John
Nevin, Rev. Alfred
Newbold, John S.
Newhall, Thomas A.
Newkirk, Matthew
Norris, George W.
Norris, Isaac
Norton, Charles F.

Ogden, Charles S.
Orne, James H.

Page, George W.
Page, James
Palmer, Benjamin F.
Pancoast, Charles S.
Parrish, George D.
Patterson, Robert
Paul, James
Penrose, Clement B.
Peterson, Henry
Phillips, Charles L.
Phillips, Henry M.
Phillips, Samuel R.
Pollock, James
Porter, William A.
Powel, Samuel
Purves, William

Queen, James W.

Randolph, Evan
Randolph, Philip P.
Randolph, Samuel E.
Rawle, William H.
Read, John M.
Reimer, B. F.
Remsen, George
Rice, John
Ringwalt, J. Luther

Ritchie, Craig D.
Ritter, Abraham
Robins, J. W.
Robins, Thomas
Robinson, Daniel M.
Roberts, Solomon W.
Rogers, Charles H.
Rogers, Fairman
Roney, C. H.
Rudder, Rev. William
Rupp, I. Daniel

Savery, John C.
Saunders, Rev. E. D.
Sharpless, Nathan
Sharswood, George
Shannon, Ellwood
Slack, J. Hamilton
Stacey, M. P.
Stansbury, Charles F.
Starr, F. R.
Scattergood, George J.
Seiss, Rev. Joseph A.
Sexton, John W.
Sheppard, W. T. J.
Sherrerd, W. D.
Smedley, Jacob
Stewart, W. H.
Stewart, W. S.
Stewardson, Thomas, jr.
Simpson, Henry
Shields, Rev. C. W.
Shipley, Augustus B.
Shipley, Samuel R.
Smith, Atwood
Smith, A. Lewis
Smith, Daniel, jr.
Smith, Ellwood M.
Smith, George Roberts
Smith, Horace
Smith, J. Somers
Smith, Rev. J. Wheaton
Smith, Richard S.
Smith, Richard Somers
Smith, Samuel Grant
Smith, W. H.
Stillé, Alfred
Souder, Stephen T.
Scott, Lewis A.
Scott, Thomas A.
Sproat, Harris L.
Stoddart, Curwen
Stokes, Charles
Stone, Frederick D.
Stone, James N.
Stone, W. E.
Stroud, George M.
Scull, Gideon D.
Stuart, George H.

Struthers, William
Shryock, Wm. Knight

Tait, John T.
Tasker, Thomas T.
Taylor, George L.
Taylor, James H.
Trautwine, John C.
Trenchard, S. Decatur
Torrey, Hiram
Tower, Charlemagne
Thomson, J. Edgar
Trotter, Charles W.
Trotter, Edward H.
Trotter, William H.
Tucker, John
Turner, John
Tyler, George F.

Vaux, Richard
Vaux, Thomas W.
Vogdes, William

Walborn, C. A.
Walker, Jerry
Wardle, Thomas
Warner, John S.
Warner, Redwood F.
Warriner, H. Ryland

Washburn, Rev. Daniel
Wattson, Thomas B.
Wharton, Henry
Welsh, John, jr.
Westcott, Thompson
Wetherill, John Price
Whelen, Edward S., jr.
Wheeler, Andrew
Wheeler, Joseph K.
Whetham, James S.
Whitney, Asa
Whitney, John R.
White, Samuel S.
Williamson, Passmore
Williamson, Isaac V.
Willing, Charles
Wildman, James G.
Wister, Casper
Wister, Mifflin
Wister, William
Wood, George B.
Wood, Richard
Wurts, Charles S.

Yarnall, Charles

Zeigler, George K.
Zeilin, John K.
Zell, T. Ellwood

www.ingramcontent.com/pod-product-compliance
Lightning Source LLC
Chambersburg PA
CBHW022105290426
44112CB00008B/562